CHINA

D1365481

CHINA
A Resource and Curriculum Guide
Second Edition, Revised

**Edited by Arlene Posner
and Arne J. de Keijzer**

**With an Introduction by
Edwin O. Reischauer**

THE UNIVERSITY OF CHICAGO PRESS

Chicago and London

The University of Chicago Press, Chicago 60637
The University of Chicago Press, Ltd., London

Printed in the United States of America

Library of Congress Cataloging in Publication Data
Posner, Arlene.
    China: a resource and curriculum guide.

Includes index.
    1. China—Library resources—United States.
I. De Keijzer, Arne J., joint author. II. Title.
Z3106.P67   1976   [DS706]   951'.007   75-9061
ISBN 0-226-67559-9
ISBN 0-226-67560-2 pbk.

ARLENE POSNER, a member of the National Committee on United States-China Relations, Inc., has been responsible for the development of the Committee's School Resources Program. She is the editor of *A Critical Guide to Curriculum Units* and of *Audio-Visual Materials on China*, and is producer of *China Conversations*, a series of audiotaped interviews.

ARNE J. DE KEIJZER, also a member of the National Committee, is a specialist in Chinese foreign policy. He has been instrumental in developing the Committee's University Field Staff Program.

Advisory Board for This Volume

Contents

Preface

Since the first edition of this guide, the number of materials on China—both written and visual—has increased dramatically. Their overall quality, however, has not kept pace with their quantity. The potential indicated by the many and varied direct contacts being developed with the People's Republic of China as well as the expansion of our academic knowledge has not yet been realized. While many of the new materials reflect the over-effusive reactions of our first acquaintance with the new China, others (new and "revised" editions) still contain cold war biases and values.

Thus, in spite of our growing awareness of China, the major overhaul of textbooks and school curricula so sorely needed is not yet underway. The burden of selection and evaluation continues to fall on the individual teacher and concerned citizens' group, and it is our hope that the guide will encourage and facilitate this task.

The guide does not attempt to be all-encompassing; it is comprehensive, however, in listing a wide range of materials currently available to the public and offering representative views of the social, economic, political, and cultural aspects of China's society and international relations, both past and present. A careful reading of this edition will reveal much that is new and some things that have been eliminated. An index has been added to aid in locating materials, and the resources section has been consolidated for easier usage. In many cases, evaluations and recommendations are more critical. Because it is important to evaluate another culture on its own terms, we also have included a special section on available materials from the People's Republic of China.

Once again special thanks are due our former colleague, Douglas P. Murray, who so willingly shared of his time and editorial skill. We also are grateful to our Advisory Board for their encouragement and helpful criticism. Our greatest debt, however, is to Shelley Metzenbaum, for her intellectual contributions, patience, and cheerful willingness to carry out the most mundane tasks of revision. This edition was produced independent of any organizational ties, and full responsibility rests with the editors.

Arlene Posner
Arne J. de Keijzer

January 1975

Introduction

Edwin O. Reischauer

The years 1971 and 1972 will long be remembered for the dramatic headlines heralding a fundamental shift in United States–China relations, culminating in President Nixon's historic visit to the People's Republic of China. The visit was a welcome symbol of relaxation in Sino-American tensions. It showed clearly that the United States no longer regarded China as the major menace it once seemed to be and that the Chinese too had changed their view of us. American acknowledgment of Peking as the capital of the great historic China was long overdue, as was Peking's rightful occupancy of the United Nations seat assigned to that country.

But one should not overemphasize the immediate gains from the new policy. Even at best, America's trade with China cannot grow to large proportions in the near future. It will certainly not exceed a small fraction of our trade with Japan, for example. Cultural and intellectual relations probably will also remain slight. The Taiwan problem will persist, to be resolved primarily by the attitudes of the government and the people on that island. The very dangerous confrontation between two highly militarized and extremely antagonistic regimes in Korea will remain almost unchanged as a major threat to world peace. The solution of the Indochina problem will depend less on Sino-American relations than on the attitudes and abilities of the people of that region. The future of the other Asian countries, while probably benefited by a thaw in Sino-American tensions, will be basically determined by other factors—first of all, their own strength and capacities, and second, the economic role of the great industrial powers, such as Japan, the United States, and the countries of Western Europe.

Despite these limitations, however, rapprochement between the United States and China is a matter of the greatest significance for the world. It is imperative that China, with close to a quarter of the world's population, become engaged in what must before long be a worldwide effort to face the dilemmas that are fast closing in on humanity. This worldwide approach will be necessary if mankind is to solve the great problems of survival in a nuclearized world—population growth, depletion of natural resources, and global pollution.

It will not be easy to enter into a meaningful dialogue with the Chinese quadrant of humanity over these great global problems. Can we develop enough mutual understanding and trust to solve them before it is too late? The time is short; the problems are great. If we are to have any hope of handling them successfully, we must make a determined and massive effort to prepare ourselves for effective communication with the Chinese, leading to fruitful cooperation. This requires some major changes in our attitudes toward China and, for that matter, toward the whole non-Western part of the world. It also will entail learning a great deal more than we now know, so that there can be real understanding and not just a dialogue between the mentally deaf.

Clearly we must do much more than we have done to develop expert knowledge, but, as a lifetime frustrated "expert," I know that this is only a beginning. As a democracy, we require not just expert knowledge, but also a considerable degree of popular understanding of other areas and the problems we face in our relations with them, if these problems are to be faced wisely over any protracted period of time. This has been shown time after time since World War II in our relations not just with China but with all of Asia. The reasons for our errors and failures have usually not been the inadequacy of expert knowledge so much as the lack of popular understanding that would have permitted a wise political use of what knowledge we did have. We face a desperate need for broad understanding by the American public of the problems involved in our relationship with China and the rest of Asia.

This is not easy to achieve. We have an educational system that even today is narrowly focused on the historical experience and cultural heritage of our own occidental branch of humanity. Such a restricted focus may have made sense in the nineteenth-century age of Western imperialism, but it is folly in the present "one world."

Efforts are being made to compensate for our lack of basic education about the non-Western world. Various foreign policy organizations, numerous study groups, and a growing number of publications attempt to fill the gap, but such activities touch only a tiny fraction of the American people. In recent years, courses on China and other non-Western areas have proliferated in our better universities and colleges. Graduate schools turn out a steady stream of specialists on Asia, and fair numbers of undergraduates take at least one course on a non-Western civilization. The percentage increase in these activities during the past three decades has been astronomical, but they still affect only a minority of each student generation. Efforts at the college and adult-education levels must, of course, be increased. But there is an even more crucial need. We must so modify elementary and secondary education that it prepares all our young people for life in the multicultural, multiracial world in which we now live.

A few secondary schools do have instruction on non-Western cultures, and some whole school systems are experimenting with additions to the curriculum for this purpose. There is danger in the latter approach, however. If the non-Western materials appear to be "additional" to the main content of the regular curriculum, this may further confirm children in their belief that any culture other than their own is somehow peripheral to true civilization, doing things in strange and backward ways. Nothing could be worse than to underline the natural human assumption that anything different from one's own norms is for that very reason exotic or even "barbaric."

Elementary and secondary education is backed up by a lot of home conditioning, which also tends to convey a very misleading impression of the human experience. The two together are likely to establish the false assumptions that the West is and always has been superior to the other civilizations of mankind and that its nineteenth-century position of dominance over the rest of the world is a natural condition which will change only as others learn to conform to Western standards. These are dangerous ideas for Americans to harbor in the latter part of the twentieth century.

A few years ago I described an imaginary schoolboy's view of world history. I am afraid it is still all too close to the picture most Americans have in mind. It ran as follows:

> Civilization got its obscure start in outlandish places like Egypt and Mesopotamia, which subsequently relapsed into barbarism, and only after it got into the hands of the Israelites and Greeks did it become true civilization. Greek civilization was passed on to Rome and the Judaic tradition to the Christianity its people adopted. Then this combined true civilization was passed to the North Europeans, and sub-

sequently it moved to the North American continent, where it achieved its final flowering in us.

Other peoples figure in the story only as the barbarians who repeatedly attempted to stamp out civilization. The Egyptians and others oppressed the Israelites; the Persians tried to destroy Greece; barbarians (and here we distinguish between our own "noble" Germanic ancestors and the truly "barbaric" Asiatic Huns) did destroy Rome; the Saracens, the Mongol hordes and the Turks all in turn threatened civilization but fortunately were repulsed. Happily the barbarians in time subsided into passive ignorance and poverty, in which state we, the bearers of the true torch of civilization, discovered them and ruled them, and now we find them a source of embarrassment and trouble, because they cause wars and revolutions and remain inconsiderately close to starvation.[1]

This picture probably is overdrawn, but I believe it is still essentially the impression many of our schools convey to their pupils. We need to restructure our concept of the world and of human history, so that children grow up learning about the whole experience of mankind that has produced the world in which we live, not just our particular corner, with its own special idiosyncrasies and prejudices. We need not slight our Judeo-Greek-Roman-North European-American heritage. It not only is our own specific line of development, but at this moment in history it is the most important one. But, by seeing that it has been paralleled and sometimes excelled by other lines of development, we will learn more about it as well as about other traditions and will become better prepared to live in our contemporary world of many cultures.

We must not go on instilling in our children the idea that there is only one true line of civilization and that all else is, if not barbaric, amusingly upside down. That sort of education may have sufficed a few decades ago, but it is not a suitable preparation for life in the last third of the twentieth century. We would not tolerate a nineteenth-century type of education in the field of the natural sciences. It should be no more acceptable in the equally important field of understanding the human experience

---

1. Edwin O. Reischauer, *Beyond Vietnam: The United States and Asia* (New York: Alfred A. Knopf, 1967), pp. 235–36. © 1967 by Alfred A. Knopf, Inc.

Introduction

and the relations between the great groupings of people in the world.

New educational approaches at the elementary and secondary levels will influence our national understanding of our foreign policies only slowly, but that should not discourage us. Our relations with China and the rest of Asia will be a problem much longer. However crucial they may be today, they will be more important a decade or two decades from now. With this in mind we should be seeking to devise an educational system really relevant to the needs of the late twentieth century. We must do this if we are to play our part in attempting to surmount the grave problems looming ahead of mankind.*

It will take time to revise curricula and textbooks to meet the needs we can now foresee. Until this is done, the burden will continue to fall on the individual teacher. But often the teacher, however well inclined, is simply too busy or too inadequately trained to develop by himself the necessary teaching materials or courses. This guide has been produced to help him, his school, or his school district in developing a meaningful program on one very large and important part of the non-Western world—the Chinese quarter of humanity. Help in locating materials, supplemented by guest lectures, films, tapes, and other materials, can enable even the inadequately trained teacher to present China effectively. This guide, of course, is no panacea for our great educational needs, but it is a long step in the right direction, leading toward the new educational approaches that must be developed further if we are going to train the next generation adequately for life in the contemporary world.

*[Editor's note: For a further elucidation of these views, see Professor Reischauer's *Toward the 21st Century: Education for a Changing World* (New York: Vintage Books, 1974).]

Part One: Essays on Teaching about China

The People's Republic of China

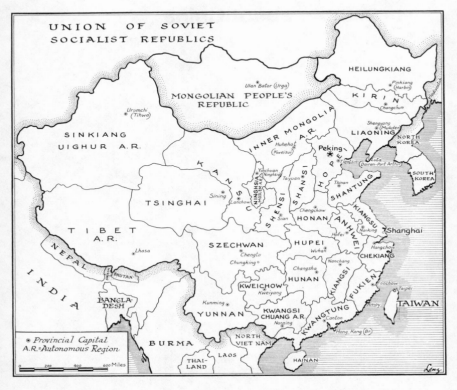

Lenz in *The Christian Science Monitor* © 1972 by The Christian Science Publishing Society. All rights reserved

1. Teaching Materials on Contemporary China: A Critical Evaluation
Edward Friedman

All teaching materials on contemporary China are biased. It is of course true that no writer can escape the influences of the general climate of opinion of his time or the perspectives of his social position. Scholarly impressions of China seem to go through distinct phases. But if we are aware of this truth, we can discount somewhat for it. We can analyze teaching materials in terms of three periods: (1) when United States policymakers took America's enemy to be monolithic communism, of which China was considered a subordinate part; (2) when the split between Russia and China became obvious, and United States policymakers worked for détente with Russia while still regarding China as America's major enemy; and (3) when United States policymakers accepted China as another nation state and dealt with it in the manner of ordinary power politics—a mixture of cooperation and competition, open-mindedness and hostility. Similarly, we can account for three distinct outlooks within the spectrum of American writers toward China: (1) antagonistic and hostile; (2) formally neutral and establishmentarian; and (3) critically receptive. While these categories are neither mutually exclusive nor necessarily chronologically sequential, such a perspective should give a teacher some control over the inevitable distortions in texts which arise from parochial interest and prejudiced misperception.

During period (1), developments in China, whatever their shape, were forced into pegholes gouged out to see Stalinist Russia. The key category was totalitarianism. There was little dissent from the idea that the cold war pitted good against evil. The enemy was seen as having no redeeming moral qualities. Indeed, for many, the enemy was not even the Chinese alone. Studies of China focused on alleged string-pulling by Russian masters, as well as on thought reform, mass murder, forced labor, inherent aggressiveness, and economic deprivation. Most of the early high-school units on China reflect this orientation, which takes China as an enemy.

Not only are such emphases misleading, they are dangerously misleading. Although this viewpoint was in part an outgrowth of our own domestic considerations—just as were the other phases—it lends itself to a portrait of the Chinese people as being one step away from revolt, ignoring the popular success of the Chinese Revolution as a nationalist movement. Chinese of all political persuasions deeply felt the indignities and humiliations of one hundred years of foreign intervention. Chinese now feel a new dignity in the ability of their government to win a place of honor and respect within the council of nations. Standing up to American military might in Korea, refusing to knuckle under to Russian pressures, developing their own atomic weapons, and moving toward becoming a spokesman for the common interests of third world nations.

Perhaps more important, the antagonistic approach to China played down the large extent to which the Chinese people have benefited in their everyday lives from the success of the revolution. First, social order has been restored. The previous one hundred years of war, famine, and chaos had split families, driven millions of people off the land, forced parents to abandon their children, and left children with little chance of marriage and adults with little prospect of a tranquil and respect-filled old age. Virtually all this abnormal misery has come to an end.

Second, the redistribution of wealth followed by successful investment and growth policies—with the major exception of the 1959–61 depression—has led to a steady and dramatic improvement in the material conditions of life. Income has increased, as have supplies of food, clothing, and shelter. Villagers increasingly can now buy sewing machines, transistor radios, chinaware, bicycles, and many other consumer goods.

Third, steps toward revenue sharing, decentralization, and local community control have given village dwellers a more immediate and participatory stake in local affairs—from reclaiming land to running schools and providing for medical care, old age, day care for children, and so on. There is great stress on action based on understanding, trust, and individual initiative at the local level of Chinese politics. In all these ways and more, the individual's experience of life does not coincide with the idea of a totalitarian state oppressing the people. Mao Tse-tung's stress on the notion "serve the people," although surely far from the whole truth, is much closer to it.

Nonetheless, this totalitarian concept of China does call our attention to at least two important features of contemporary Chinese life: the power of the state and the mobilization of the people. First, in contrast to the weak government of the past which could not defend the independence of China there is now a strong, centralized state much as in any other nation. Second, the hopes raised by successes already achieved do establish a popular basis for mobilization on behalf of particular objectives—planting trees, erecting dams, building small industries, reclaiming wastes, training militias—which is the envy of many other governments, especially when this has provided China a degree of self-sufficiency which has permitted it to avoid much of the havoc of international inflation and energy crises.

By the 1960s, with liberalization seemingly taking place in post-Stalin Russia and relations with the United States improving, a younger group of American social scientists began to change the major categories used to understand communism, and, as a by-product, China. Notions were applied which had been applied to other societies, not just enemy societies: political socialization, military modernization, pluralistic politics, psycho-history, organization theory, and so on. The virtues of these approaches over the earlier one are manifold. They permit a more rigorous and dispassionate view of Chinese events to replace the earlier demonology which knew the truth so well in advance—totalitarians, after all, were totalitarians—that it seemed unnecessary, even wasteful, to examine the data. This more formally neutral approach makes China comprehensible by interpreting it within the context of categories at one with our own experience of life: power, conflict, interest, bureaucracy, careerism, and so on.

Nevertheless, while our societies may in many ways be similar, surely it is the manner in which we differ that most attracts our interest. Yet once social science is defined by the evaluative norms of our own society's experience, then whatever does not reflect our own society may too hastily be dismissed as a mad distortion or rejection of human nature. Thus this approach tends to write off as impossible utopianism what does not harmonize with established values in the United States.

For example, the Maoist effort to downgrade individual material incentives as the carrot to induce hard work was written off as an impossible attempt "to change people" into something they are not. Yet a moment's reflection tells one that many American factories suffer from low morale, high absenteeism, rapid turnover, sabotage, and theft, whereas observers of Chinese affairs report almost unanimously that such problems do not exist in Chinese factories, which are marked by great energy and elan among workers.

These formally neutral social scientists tend to accept the most optimistic assumptions about American society as a basis for judging the Chinese. No one is an expert on everything, and perhaps it is only natural that scholars sustain ongoing prejudices in matters about which they are uninformed. Nonetheless, we should note that the prejudices tend to be consistently anti-Maoist. Because they are biased in favor of technological solutions, they denigrate these Chinese attempts to solve difficulties through social rearrangements. Such mobilization is usually written off as romanticism. Yet in such matters as combating venereal disease and drug addiction, the Chinese approach of stressing reform of habits and modes of conduct has worked, whereas the American search for technical solutions has failed, as medical specialists increasingly agree.

Yet we must emphasize the contribution of these social scientists. At a time when China was portrayed as the most dangerous nation in the world, they painstakingly gathered massive evidence to negate the false and unsubstantiated proposition that China was inherently aggressive. At the same time, they offered alternatives to the model of an alleged totalitarian China composed of inhumanity piled on irrationality.

More recently, America's military intervention in Asia, and the inability of Washington to deal successfully with problems at home, has led a new generation of scholars to a more critically receptive approach to China. These scholars found a more humane truth in sympathetic, detailed, firsthand reports by Jan Myrdal, William Hinton, Han Su-yin, and Edgar Snow which depicted the Chinese struggling to change China for the better, in contrast to the abstract and often condescending efforts of their academic colleagues.

Of course there is always a danger that an approach to China based on the discovery that America is not living up to its own promise will be based somewhat on wishful thinking. Even then, considering the established influence of anti-Chinese scholarship and teaching, which holds that there is nothing humane or worthy of emulation in China, such a new approach may be a useful antidote. But although the search for Chinese answers to American problems might be understandable—particularly given the exciting social experiments taking place in China—the differences between a predominantly semiindustrial, rural, socialist, Buddhist China and our technological, urban, capitalist, Christian society preclude mechanical borrowing in most areas. The Chinese model does, however, demand our understanding.

The new approach by critically receptive scholars has made major contributions to this understanding. Their studies have tried to help us see the Chinese people as confronting some of the most serious issues of our times: the roles of economics and ideology in society (in China, premised on egalitarian distribution, factory democracy, and so on), education for rural or culturally deprived citizens, the role of women, popular participation in all aspects of decision making, administration of the law, and others. Certainly they do not find in China perfect answers, any more than Tocqueville found in America a perfect democracy. Rather, they find that which is special and instructive in the continuing Chinese revolutionary experience, and thus they throw light on our own unstated assumptions and hitherto little-explored potentialities. The Chinese experience insists that to practice democracy genuinely, a society must deal seriously with undemocratic practices: for example, expertise which precludes knowledge of and responsiveness to popular needs; meritocracy which perpetuates inequality; and bureaucracy which obstructs the efficient implementation of popular policy. Rather than assuming, as do their formally neutral colleagues, that they are objective outsiders who can dispassionately dissect the living people of China, these receptive critics assume there is much of value to be learned by opening oneself up to the vital Chinese human project.

The Chinese people will long continue to struggle and change. Official United States relations with, and political perspectives on, China will also change. Given the rapidly changing international economic crisis, relations could swiftly change. China could become a scapegoat for U.S. problems; alternatively, its role in the early 1970s as a source for America earning foreign exchange could possibly enhance its place in the American scheme of things. Consequently, new American scholars will continually find other angles, unmask old prejudices, and reveal new truths. So far, unfortunately, two decades of America's cold war policies toward China have minimized genuine contact and mutual respect and maximized studies of "the enemy": military-industrial capacity, elite shifts, nuclear prospects, international maneuvers, and so on. It is hoped that we will learn more about these people in the future. The recent spate of eye-witness accounts—at times a bit starry-eyed—of such matters as child care in China, family planning, ecology, medical services, and the educational system suggests that real knowledge is increasing. For the present, teachers who are willing to approach existing materials critically and who are aware of their limitations and biases can still do much to guide their students wisely.

Teachers should remember that they are subject to many of the same pressures as the scholar. They can moderate the consequences of these pressures by facing up to them. In what ways were their images of China formed? What reference groups, career experiences, and value assumptions led them to prefer, and proffer to their students, only certain views about China? Perhaps in the American teacher's self-awareness lies some basis for understanding the biases of most American scholarship on China and also for a better comprehension of the lives and hopes of the Chinese people.

2. Adapting Scholarly Work to the Needs of Educators
Jonathan Spence

There is often a gap of a decade or more between the scholar's research and its reflection in the secondary school classroom. The reasons for this gap are various. Research findings are in technical or opaque language, and the most important findings often appear first in unpublished doctoral theses, in collections of conference papers, or in learned journals that are not generally available outside a few university libraries. Even if such findings appear in published monographs, these are expensive to obtain and time-consuming to read. In the field of late nineteenth- and early twentieth-century Chinese history alone, for example, nearly twenty interesting monographs were published by university presses in 1973 and 1974. Few schoolteachers, however fascinated they might be by the subject, would have the time to read such a load in the hope of improving their classroom presentations. Very few schools are in easy reach of a university library, and no school could possibly afford—nor should it try to purchase all the scholarly monographs in a given field.

The conventional textbook, moreover, is not a medium well designed to overcome this ten-year lag. The textbook writer, be he high school teacher, college professor, or professional author, is nearly always a man in a hurry. He has to be a generalist, a synthesizer, and an organizer, and he can function only by making good use of his predecessors' works. It is most unlikely that he will be able to incorporate ideas from more than a handful of exciting and newly published works in his own book. Moreover, the textbook format—a specific body of knowledge frozen between covers—means that any new and exciting material that he did not include will remain unknown to his readers until that textbook is abandoned or rewritten, at which point the process begins again!

The remedy does not lie in specifically adapting scholarly work to the needs of educators, if by "adapting" we mean simplifying. Scholarly work must be presented in the form the scholar finds most appropriate to the expression of his ideas and discoveries: this generally means a cumbersome system of notation, masses of detail, a careful bibliography, and a style of delivery that incorporates modifications and anticipates criticisms. It is hoped, of course, that scholarly work will also be readable in a broad sense, and sometimes it is, but to insist on general readability as a key criterion at the stage of initial research presentation is to overstate the argument—for the qualities of coherence, honesty, thoroughness, and analytical sophistication are all more important. Furthermore, even if every scholarly work were presented in a form and with a vocabulary that could be immediately understood by a high school junior, we would still be left with the problem of dissemination. The schools would sink under a deluge of data.

There are two interrelated areas that we must now consider: first, teaching material format; second, high school and college teacher interactions.

The textbook format is inherently inflexible, and most colleges and many secondary schools acknowledge this by assigning one textbook and adding books of supplementary readings. The books of supplementary readings—reprinted articles, condensed or annotated source materials—may often be as outdated from the scholarly point of view as the textbook itself. This does not necessarily mean that either textbook or supplements are inadequate. It means simply that they will not be at that forefront of knowledge where discoveries are being made. The student needs to have the feeling, from time to time, that he is among the pioneers, that learning is an ongoing process of discovery; if we teachers deny him that experience, we are shrinking the value of his education.

There are a great number of teachers, of course, who show immense resourcefulness and imagination in hunting up exciting material for their students, and they do not need much help from the scholar. But teachers with very limited time for a topic such as China, with restricted budgets, and perhaps also with a bored or hostile student body, could be helped greatly. Probably the most useful thing that the scholar can do for them is to draw attention to new materials that relate to matters of contemporary student concern. By this I do not mean "relevant" material as that is now understood, material drawn from the students' immediate culture and physical environment, often with a core of racial identification. I mean, rather, the selection of material from a completely different culture that nevertheless echoes our own concerns.

Specific examples will be more useful at this point than the continuation of a general discussion. Let us take some recent scholarly monographs and look at them from a high school angle. First, *The Comprador in Nineteenth Century China: Bridge between East and West*, by Hao Yen-p'ing (Cambridge: Harvard University Press, 1970), is hardly an encouraging title or topic for the schoolroom; yet from this book one could draw vivid details to show just how individual Chinese businessmen were able to build their fortunes at the expense of *and* with the connivance of their British and American "employers." As well as telling something important about Sino-Western relations and the structure of the Chinese economy in the nineteenth century, this book could lead to lively discussion about business roles in different communities, and the contrasting patterns of exploitation and adjustment among different racial groups. Similar use could be made of the sections on the seventeenth-century Dutch misunderstandings with the Chinese, which can be found in John E. Wills, Jr., *Pepper, Guns, and Parleys: The Dutch East India Company and China, 1662–1681* (Cambridge, Mass.: Harvard University Press, 1974).

Second, let us take *The City in Communist China*, edited by John W. Lewis (Stanford: Stanford University Press, 1971). At one level, this is a formidably technical book, taking a long time to read and even longer to digest. Yet within it there is a variety of data on such things as neighborhood organizations, public transport, jobs, education, and law and order, which might have a direct impact on children from an American urban ghetto background. The impact would not be in the sense of clear parallels; it would rather be in the area of shared problems and contrasting solutions (or failures).

A third example will suffice to emphasize my point: *Early Chinese Revolutionaries: Radical Intellectuals in Shanghai and Chekiang, 1902–1911*, by Mary Rankin (Cambridge: Harvard University Press, 1971), is a readable but highly technical analysis of one area of the prehistory of the 1911 Revolution. As such, few teachers would hear of it or ever think of using it. Even if they were interested in devoting a unit to the 1911 Revolution, they would be more likely to dip into a biography of Sun Yat-sen, or to read from an accepted textbook. But one of the themes in Mary Rankin's book concerns Ch'iu Chin, a revolutionary executed in 1907. The story gains particular interest from the fact that Ch'iu Chin was a woman. Case studies of women in China are extremely rare, and Ch'iu is especially fascinating: we can follow her as wife, schoolteacher, feminist, revolutionary organizer, and martyr, learning about her society and speculating on our own as we go.

And if students began to get involved in these problems of rebelliousness and "outsideness," they could follow them up by reading about a man on the run a few years after Ch'iu Chin's death—"White Wolf," who is colorfully described in Edward Friedman's *Backward Toward Revolution: The Chinese Revolutionary Party* (Berkeley: University of California Press, 1974).

Consideration of Rankin's and Friedman's books leads to another area in which the scholar has access to information, namely the specialized research conference. Thus an earlier version of Mary Rankin's account of Ch'iu Chin and other analyses of the Ch'ing fall appear in a book composed of the expanded and edited papers of a conference held in 1965: Mary C. Wright, ed., *China in Revolution: The First Phase, 1900–1913* (New Haven: Yale University Press, 1968). Behind the research papers for such a conference there often lies a Ph.D. thesis or an extended paper written for some research seminar. Thus the alert and well-informed scholar is often aware of vast amounts of intriguing research long before it reaches the scholarly community as a whole, let alone the general reader. The teacher, too, could profit by being alert to such uncommon sources.

It is easy enough to describe this situation, but it is extremely hard to know what to do about it. Here are some possible options:

1. Scholarly material can be systematically scoured by people who understand the problems of secondary education. (Who these people are, how they might be funded, and where their time would come from are all problems awaiting solutions!)

2. Since secondary schools are in no way homogeneous, and have totally different needs, the teachers should have some way of making their desires known to the people doing the scouring.

3. Those with a common interest in Chinese studies who teach at different levels should have a common medium of communication (along the lines of *Focus on Asian Studies*, edited by Franklin Buchanan—see chapter 7); perhaps a quarterly periodical devoted both to research and to curriculum should be established. Such a periodical should have a large correspondence section for exchange of views and sharing of problems.

4. Means of making new material rapidly available are needed. The answer might be to use pamphlets that could be accumulated and indexed, or clusters of pages that could be adapted to

different lesson plans.

5. Informal communication between university and school should be encouraged. The Association for Asian Studies already has its Committee on Secondary Education and its panels on curriculum. Such contacts should be extended to urban areas to supplement the annual national conferences. This would ideally lead to a continuing dialogue in which scholarly work would come out into the open, as it were, and confront the opportunities and challenges of the crowded classroom.

3. Teaching about China in the Classroom: What We Look for beyond Seeing

David L. Weitzman

To write an essay on teaching about China in the classroom at first appears deceptively simple. We have, after all, become quite sophisticated on the subject of Asia. Such an assignment, then, seems to call for a guide to materials, or a list of key topics in Chinese history around which a course might be built, or an analysis of ways to organize the course much like the middle game in chess. Although these are certainly vital concerns, they are not central. None has yet caused any significant improvement in the teaching of Asian studies, because they simply miss the point: emphasis must be placed on improving the quality of our *teaching*.

Teachers teaching about China are part of, and inseparable from, the larger problem of teachers teaching about anything. Teacher selection and training, instructional strategies, and materials can no longer be treated as discrete concerns. Materials are as effective as the teachers who manipulate them, and teachers are only as effective as their training and experience make them. Because most publishers design instructional materials to complement rather than develop and improve teacher skills, something of a cycle endures, and the problem becomes one of deciding at which point we can most effectively intervene. Although this cycle demands that we consider these issues simultaneously, a difficult task at best, we will have to deal sequentially with synchronous ideas. Our concern, then, should be: (1) materials and what they have revealed about (2) the teacher, whose immediate problem will be (3) the focus of a course designed to accomplish nothing less than reconditioning high school teachers and students to accept the unity of the human experience—specifically, the place of Asians in the history of mankind.

At first the state of Asian studies in the schools was attributed to a paucity of readable materials and the inadequacy of the few materials then available. There were a few paperbacks on Chinese poetry and philosophy, but our first interest in China—like our first interest in the Soviet Union a decade earlier—was political. While authors debated the fine points of Maoist strategy (is he a Marxist Chinese or a Chinese Marxist?), whole areas of Chinese accomplishment in literature, the arts, music, poetry, philosophy, and government were ignored.

But this was soon to change. The paperback revolution discovered China in the mid-sixties, and each weekly or even daily visit to the bookshop was rewarded by the appearance of a brightly colored new volume or, more accurately, a reprint of an earlier book. The teacher's dilemma became one of having too many books to read and evaluate for classroom use. To meet this delightful problem, there appeared bibliographies and resource guides from groups such as the Asia Society, the American Society for Eastern Arts, the National Committee on United States–China Relations, libraries, museums, and most notably the Asian Studies Project at Ohio State University, now the Service Center for Teachers of Asian Studies (see chapter 8). This last-mentioned name change reflects the most recent (March 1971) and potentially most significant development in Asian studies, the acknowledgment by the Association for Asian Studies of their responsibility to teachers.

More recently, the challenge of developing classroom materials for high school readers has been met, though by no means mastered. Although publishers are turning out more materials on Asia, most of these are supplementary (a revealing word in the school vocabulary) and not only fail to reflect recent developments in social science teaching strategies, but more closely resemble materials produced twenty years ago in their tired, dull format and style. An exception is the Asian Studies Inquiry Program, which emerged from the USOE-financed Asian Studies Curriculum Project at the University of California, Berkeley (these units are reviewed in part 2). Based on the inquiry mode of teaching and using primary historical sources, this program was an important beginning and should point the way for further developments in classroom materials.

These were some of the first tentative answers to classroom problems, but like most solutions, they revealed problems even more complex. The books, the resource guides and bibliographies, and the new classroom materials were, by the late sixties, as good as if not better than any other high school materials; yet the quality of classroom instruction remained largely unchanged. An inflexible teacher, uncomfortable among the ambiguities of the modern social studies class, will not be fundamentally affected by a few course outlines, books, or teaching materials. As similar efforts in developing and testing materials in other fields such as biology, mathematics, and anthropology have shown, the key to better instruction is not materials, but *the teacher*.

Preparation of high school teachers for Asian studies has been considered basically an intellectual problem. Preparing teachers, it is thought, is simply a matter of exposing them to university courses on Asia and encouraging them to read. It was to this end that Asian scholars proposed, organized, and conducted summer institutes for secondary school teachers. The approach of these institutes has been almost entirely intellectual, little attempt being made to deal with the participant's inherent resistance to things Asian, or to anticipate predictable conflicts in values. This is not to condemn these institutes; to the contrary, they are remarkable institutions in the history of American public education and one of the too few examples of cooperation between professors and teachers. I mention them now because they suggest a lesson unlearned and an essential priority in the planning of future programs for teachers. I know of no program to date designed to deal with the teacher's state of mind, though it is well within our experience and ability to do so.

Preparing to teach about Asia includes coming to grips with this "state of mind," a term deliberately chosen because it transcends intellectuality. It is a fragile, unpredictable, very human thing almost entirely the product of our environment, conditioned by everything with which we come in contact. Unfortunately, it can also be conditioned by what it does *not* know, what it has not contacted. This is what happens when the mind must deal with things beyond its experience; for example, Asian thought and values. If we want to know why, even in the educated and analytical mind, conflict, defensiveness, and resistance are aroused by ideologies antithetical to its own, the answer lies not in the intellect.

The first task for teachers of Asian studies, then, is to deal with their Westernness, that part of them deep inside which, while allowing them to pursue with excitement and considerable intellectual commitment their interest in China, prevents them from absorbing or being absorbed by Asian thought and feelings. What is essential to this task is to understand how one acquires beliefs and values, and develops affinities for some ideologies while rejecting others.

To begin, beliefs and ideologies often have little to do with reality. The acquisition of ideologies is largely an accidental and irrational process, and the implications of this for the teaching of Asian studies are enormous. Once we accept the fact that values and beliefs are not immutable, that people can and have adapted to ideas and values very different from those with which their lives began, we realize how fortuitous differences in humanity really are. It is the accident of birth, and little more, that determines what one believes, whether one is a Christian or a Buddhist, a capitalist or a communist, a painter in oils on canvas or a painter in ink on silk. If you happen to be born in the United States, you will, more than likely, eat with knife and fork, acquire a deep commitment to ideas of individualism, and be moved by harmonies of twelve tones. Born in China a century ago, however, you would pick up your food with *k'aui tzu* and accept without question the Five Relationships and the sounds of the pentatonic scale.

Our view of history too is irrational, and the effects of this reach far beyond the classroom. Student reaction on hearing the Chinese concept of the "Middle Kingdom" is often one of mild amusement; yet there is little doubt where our own country lies in the American scheme of history. Professor Reischauer's imaginary schoolboy view of world history in the introduction to this volume describes a state of mind that has caused vibrations across the world that are far from imaginary. In this day of optimism and promise for United States–China relations, it would be well for teachers and students to be aware of the effect that our ethnocentrism has had on the Chinese, who view it with something less than amusement. Unfortunately, ethnocentrism affects not only the way we think about people but also how we behave toward them. The modern Chinese historian Liu Ta-nien makes very clear the violence done to both peoples by such a view of history in the angry comments that open his essay, "How to Appraise the History of Asia":

Histories of Asia, of the East, and of the various Asian countries written by such Western bourgeois scholars usually propagandize two concepts. Firstly, that Asia has been "bar-

barous," "backward," "immoral," and "uncivilized" in all its ages. Secondly, that the progress and civilization of Asia in modern times have been favours generously bestowed on her by the West. Deliberately distorting Chinese history in the U.S. White Paper of 1949, Dean Acheson, the former U.S. Secretary of State wrote: "Then in the middle of the 19th century the heretofore impervious wall of Chinese isolation was breached by the West. These outsiders brought with them aggressiveness, the unparalleled development of Western technology, and a higher order of culture which had not accompanied previous foreign incursions into China." . . . Did the West brutally invade Asia? This is not, apparently, what happened; the West "brought . . . a high order of culture" with it to bestow on Asia.[1]

Teachers about to prepare for teaching Asian studies could profitably read this and similar essays by modern Chinese historians and, through reflection, learn about their own values. Acquiring some perspective about our beliefs does not mean we need to reject them; it does, however, allow us to step away from them momentarily, to hold them up alongside Chinese values, and to see where they diverge and where they touch, where they interfere and where they reinforce each other. It is as if you were a third person, viewing the interaction of your own values and those of a Chinese. Understanding China intellectually is not difficult in this age of instant information; behaving with understanding, and developing this ability in students, is the beginning of an Asian course of immeasurable value.

The focus of such a course would be people. The current process of isolating Asians from our curriculum and our world view has developed into a subtle psychological device of dehumanization. Social science courses which emphasize events, abstract ideas, and generalizations about people, indeed about entire nations, are dehumanizing in that they teach students to see people only as adjuncts to, or agents of, changing events. In this way, social science teachers and writers may be said to have created a new grammatical form—the transitive noun. Here are some examples:

1. Liu Ta-nien, "How to Appraise the History of Asia," in *History in Communist China*, ed. Albert Feuerwerker (Cambridge, Mass.: MIT Press, 1968), pp. 356–57; originally printed in the *Peking Review*, no. 45, 5 November 1965.

Teaching about China

Tung Ch'i-ch'ang created a new style of painting.
Nationalist armies, led by Chiang Kai-shek, moved southward.
This poem was written by Li Po.

Notice some characteristics of the transitive noun. It may appear at the beginning, in the middle, or at the end of a sentence. Sometimes transitive nouns are found under old, scratchy photographs and, sprinkled about the page, they explain how paintings got painted, who led armies, and who expounded this or that philosophy. I have even seen transitive nouns behind red arrows sweeping across a map of some military campaign. Most transitive nouns are followed by numbers in parentheses— "Sun Yat-sen (1867–1925)"—to show when they began and when they ceased to be transitive. Transitive nouns, unlike adjectives and verbs, have no moods, no feelings, no color or personality, no movement.

Asians, reduced to abstractions and dehumanized, cannot possibly be understood. But Asians presented as humans can become part of our experience. The motives which impelled a Chinese painter, poet, or writer to express himself with his brush are reflected in his work, and human nature being essentially the same the world over, there is no reason why an American cannot infer something of the man behind a scroll, a short story, or a ceramic figure.

If our concern is people, then let them appear as real people with motivations, emotions, ambitions, and a sense of purpose to their lives. The dehumanized figure in the history text, known to the student only as a name, is a mask behind which some puppetlike figure lurks without revealing anything of its substance. Mao Tse-tung is a name; pictured standing with his hand raised before an adulating crowd, he acquires a face; but he comes alive in the student's mind with his remarks to Edgar Snow: "My father had two years of schooling and he could read enough to keep books. My mother was wholly illiterate. Both were from peasant families. I was the family scholar. I knew the classics but disliked them. What I enjoyed were the romances of old China, and especially stories of rebellions. I used to read them in school, covering them up with a Classic when the teacher walked past. So also did most of my classmates." I have seen knowing smiles move across students' faces as they read this, and there were few among them who could not in that moment relate to the leader of the world's most populous nation. Mao the abstraction had become Mao the man. For this effect alone the passage would be a valuable source, but for the observant, alert teacher it has much greater meaning. In these few words students can discover a clue to the fate of China's last dynasty and of Confucianism, and begin to see the subtle changes in Chinese life, a process which Joseph R. Levenson called "the making of an anachronism."

One step toward understanding Asians, then, is to let them speak for themselves, whenever possible using materials in translation. Teachers of Asian studies should be skilled in the use of historical materials, all kinds of historical materials: dynastic histories, biographies, letters, diaries, imperial decrees, and also poems, novels, short stories, woodcuts, paintings, and sculpture. The official histories of China, produced by court historians, are capital-centered and elitist, just as is most of the painting. But the romances enjoyed by young Mao and his classmates, and ceramic figures of people, houses, buildings, animals, vehicles, and implements provide vivid images of everyday life in ancient China. These, combined with novels, anthologies of literature, and biographies, many well within the reading and comprehension level of secondary students, could be the substance of an exciting Asian experience.

An example of one of these experiences is provided by a short poem. Students should be given the opportunity to obtain information for themselves from a historical source and should be encouraged to speculate on ideas not evident in the text. There are, for example, several good books describing life in early China, but not even the best of the expository histories holds the vividness of these lines from the *Shih Ching, Book of Songs,* compiled around 600 B.C.[2]

In the seventh month the Fire ebbs;
In the ninth month I hand out the coats.
In the days of the First, sharp frosts;
In the days of the Second, keen winds.
Without coats, without serge,
How should they finish the year?
In the days of the Third they plough;
In the days of the Fourth out I step

2. Cyril Birch, *Anthology of Chinese Literature* (New York: Grove Press, 1965), pp. 24–26.

Teaching about China

With my wife and children,
Bringing hampers to the southern acre
Where the field-hands come to take good cheer.

In the seventh month, the Fire ebbs;
In the ninth month I hand out the coats.
But when the spring days grow warm
And the oriole sings
The girls take their deep baskets
And follow the path under the wall
To gather the soft mulberry-leaves;
The spring days are drawing out:
They gather the white aster in crowds.
A girl's heart is sick and sad
Till with her lord she can go home.

In the seventh month the Fire ebbs;
In the eigth month they pluck the rushes,
In the silk-worm month they gather the mulberry-leaves,
Take that chopper and bill
To lap the far boughs and high,
Pull towards them the tender leaves.
In the seventh month the shrike cries;
In the eighth month they twist thread,
The black thread and the yellow:
"With my red dye so bright
I make a robe for my lord."

In the fourth month the milkwort in spike,
In the fifth month the cicada cries.
In the eighth month the harvest is gathered,
In the tenth month the boughs fall.
In the days of the First we hunt the raccoon,
And take these foxes and wild-cats
To make furs for our lord.
In the days of the Second is the great Meet;
Practice for deeds of war.
The one-year-old boar we keep;
The three-year-old we offer to our lord.

In the fifth month the locust moves its leg.
In the sixth month grasshopper shakes its wing,

Teaching about China   *21*

In the seventh month, out in the wilds;
In the eighth month, in the farm,
In the ninth month, at the door.
In the tenth month the cricket goes under my bed.
I stop up every hole to smoke out the rats.
Plugging the windows, burying the doors;
"Come, wife and children,
The change of the year is at hand.
Come and live in this house."

In the sixth month we eat wild plums and cherries,
In the seventh month we boil mallows and beans.
In the eighth month we dry the dates,
In the tenth month we take the rice
To make with it the spring wine,
So that we may be granted long life.
In the seventh month we eat melons,
In the eighth month we cut the gourds,
In the ninth month we take the seeding hemp.
We gather bitter herbs, we cut the ailanto for firewood,
That our husbandmen may eat.

In the ninth month we make ready the stack-yards,
In the tenth month we bring in the harvest,
Millet for wine, millet for cooking, the early and the late,
Paddy and hemp, beans and wheat.
Come, my husbandmen,
My harvesting is over,
Go up and begin your work in the house,
In the morning gather thatch-reeds,
In the evening twist rope;
Go quickly on to the roofs.
Soon you will be beginning to sow your many grains.

In the days of the Second they cut the ice with tingling blows;
In the days of the Third they bring it into the cold shed.
In the days of the Fourth very early
They offer lambs and garlic.
In the ninth month are shrewd frosts:
In the tenth month they clear the stack-grounds.
With twin pitchers they hold the village feast,

Killing for it a young lamb.
Up they go into their lord's hall,
Raise the drinking cup of buffalo-horn:
"Hurray for our lord, may he live for ever and ever!"

After reading the poem, the first step is to stimulate a dialogue between the students and the source. Teachers can help students develop this skill by asking questions of the source for them to answer. Students can then work alone or in small groups to develop their own dialogue with the poem. The teacher might begin with a few questions which require students to search for answers: Describe a typical peasant meal. Can you list the steps in silk production? What crops did the people of this village grow? What kinds of implements did they have? From these simple data-gathering questions, students can progress to questions that require synthesizing several bits of information into an idea not explicit in the poem: Can you describe the organization of this village? Compare the roles of men and women. How were the labors and responsibilities of the villagers divided? Can you draw a picture of a Chinese house? How was the village governed? The amount of information that can be drawn from this one poem is virtually unlimited, and students usually accept the challenge with considerable excitement. On their own, many students go on to extract information about farming methods, climate, family structure, religious practices, marriage customs, and even the social background of the writer.

Later, after many experiences like this, students will no longer need someone else to interpret the Asian mind for them, for they will be more at one with it. And the teacher will begin to realize, as did Lao Tzu, that

A leader [Teacher] is best
When people barely know that he exists,
Not so good when people obey and acclaim him,
Worst when they despise him.
"Fail to honor people,
They fail to honor you."[3]

3. Witter Bynner, trans., *The Way of Life* (New York: Capricorn Books, 1962), © 1962 by G. P. Putnam's Sons, pp. 34–45.

Part Two: Materials on China

4. Curriculum Units

1. INTRODUCTION

As was emphasized in the essays that open this volume, classroom instruction about societies with different political and economic systems raises many difficult problems of method and content. This is especially true in the case of China, where social studies teachers may find little to satisfy them in conventional textbooks. These, as Jonathan Spence notes, tend to be specific bodies of knowledge frozen between two covers. In addition, texts on world history often make only passing mention of China and usually introduce the Far East through India and Japan. Texts which do discuss China at some length—usually written by nonspecialists—have generally revealed two serious shortcomings: errors of fact or misrepresentation, and a rather ethnocentric viewpoint. It will take time to revise these texts; until this is done, the responsibility for better instruction will continue to fall primarily on the informed teacher.

Fortunately, to help teachers look beyond the textbooks, special curriculum units have been developed to explore particular areas of the world in greater depth. Through commercial publishers and federally financed projects, a number of curriculum units on China have been produced in the past few years. A curriculum unit generally consists of two manuals: the student's manual, which includes selected primary sources, a general expository text, or both; and the teacher's manual, which attempts to provide the nonspecialist with extra background information and suggestions. A unit differs from a text in that it is shorter (designed for use as part of a larger course), tends to focus on one main problem, and is often flexible enough to be used in several different courses. It may include bibliographies, teaching games, project guidelines, and so on, and occasionally may be accompanied by filmstrips and recording tapes.

This chapter is designed to assist teachers in selecting and interpreting curriculum units. General textbooks that present China as part of a larger world area are not reviewed or listed. Sorely needed textbook evaluation projects in this area are underway, however, and those interested should write directly to the following: The Asia Society (112 East 64th Street, New York, New York 10021); Bay Area China Education Project (P.O. Box 2373, Stanford, California 94305); Texas Field Staff of the National Committee on U.S.-China Relations (Center for Asian Studies, University of Texas, Austin, Texas 78712); Project on Asian Studies, (300 Lane Hall, University of Michigan, Ann Arbor, Michigan 48104). In addition, a number of resource centers listed in chapter VIII can be of assistance.

The units selected are readily available, specially designed for teaching about China, and in most cases already widely in use. The names of the publishers have been listed, and addresses for complete ordering information can be found in the Appendix. The information under "Author's Professional Background" is accurate as of the time of publication of the unit.

As our evaluators have noted, the reader will discover in some units a rather narrow approach to traditional China, often coupled with a parochial political perspective on modern China. In both cases, the effect, perhaps unintentionally, is to reinforce old stereotypes rather than to educate students to better understand and interpret the history, culture, and recent development of Chinese society. Some authors have evaluated China in terms of Western social experience, often drawing idealized pictures. This more subtle, but important, problem is treated by David Weitzman in his essay.

The judgments and evaluations in this section represent the considered views of several people, and are based on an assessment of the reliability and relative objectivity of the materials—no comprehensive attempt has been made to evaluate units on pedagogical grounds. Special thanks are due to Richard Kagan, Karen Burke, Richard Sorich, Janet Cady, and Francy Hays.

Units particularly recommended are marked with a ●.

2. MAJOR CURRICULUM UNITS

● *Asian Studies Inquiry Program*
John U. Michaelis and Robin J. McKeown, coordinators
Field Educational Publications, 1969
Distributed by: Addison-Wesley, Inc.

The series, which resulted from the federally financed Asian Studies Curriculum Project at the University of California, Berkeley, consists of twelve units. The units, identified by †, are reviewed on the following pages.

Teaching Approach and General Evaluation. The teaching approach common to all these units is the inquiry method. This method seeks to guide students to the following five objectives: a basic knowlege of Asian cultural patterns; a joint awareness of universal issues and the rich variety of Asian experiences; an empathetic understanding (by judging human behavior from another perspective); the development of inquiry skills; and the development of positive attitudes toward Asia and Asians.

The individual units, which are relatively short (50–64 pages), consist of a selection of readings by actual observers of the events and experiences described rather than the single perspective of a scholar-synthesizer. The readings are linked with short explanatory paragraphs; there is no long, descriptive text. The units are therefore an effective departure from both the standard text and the traditional curriculum unit.

The units fall within three general clusters: Asian Thought; Changing Patterns of Asian Life; and Traditional Patterns of Asian Life. A teacher's manual which accompanies each cluster explains the appropriate method of teaching and also contains suggested questions and activities for each unit.

The units demand a high degree of involvement from both teacher and student. Since they are largely self-teaching, their value depends strictly upon the limits and potentials of the inquiry approach itself. This implies meaningful interpretation and analysis of how the readings actually relate to the larger Chinese society; the historical process is left to (unguided) deduction. Unless a teacher is willing to do adequate background reading and lead the class in a spirit of free inquiry, the units may not achieve their full educational potential.

Yet even in themselves the readings are valuable. The limitations of these units (including lack of maps and transitional readings) are far outweighed by their exciting potentials. The inquiry approach seems closer than any other to generating empathetic understanding and avoiding, in David Weitzman's words, reliance on the "transitive noun." The units rarely reinforce the stereotypes which creep into the standard units and textbooks dealing with China.

† *Buddhism*
Everett B. Johnson, Jr.
Field Educational Publications, 1969, 64 pp.
Price: $13.88 for 10

Author's Professional Background. Everett B. Johnson, Jr., is a history teacher at Oakland High School, Oakland, California.

Scope and Emphasis. Buddhism is presented both as a general set of beliefs about human existence and as a worldly religion which has adapted to the individual cultures of Asia. The unit is introduced by an interview with a Thai monk who explains his style of life as well as his beliefs. The religion is then placed in historial perspective through a biographical sketch of the Buddha and an explanation of the Four Noble Truths. An excellent discussion of the differences between Hinayana (basically Southeast Asian) and Mahayana (Northeast Asian) Buddhism introduces the last two-thirds of the book which explains the various paths taken to achieve enlightenment, from monks in Saigon to an American Zen initiate.

This unit, which contains twenty-four photographs, has only a two-paragraph story and one Chinese landscape painting to remind us that Buddhism is also part of the Chinese tradition. The readings are linked together with one-paragraph transitions.

Unit Evaluation. The editor has presented a generally successful, but occasionally confusing blend of the basic tenets of Buddhism and its particular national adaptations. Perhaps there is an overemphasis on Zen, but the selections chosen (Haiku, Zen riddles, and so on) are likely to be of great interest to students.

The general approach is excellent, though often not fully exploited; concepts such as "karma" and "nirvana" probably deserve more discussion, since they are among the elements of Buddhism most alien to Western religious ideas. Chinese Buddhism might have been presented at somewhat greater length. The Chinese contemporary criticism of Buddhism for its emphasis on otherworldliness, superstition, and organizational autonomy would help illuminate some of the features of Chinese society as well as highlight the religion's evolution into Ch'an (later Japanese Zen) with its emphasis on this-worldliness.

Outstanding Contributions. The variety of means employed by the author to express the elements of Buddhism provide one of the best expositions of these principles available. The Zen selections and the opening interview with a Thai monk particularly stand out for giving one a feeling for the actual working Buddhist values in Asian life.

Contents. 1. "Happiness Is My Duty"; 2. Life of Buddha; 3. The Four Noble Truths; 4. Mahayana and Theravada; 5. Buddhists in Saigon; 6. An Introduction to Zen; 7. Life in a Zen Monastery; 8. The Satori of Mrs. L. T. S.; 9. Zen Stories; 10. Haiku; 11. "Me and Mine"; Conclusions; Suggested Readings

† *China and the United States*
David L. Weitzman
Field Educational Publications, 1969, 64 pp.
Price: $13.88 for 10

Author's Professional Background. David L. Weitzman is Social Studies Department chairman at Oakland Technical High School in Oakland, California, a demonstration secondary school of the University of California, Berkeley.

Scope and Emphasis. "When you think of China, what comes to your mind?" (p. 7). This is the question the unit seeks to explore in historical context, and the readings help us see perceptions which often had little to do with Chinese reality.

The readings begin with an account of the first American ship to land in Canton in 1784. Crew members of this ship returned home with an image of quaint Chinese and a fat profit—twin lures which continued to shape the interaction between the two countries to the present day. Further readings tell of commerce (from opium to "coolie cargoes") and of American impressions of the Chinese who came to this country ("Gentle, Inoffensive Chinese" and "Chink, Chink, Chinaman").

The period from 1900 to 1940 is omitted; the unit continues with the postwar period and our involvement in the Korean War. The readings conclude with an essay on our tendency to dehumanize international relations, and an implicit plea for us to understand the Chinese as fellow human beings, on their own terms.

Unit Evaluation. The section on the nineteenth century is particularly well presented, and all the selections are open-minded and sensitive. Through a well-chosen group of readings, many of the images and realities from the American point of view are presented. The selections on the McCarthy period and on U.S.-China relations in the 1950s are especially provocative and interesting. (It may be argued, however, that a single speech by Harry Truman to explain the Korean War is as inadequate as one speech by Lyndon Johnson about Vietnam.)

Criticism of the unit can be restricted largely to its omissions, notably the lack of readings for the period 1900-1940. Perhaps more important, there are no readings to help us understand the other side of a relationship which after all was not one-dimensional; *Chinese* expectations and misperceptions also contributed to the lack of intelligent interaction. It was these combined misperceptions which often led to unpleasant reality.

Outstanding Contributions. The readings are vivid and unusually interesting, and the unit breaks new ground by confronting unpleasant but real pages of the past. The unit is especially effective in dealing with the influences which shaped American views of China (e.g., trade and missionary activities).

Contents. 1. China Ho!; 2. White Sails and Black Gold; 3. "The Way of Heaven Is Fairness to All"; 4. A Mission of Faith; 5. Coolie Cargoes; 6. "The Gentle, Inoffensive Chinese"; 7. "Chink, Chink, Chinaman . . . "; 8. Expel the Foreign Bandits; 9. The Open-door Policy Reaffirmed; 11. Death in the Snow; 12. Fallen Heroes; 13. China Crosses the Yalu; 14. Hysteria; 15. The Formosa Question; 16. Soy Sauce and Prawns; 17. Human Nature and International Relations; Conclusions; Suggested Readings

† *Chinese Painting*
David L. Weitzman
Field Educational Publications, 1969, 48 pp.
Price: $13.88 for 10

Author's Professional Background. David L. Weitzman is Social Studies Department chairman at Oakland Technical High School in Oakland, California, a demonstration secondary school of the University of California, Berkeley.

Scope and Emphasis. "Painting," the author says in his introduction, "is recorded history." For Western art, this may be an exaggeration, but for China it is nearer the truth. Chinese painting is closely connected with all the other arts: poetry, fiction, calligraphy, and even the art of ruling.

The author surveys traditional Chinese painting, emphasizing landscapes. He attempts to take the student beyond first impressions to an "understanding and appreciation for the aesthetic, philosophical, and religious values of Chinese society through the medium of painting." Readings are included which contrast Eastern and Western styles, and explicate on "the Way" of painting, the language of painting, and its instruments and techniques.

The unit contains ten readings, and has three photos and seven illustrations which considerably enhance the text.

Unit Evaluation. The contrastive approach which the unit takes to Chinese and Western art is singularly effective, and the readings are well chosen. Superb illustrations serve to demonstrate points of mutual influence; e.g., the ram painted in the fourteenth century in China by Chao Meng-fu and the ram painted by Picasso in this century.

The section which deals with the ideas and values behind Chinese painting tends to be abstract and may prove difficult for lower-level high school students. Moreover, the brevity of the unit forces the author to gloss over other cultural factors which influenced Chinese painting (e.g., Buddhism, Taoism, and Confucianism). The impression is also given that Chinese art has been in a "static state." Actually, Chinese painting went through many phases, and the refinements of one school were endless. We are also left wondering what happened to Chinese art in this century, and particularly its role in the People's Republic.

The last section, "Instruments and Techniques of Painting," has a valuable reading on calligraphy and its relationship to painting.

Outstanding Contributions. By focusing in detail on aspects of Chinese landscape painting, the editor takes us "behind" the works of art to examine the perceptual framework of the Chinese artist—how he sees the world, and what it is that represents beauty. Relating this to familiar Western forms helps the student question his exclusive reliance on Western standards of beauty and art.

Contents. Introduction; East and West: Contrasts and Parallels (1. Ling to A.D.; 2. China Anticipates Modern Europe; 3. They All Look Alike to Me); The Way of Painting (4. On Tao and the Tao; 5. The Painter Views Nature; 6. Comments on Landscape); The Language of Painting (7. Fundamentals of Painting; 8. The Artist's Choice of Materials); Instruments and Techniques of Painting (9. The Four Treasures; 10. Chinese Calligraphy); Conclusions; Suggested Readings

† *Chinese Popular Fiction*
David L. Weitzman
Field Educational Publications, 1969, 64 pp.
Price: $13.88 for 10

Author's Professional Background. David L. Weitzman is Social Studies Department chairman at Oakland Technical High School in Oakland, California, a demonstration secondary school of the University of California, Berkeley.

Scope and Emphasis. This unit presents eight selections from Chinese popular literature chosen not only because of their intrinsic interest and insight into Chinese culture and history, but also because they illustrate the common thread of humanity underlying all cultures. Because of his excellent choice of selections, the author generally succeeds in his goals.

The clear division between classical novels, the modern literary revolution, and communist fiction accurately reflects the major trends in the history of Chinese popular fiction. Notes in the text introduce extraneous characters who appear and explain some of the technical terms. A brief introduction to each reading outlines its historical and literary significance (the three individual sections of the book have longer, one-page introductions which are particularly helpful). The introduction to Chinese communist literature, for example, traces its roots and importance back to the Yenan Forum (1942) and presents a short, balanced account of the role of fiction in the service of the Chinese revolution.

Unit Evaluation. The selections represent the best of Chinese literature, especially those from the older classics and the writings of the twentieth-century writer. The analytical prefaces tie the readings to the larger historical events that surrounded them, and the writings themselves reflect the basic social and political concerns of their authors (especially those of the literary revolution period).

One could have wished for a clearer separation of the dual historical trends of Chinese literature: court and popular literature. Popular literature was often classified as subversive, and was one dividing line between ruled and rulers. This was the background for the literary reform movement which began in the late nineteenth century and crescendoed in the first decades of this century. The author could have better explained the larger social aims behind literary reform—the desire to be relevant to and reach the common people (e.g., the argument over the writing of literature in the vernacular, *pai-hua*, instead of the classical language) in order to mobilize them against the old traditions for the cause of modernizing China.

Although he does not adequately explain this background, the author does note why Mao's appeal to many intellectuals was effective even though they were asked to serve in highly structured and totalitarian ways. The author might well have explained the importance of literary dissent in China, and placed greater emphasis on the link between literature and the social-political concerns of the Communist leadership.

Outstanding Contributions. The book gives students a unique sense of the change and variety in Chinese culture, and thus, like few other units, challenges the common view of China as a monolithic, static, Confucian entity.

Contents. Introduction; Classical Novels (1. Romance of the Three Kingdoms; 2. The Water Margin; 3. Dream of the Red Chamber); The Literary Revolution (4. Call to Arms, Preface; 5. Medicine; 6. The Family); Communist Fiction (7. A National, Scientific, and Mass Culture; 8. Wheelbarrows); Conclusions; Suggested Readings

† *Confucianism and Taoism*

A. Jeff Tudisco
Field Educational Publications, 1969, 64 pp.
Price: $13.88 for 10

Author's Professional Background. A. Jeff Tudisco is Social Studies Department chairman at Berkeley High School, Berkeley, California.

Scope and Emphasis. This unit presents traditional Chinese thought through excerpts from the works of Confucius and Lao-Tzu, whose ideas became the major themes of traditional Chinese philosophy. The unit contains seventeen readings which directly contrast these two philosophers' views on government, human conduct, learning, war, and the arts. Eighteen excellent illustrations complement the text.

Unit Evaluation. The author correctly notes that Confucianism and Taoism were the dominating philosophies of traditional China, but does a disservice by not giving even passing mention to other strains of thought: specifically Legalism, which played a crucial role in the development of Chinese political theory as well as Maoist ideology, and Buddhism, which had a powerful impact on the evolution of Confucianism as well as on the religious practices of the common man. Similarly, later developments in Confucianism and Taoism are not mentioned, leaving the overall impression that these philosophies remained unchanged. Chinese philosophy, like philosophy everywhere, was not a fixed entity; it was constantly adapting to changes in the environment.

Beyond the treatment of the civil examination system, the book might have tried to systematically relate Confucianism and Taoism to social institutions. This problem becomes serious when one considers the ultimate fate of these philosophies. The author implies that they abruptly changed in 1949, whereas in actuality the decay of traditional philosophy was closely connected with general social decay and unrest in China during the past several centuries, going through its "last stand" in the mid-1800s. The questions of how and why this happened are not raised.

These criticisms, however, are a function of the brevity of the unit, and the teacher will have a difficult time finding a better or more concise description of Confucianism and Taoism.

Oustanding Contributions. In capturing two of the basic elements of Chinese philosophy, these well-chosen passages from the philosophers themselves give the student an opportunity to test his own views against theirs on such matters as government, the family, war, and the arts.

Contents. Introduction; On Government (1. Virtue and Leadership; 2. The Sparrow and the Phoenix; 3. Division of Labor and Social Stratification; 4. Govern the State with Correctness; 5. Horses' Hoofs); On Human Conduct (6. Filial Piety; 7. The Meaning of Jen; 8. To Yield Is to Be Preserved Whole; 9. The Tale of Chi'ienniang); On Learning (10. Education; 11. A Palace Examination; 12. Abandon Learning; 13. Do-Nothing Say Nothing); On War (14. Soldiering Is Our Lot; 15. The Strong and the Great Are Inferior); Confucian and Taoist Impacts on the Arts (16. Confucian Elements in Painting; 17. Taoist Attitudes in Painting and Poetry); Conclusions; Suggested Readings

† *Cultural Patterns in Asian Life*
Everett B. Johnson, Jr.
Field Educational Publications, 1969, 64 pp.
Price: $13.88 for 10

Author's Professional Background. Everett B. Johnson, Jr., is a history teacher at Oakland High School in Oakland, California.

Scope and Emphasis. This unit offers readings on Asian philosophy, religion, government, family life, education, and so on, in order to impart general knowledge about Asian customs, and to develop in the student an understanding of ethnocentrism.

There are only three readings on China, however, and these deal with burial customs (very briefly), religion and ancestor worship, and class structure. Each of these readings contrasts American and Chinese attitudes.

Unit Evaluation. Although the author does a good job in illustrating the variety of Asian cultural patterns he shows little about China, which, after all, had a considerable influence on other Asian societies. Moreover, the effectiveness of his presentation is limited by taking all three of the readings on China from one book (Francis L. K. Hsu, *Americans and Chinese*). While Hsu has a knack of explaining some of the apparently more exotic aspects of traditional Chinese culture in understandable terms, he provides only one man's viewpoint (e.g., his discussion of social class). Hsu clearly is discussing *traditional* Chinese culture; there is not a word on the contributions—or alterations—made by the Communist government. The result, at least in the case of China, is to present almost as misleading an impression as that he seeks to dispel.

Outstanding Contributions. The readings about China provide a good basis for comparison with American customs, allowing the student to approach Chinese traditional culture by relating it consistently to his own familiar environment. The reading on Chinese religion is especially useful in answering the generally elusive question "What is the religion of China?" (at least for the pre-1949 period).

Contents. Introduction; 3. Two Ways of Life; 7. The Chinese Way in Religion; 9. Class; Conclusions; Suggested Readings

† *East Meets West*
David L. Weitzman
Field Educational Publications, 1969, 64 pp.
Price: $13.88 for 10

Author's Professional Background. David L. Weitzman is Social Studies Department chairman at Oakland Technical High School in Oakland, California, a demonstration secondary school of the University of California, Berkeley.

Scope and Emphasis. This compilation, which covers the period before 1900, deals with the initial contacts—and collisions— between Westerners and both Chinese and Japanese. The book emphasizes the way their perceptions initially were formed, and begins with impressions (told in his own words) of Marco Polo, the early Christian missionaries, and the growing number of Western seamen and traders.

Turning to the nineteenth century, the unit describes the

reaction of the Chinese to Western commercial demands (see reading 7, "An Imperial Edict to the King of England"). A unique contribution of the unit is the three readings on how the Chinese looked upon the West and Westerners. The final reading—which seems rather randomly thrown in—reflects the period at the end of the nineteenth century when the Chinese were at a stage of "self-strengthening" by attempting to blend Chinese values and Western technology.

Unit Evaluation. The unit is a unique and generally successful compilation dealing with the process of cultural contact and perceptions. Interesting selections, careful analyses, and well-chosen illustrative materials (especially reading 11, which contains reproductions from a hand-painted Japanese scroll depicting the landing of Commodore Perry) make it especially valuable, particularly in the context of the full Asian Studies Inquiry series.

It is not, however, a comprehensive presentation of the issues involved in the meeting of East and West. The omissions are certainly due to limitations of space, but they should not be ignored in classroom discussion.

On balance, the positive aspects of the unit can be emphasized. The selections are well chosen for their relevance to American students (such as the fascinating early Chinese account of the U.S.), and the editor lets the student view some of the Eastern preconceptions of the West as well. This results in a well-balanced account of how each culture was shocked and amused by the habits of the other.

Outstanding Contributions. The readings are an excellent collection of fresh materials which can be revealing even for well-read students of East Asia. The illustrations (twenty in all) enhance the text, and the pictures of the Japanese impressions of Westerners at the time of Commodore Perry (1853) are particularly appropriate. The unit illustrates that misconceptions result not only from faulty observation or poor data collection, but also from different cultural values and experiences.

Contents. Introduction; 1. The People of Kytay; 2. The Description of the World; 3. "The Best Race Yet Discovered"; 4. "Ritcheness and Plentiffulnesse"; 5. Novissima Sinica; 7. An Imperial Edict to the King of England; 8. America; 9. The

Distant and Strange Continent of Europe; 10. Among the
Western Tribes; 12. Toward Self-strengthening; Conclusions;
Suggested Readings

† *Food and Survival in Asia*
Robin J. McKeown
Field Educational Publications, 1969, 64 pp.
Price: $10.33 for 10

Author's Professional Background. Robin J. McKeown was a
coordinator of the Asian Studies Inquiry Program and a codirector
of the Asian Studies Curriculum Project at the University of
California, Berkeley.

Scope and Emphasis. The unit deals with the general problem of
hunger and poverty in Asia and poses a series of questions: What
are their actual effects? Their causes? What can be done to
eliminate them? All the readings are by firsthand observers of the
scenes depicted. Four of the fourteen selections are on China.
  The first reading on China depicts famine conditions during
different periods and places the problem in historical perspective.
The solution (in part) for the new China has been the commune
system, and this is described in a rather critical fashion by a
French observer who visited China in 1966. The results of
population crowding are vividly depicted in a story about Hong
Kong. Resistance to change in a tradition-bound society is
discussed in the last China reading; it is strange, however, that
this was written by Mao Tun, who, although certainly admired by
the present government, was describing conditions in the 1920s.
  The unit concludes with two readings by the editor detailing the
problems of waste and population growth. There are ten pictures.

Unit Evaluation. The various case histories in the unit are easy to
read and are deeply interesting from an emotional and human
point of view.
  The approach is one of overview, however, and the special
problems of different areas and the individual solutions being
attempted could have been more clearly pointed out. This is
particularly true for China, where the generally successful program of flood control, the virtual elimination of hunger and

waste, and the general increase in the standard of living are completely ignored.

The unit presents Asia as tradition-bound. Although it is obviously true that hunger and poverty exist there, and that there are social roots and consequences of these conditions, more could have been said about the process of modernization and development.

Oustanding Contributions. This unit effectively describes human conditions that have prevailed in most of Asia and gives the student an excellent perspective from which to study the impediments to social change.

Contents. Introduction; The Impact of Hunger and Poverty in Asia (3. The Chinese Agricultural Communes; 6. The Poor of Hong Kong); The Causes of Hunger and Poverty in Asia (8. Climate and New Techniques); Conclusions; Suggested Readings

† *Life in Communist China*
Daniel R. Birch
Field Educational Publications, 1969, 64 pp.
Price: $13.88 for 10

Author's Professional Background. Daniel R. Birch is assistant professor of education at Simon Fraser University in Vancouver, Canada.

Scope and Emphasis. This unit is a series of twelve readings ranging from the personal diary of a peasant in northern China (1962) to a foreigner's account of his visit to a large automotive plant in Peking (1967). All the readings are either by personal participants or by people actually witnessing the events they describe.

The emphasis here is on the comparative approach; the intent is to have students draw inferences about the standard of living, working conditions, personal and family life, and hopes and ambitions of Chinese people. Comparisons are made between life in the cities and life in the countryside.

Unit Evaluation. By his excellent selection of readings—which range from sympathetic to critical views of the present way of life in China—the author goes far toward encouraging students to ask their own questions about life in the People's Republic of China. The introduction rightly raises the question of the accuracy of the reports, and, although the author's introduction emphasizes the "totalitarian" aspects of the government and its "attempts to control" and suggests a picure of China in confusion and turmoil (a view not inaccurate for the period about which it was written), the overall impression is rather sympathetic. The author encourages students to consider what might be best for China, not our own image of what China should be.

There are some minor technical problems. With respect to footnotes, there was no *one* Red Guard organization (presumed on p. 23 and p. 38). Although he explains the term *ganbu* correctly in one place (p. 38), the author fails to mention that it means "cadre." He does translate it on p. 54, but then erroneously tells us that cadres are simply personnel in charge of training.

The introductory paragraphs tend to be rather weak, and the material in the last section (pp. 50–53) might have been more useful earlier. Concerning the introductory paragraphs that emphasize China's totalitarian aspects, the author might have let the student reach his own conclusions, especially since he has presented a fair range of relevant materials.

Outstanding Contributions. This unit gives the student a rare opportunity to read firsthand accounts of visitors to China, thus breathing life into the usual scholarly generalizations about Chinese society today. The author has identified people and jobs which are familiar to American students (such as a worker in an automobile plant), thus encouraging comparisons which may lead to a better understanding of what life is like for the Chinese people.

Contents. Introduction; Life in Rural China (1. Life in Liu Ling Village; 2. Pride of Poor Men: Willow Grove Commune); Life in Urban China (3. What It Is Like to Live in Peking Today; 4. In Automobile Factory Number One; 5. Letters from Red China); The Effect of Mao Tse-tung's Thought in Rural China (6. A Family Meeting; 7. Thirteen Months in a Rural Commune; 8. Students and Peasants); The Effect of Mao Tse-tung's Thought in

Urban China (9. The Thought Revolution; 10. Theater and Thought Reform); The Effect of Government Policy on Progress in Modern China (11. Bamboo H-Bomb; 12. Report from a Long Nose); Conclusions; Suggested Readings

† *Man and His Environment in Asia*
Christopher L. Salter
Field Educational Publications, 1969, 64 pp.
Price: $13.88 for 10

Author's Professional Background. Christopher L. Salter, a specialist in Asian geography, has taught at the University of California, Los Angeles, and is currently in the Department of Geography at the University of Oregon.

Scope and Emphasis. The ten readings in this booklet are designed to present Asian areas on a comparative basis. Four of the readings deal with aspects of Chinese geography.

It is stressed that, particularly in Asia, no man can escape the land; his dependence on it is nearly total and the life of Asians is primarily agricultural. This is depicted in a series of firsthand descriptive passages which improve upon the standard geographic analyses. The unit includes twenty-one photographs.

Unit Evaluation. The unit is an excellent supplement to a basic text on the geography of Asia. Unfortunately, the unit contains no maps or charts; but, these limitations aside, it puts much-needed flesh on the general bare-bone descriptions of Asia. The selections on China deal with the basic problems of the Chinese peasant: land and its reclamation, drought, and water control. Although these are vividly presented, the readings do not adequately indicate that China itself contains a variegated pattern of geography and related problems.

Outstanding Contributions. The unit points to the problems of change in societies which are highly dependent on their physical environment. This is done most effectively through firsthand description rather than textual narration.

Contents. Introduction; Asia's Physical Diversity (4. Parched

Earth); Asian Man and His Environment (6. An Irrigation Project for Hunan; 7. Reclaiming Dead Land in China; 9. Violence among Villagers); Conclusions; Suggested Readings

† *Man and Woman in Asia*
Robin J. McKeown
Field Educational Publications, 1969, 64 pp.
Price: $13.88 for 10

Author's Professional Background. Robin J. McKeown was a coordinator of the Asian Studies Inquiry Program and a codirector of the Asian Studies Curriculum Project at the University of California, Berkeley.

Scope and Emphasis. Man and Woman in Asia focuses primarily on the role of women and their relationship to the family. From this, the student is expected to gain insight into the paths of life which the Asian woman must follow, and to reflect on the appropriate standards of human behavior in different parts of the world—some of which may be similar to his own experience and some not. The unit has nine photographs.

Three of the sixteen readings are on the role of women in China. One deals with women generally, another with parents-in-law; a third describes the role of women in China today and the efforts to liberate women from the "feudal depravity" of the past into a new equality with men and full participation in the Chinese economy. This reading is an important contribution to a unit which otherwise describes only traditional roles.

Unit Evaluation. Although this unit has little material on China, the general approach is a novel one and relevant for the high school student's approach to Asian life. The selections are easy and enjoyable to read, and generally sustain interest. The traditional patterns of male-female relations are vividly presented.

The author might have included more material to suggest the link between women and the larger society. In the case of China, for example, the social forces bearing on marriage are relegated to a few paragraphs in one reading. Neither is it noted that the social treatment of women did have some important variations; it is generally agreed, for example, that women's status was higher in pre-Sung China, just as it was higher in pre-Kamakura Japan.

One may also question the overemphasis on traditional China; only in the last reading (from Edgar Snow's *The Other Side of the River*) is there mention of post-1949 changes.

Outstanding Contributions. By focusing on the role of women in Asian life, the author has brought a unique perspective from which to view patterns of Asian society. The readings are vivid, and bring into the classroom a neglected and important topic.

Contents. Introduction; Traditional Marriage Patterns; Traditional Roles in the Asian Marriage; Traditional Roles in the Asian Family (9. The Birth of Sons and Daughters; 10. The Roles of the Chinese Female); Changing Roles in the Asian Family (15. A Chinese Family in Singapore); Conclusions; Suggested Readings

† *Mao Tse-tung and the Chinese Revolution*
David L. Weitzman
Field Educational Publications, 1969, 64 pp.
Price: $13.88 for 10

Author's Professional Background. David L. Weitzman is Social Studies Department chairman at Oakland Technical High School in Oakland, California, a demonstration secondary school of the University of California, Berkeley.

Scope and Emphasis. In the brief space of sixty-four pages, the author traces some of the more important causes and characteristics of the Chinese Revolution. The three initial readings set the social context (famine, the misery of the peasant, and chaotic city life); the unit then traces the revolution from its ideological and political origins through the birth of the Communist Party, the KMT-CCP split, and ends with the "Roots of Mao's Victory."

The unit outlines the history of the Chinese Revolution through a series of descriptions of critical events. Comparison with the American Revolution (made in the introduction in the spirit of inquiry rather than as bold comparison) seeks to encourage the student to raise questions about the meaning of revolutions in general.

Unit Evaluation. The editor has done an outstanding job of making certain aspects of the Chinese Revolution come alive and acquire meaning for the reader. The readings by actual participants in or witnesses of the events described are vivid and generally sympathetic. On the negative side, the readings could have been better tied together to give a broader perspective on the revolution by noting its appeal to various social classes, the interplay of modernization and political integration, and the simultaneous confrontations with internal unrest and foreign aggression. This might have reduced the sense of jumping from one major event to another. Some critics would find the unit biased in linking the events of the twentieth century solely to the cause of Communism.

The description of the origins and progress of the Chinese Revolution may also be faulted for its exclusive focus on poverty and misery among the peasants. A noticeable omission is the rise of nationalism and the central role of the military. Although these and other points were perhaps necessarily omitted owing to space constraints, they should not be overlooked in a general presentation of this topic in the classroom.

In general, the book is most useful as an account of the basic features of Mao's career, the Communist rise to power, and the revolutionary and egalitarian aspects of the Communist Revolution. Most important, it is a landmark contribution to correcting our ethnocentric bias toward the Chinese Revolution and the misinterpretations which have long been perpetuated in the classroom. The author shows that it was conditioned by disorder and discontent in Chinese society and was not simply the product of an elite mastermind whose cues came from Moscow. He indicates that the revolution involved changes in intellectual perspectives and consciousness among all segments of Chinese society, and was a natural outgrowth of various historical factors. In short, the unit demonstrates that the Chinese Revolution was Chinese.

Outstanding Contributions. By challenging the common view that an outside force concocted and led the Communist Revolution, and by illuminating the pattern of twentieth-century Chinese history, the editor has made a unique contribution to classroom materials. Choosing excerpts from Mao Tse-tung's life and writings and drawing on the vivid eyewitness accounts of Western observers prove successful from both the pedagogical and substantive points of view.

Contents. Introduction; The Social Context (1. Famine; 2. The Peasant; 3. City Life; 4. The Pleasures of Life); Revolution (5. Genesis of a Communist I; 6. Revolution; 7. The May Fourth Movement); The Birth of Chinese Communism (8. Genesis of a Communist II; 9. First Manifesto of the CCP; 10. The Peasant Movement in Hunan); The Kuomintang-CCP Schism (11. The Shanghai Coup of April 12, 1927; 12. The Long March); The Roots of Mao's Victory (13. Memoranda by Foreign Service Officers in China; 14. General Wedemeyer Reports on China); Conclusions; Suggested Readings

China
Edward Graff
Oxford Book Company, 1972, 156 pp.
Price: $1.65

The unit is part of the Regions of Our World series.

Author's Professional Background. Mr. Edward Graff is Director of Social Studies for the Long Beach School District in New York. He has also written on Southeast Asia and Africa in the same series.

Scope and Emphasis. This unit, written for the 8th and 9th grades, covers geography, traditional history, the period of contact with the West, the rise of nationalism, and the People's Republic as well as Taiwan. Its focus, however, seems to lie somewhere in the 1930s. Although different facets of the People's Republic are covered, the overall picture drawn of the Chinese people is that of unchanging, tradition-bound masses. The book appears to be patched together from an eclectic set of research materials, giving it a curiously distorted scope and emphasis.

Teaching Approach. The author expects the student to deal with broad concepts as well as with factual information in order to see history and culture as a "gradually developing, organized process." Broad topics (religion, way of life, the arts, government) are elaborated in narrative style. The unit touts "eyewitness reports" to "develop interest and dramatize the presentation," yet only two are used, and both refer to the pre-1949 period.

Unit Evaluation. The unit fails by almost every criteria. It asks us to "understand each other, to appreciate each other, and to help each other" if the "inhabitants of the planet Earth are to avoid disaster." Unfortunately, the book may contribute to greater misunderstanding through its view of the Chinese people as dominated by Confucianism, traditional festivals, and an unchanging class system (the gentry system is discussed in between sections entitled "Communists and the Chinese Family" and the "Population Explosion"). The People's Republic is written in as if it were "one more burden" for an unchanging China.

Conceptual distortions are mixed with factually jumbled descriptions. In the two paragraphs devoted to religion in China today, the author talks about the elimination of the old forms, with statements such as: "Islamic groups were forced to give up Arabic education and accept social reforms, such as the elimination of veils for women." He notes (correctly) that especially harsh treatment was reserved for Christians (without saying why), but again resorts to extremes: "Christians were forced to pray to Marx and Mao. Christ was looked upon as a carpenter who was a great communist leader." This kind of prose does little to contribute to our understanding of a complex subject.

On the political side, although occasional credit is given for post-1949 progress ("The overall picture of Communist Chinese public health, medical care, and sanitation is infinitely better today than it was in 1949," p. 75), the overall impression conveyed by the unit is a China ruled by "Little Red Book" dictators who "have not shown a great effort to improve the living standard of the individual," (p. 72), and for whom " 'merit' means denunciation of others and 'great merit' refers to the denunciation of major opponents (p. 101)." The political and social experiments of the past twenty years are described with little understanding of their implications.

The numerous and glaring factual errors obliterate what worth the unit may have: Peking is said to be 12 miles west of the "Pes River"; Liu Shao-chi is spelled "Kio Shao-chi"; Shenyang is called by its pre-1949 name of Mukden; the assertion is made that "there is no common language in China"; and so on. Debatable historical judgments are stated as fact (e.g., "The Chinese invaded India"). Subtle distortions are also carried through the pictures—rural and peasant scenes with "hardship" captions for the People's Republic, modern highways and shipbuilding for Taiwan.

Outstanding Contributions. This unit makes little contribution to our understanding of China.

Contents. "The Land and the Climate," "China: Ancient Times to 1918," "China: Contact with the West," "Chinese Nationalism and Independence," "Religion," "Ways of Life," "Economy," "Government," "The Arts," "Taiwan—The Other China," "China and the World"

Illustrations. "Physical Features: China," "Ancient China and India," "T'ang China," "Highlights of China's History," "Agricultural and Mineral Resources," "Structure of Government and Party," "U.S.-Red China Comparison"

China
Hyman Kublin
Houghton Mifflin, 1972, 256 pp.
Price: $3.45; paperback, $1.95

This unit is one of seven texts in Houghton Mifflin's World Regional Studies series. *China: Selected Readings* accompanies the text (1972, 256 pp., $2.96; paperback, $1.95).

Author's Professional Background. Hyman Kublin, a specialist in East Asian history, is professor of history at Brooklyn College.

Scope and Emphasis. One-third of the text is allotted to traditional China and two-thirds to modern China. It is basically a chronological narrative of China's political and institutional history with a focus on Western relations with China and the attendant revolutionary changes. The unit stresses factual narrative rather than developing analytical generalizations. This occasionally results in artificial separation of historical concepts; for example, the book might have related feudalism and Confucianism more analytically rather than treating them as separate topics.

Teaching Approach. The text is divided into short descriptive passages on important aspects of Chinese history. After every three or four pages there is a "Check-up" which quizzes the student's memory on the preceding details. At the end of each chapter is a "Summing-up" and a "Chapter Review" which includes identifications, general discussion questions, and several research topics. "Timetables" which assemble important dates are scattered throughout the unit. Visual features include twelve maps, eighty-nine photos and illustrations, and two economic output charts. A three-page annotated bibliography (slightly revised since the first edition in 1968) and an index complete the work.

Unit Evaluation. Factual errors frequently occur (p. 58 on Islam, p. 96 on Taoism, and p. 100 on queues), and some of the unit's interpretations seem debatable. The unit apparently does not take into consideration recent research on China by Japanese and Western scholars. Changes in the later (1972) edition are only in the section on Communist China, and these are largely cosmetic. Consequently, the unit confirms many stereotypes. It over-emphasizes the unity and strength of Confucianism in premodern China and views traditional China as basically unchanged. The Opium War is interpreted only as a result of an economic problem. Psychological, legal, and cultural factors, which might have broadened the student's perspective on the unit's themes, are not adequately described.

The unit's approach to Communist China tends to be hostile, although some of the more controversial statements have been omitted from the recent edition. Little has been added that reflects the great increase in our knowledge about China since 1968. The readings include the use of Chinese Communist documents, which could have been more meaningfully integrated if a less apologetic tone had been taken in presenting them and if the Communist case had been presented less defensively. Instead of allowing the reader to reach his own conclusions inductively, the presentation of the issues encourages the student to support the unit's assumptions.

The *China: Selected Readings* volume which accompanies the

unit might have been improved if there was a juxtaposition of different views on the same major issue. The materials tend to overemphasize the importance of Western contact, overrepresent the views of the Nationalist Party in the "New China" section, and neglect the nonmilitary and less militant aspects of the People's Republic. Four selections were added in the 1972 edition which deal with the decisive role of politics, but overall, the selection and emphasis of the materials tend to restrict the student's opportunity for both inductive reasoning and lively discussion.

Outstanding Contributions. As a full-length treatment of China in the standard textbook genre, it serves both as an introduction to the vocabulary of Chinese history and as a reference work providing background for the student studying a particular topic. Overall, however, this unit is not recommended for a student's only exposure to China.

Contents. Introduction; 1. China and the Chinese; 2. The Ancient World of China; 3. The Early Imperial Age; 4. The Late Imperial Age: From Sung to Ming; 5. The Late Imperial Age: The Manchus; 6. The End of the Chinese Empire; 7. The Struggling Republic; 8. China: From Nationalist to Communist; 9. China under the Red Flag

Maps. North and South China; The People's Republic of China; Land of Almost 800 Million; Ancient China; The Early Imperial Age; The Mongol Empire; The Manchu Empire; Imperialism in China; The Struggle for National Unity; The Triangular War; The Communist Victory; Transportation and Natural Resources

Contents of *China: Selected Readings.* Foreword; Map of China; Part I, Foundations of China (Introduction; 1. The Land under Heaven; 2. Forests and Floods; 3. Men and Goods on the Move; 4. Fields and Farmers; 5. Dragon Bones and Royal Tombs; 6. The Written Word; 7. Honor Thy Father and Mother; 8. Keeping in Tune with Nature); Part II, Early Imperial China (Introduction; 1. The Three Kingdoms; 2. The Western Paradise; 3. A Hike through T'ang China; 4. How Scholars Reigned; 5. Poets and Poetry; 6. The Family Web); Part III, The Late Imperial Age (Introduction; 1. The Flowing Brush; 2. Marco Polo in the Mongol Empire; 3. The Food Revolution; 4. Ch'ien-lung and King George III; 5. A Voyage with Opium Smugglers; 6. "Unequal Treaties"; 7. China from the Inside); Part IV, The Emergence of a New China (Introduction; 1. The Warriors of the Heavenly Peace; 2. How to Save China; 3. The End of Imperial China; 4. The Father of the Revolution; 5. Reading and Writing for All; 6. The Dynamics of Revolution; 7. The Hour of Decision); Part V, The Surge of Communism (Introduction; 1. Techniques of Guerrilla Warfare; 2. The Communist Victory; 3. Towards a One-Party State; 4. Manchuria: Hub of Industrialization; 5. The Good Earth and China's Future; 6. The Commune System; 7. A Low-Risk Foreign Policy; 8. The Sino-Soviet Split; 9. The Shaper of Red China; 10. "Let Politics Take Command"; 11. "People Are the Decisive Factor"); Questions for Study and Discussion; Index

● *China: A Culture Area in Perspective*
James E. Sheridan
Allyn & Bacon, Inc., 1970, 81 pp.
Price: $2.10

This unit has replaced one with the same title written by Leften Stavrianos and Roger Hackett (1966). It is part of a large World History Project which has produced the textbook series: *A Global History of Man.*

Author's Professional Background. James Sheridan is professor of history at Northwestern University in Chicago, Illinois.

Scope and Emphasis. Organized topically, four chapters ("Basic Facts," "Politics," "Economics," and "Culture") cover the major areas of Chinese life from a social scientist's point of view. Although present-day China is the main focus of the unit, the author gives particular emphasis to the period of Western presence in China during the nineteenth century and the period of internal disunity from 1900 to 1949. Frequent comparisons with other Asian countries and the United States help give the student perspective, and a generally sympathetic approach to China's problems encourages the student to see the underlying themes and ideas behind the People's Republic.

Teaching Approach. Each section of the unit emphasizes concepts rather than factual detail. A unique feature is the use of the "flashback" technique which illuminates the present by introducing historical origins, thus providing the student with a solid historical background. The text is interspersed with well-produced pictures, maps, charts, and diagrams. At the end of each chapter is a section entitled "Reviewing the Essentials" which includes a series of questions and terms to be explained, identified, or located. Eleven unit activities, including reports and discussion topics, and an excellent reading list are offered in the conclusion. The reading level of this unit makes it most suitable for good readers in the upper grades.

The *Readings in World History* volume supplements the four major themes of the book and, on the whole, provides a selection of materials on traditional society, politics, and economics. Only the section on culture includes contrasting descriptions of traditional and contemporary China.

Unit Evaluation. The judicious revision of this unit made by Professor Sheridan in 1970 makes it one of the better available curriculum materials. One is often struck by the balanced tone on such controversial subjects as religion in China today (p. 11), the reasons for the Communist victory in 1949 (p. 43), and the attempt to explain the philosophy underlying some of China's economic and social movements (e.g., the section on the Cultural Revolution, p. 46). The section on economics, particularly on the Great Leap Forward, has been greatly improved.

Nevertheless, some stereotyping and obvious subjectivism remains. In part, this may be caused by the author's apparent need to link his text with some awkward and misleading selections from the *Readings in World History* text intended to accompany the unit. How else are we to explain why he ends a balanced discussion of the Red Guards with a reference to "monster rallies" addressed by Chairman Mao which led to renaming so many streets "Anti-imperialist Avenue" that finally "nobody knew his address and the old names had to be restored" (p. 49)? In addition, the text has such obviously subjective comments as: "In the case of communes we have seen that the women perhaps were freed more than they wished" (p. 67); and the role of the family in the past "was marked by solidarity," while today it is seriously weakened (p. 65). The past is distorted because it is seen as a totally stable society based on Confucianism; the present is maligned because, according to the unit, today's society is in chaos because it rejects Confucianism.

Outstanding Contributions. Despite distortions of some aspects of life in China today, the unit is comprehensive and solid enough to be used as a basic introductory framework to China. It stands well by itself, thus making the corresponding materials in the *Readings in World History* volume optional—indeed, the teacher would be wise to employ other, more current source materials. Such adaptation would make this an excellent unit for classroom use.

Contents. Basic Facts (Geography; Peoples; Languages; Religions; Historical Periods; Traditional China); Politics: The Rebirth of China (Present State; Westerners in China; The Future); Economics: Great Leap and a Stumble (Historical Origins; The Future); Culture: Anti-Western Westernizers (China and World Culture; New Ways and Old; The Family; The Position of Women; Social System; Literature; Fate of Confucianism; The Future)

Maps, Charts and Diagrams. Climate of China, Physical-Political Map of China and East Asia; Population of China; Periods of Chinese Expansion; Government and Party Structure; Time Chart; Divided China, 1941; Land Use in China; and, Area Comparison: U.S.–China

China: Emerging Asian Giant
Charles L. Cutler, George P. Morrill
Xerox Education Publications, 1972, 47 pp.
Price: $0.50

This unit is one of a series of Area Study Unit Books and is a revision of *China: Troubled Asian Giant* (American Education Publications, 1967) reviewed in the first edition of this guide (p. 55).

Authors' Professional Background. None listed.

Scope and Emphasis. As in the former edition, the unit emphasizes the troubles China has inherited or created. It is extremely limited in scope, giving only superficial insight into geography, population, human conditions, Confucianism, Red Guards, education, and the Sino-Soviet dispute. U.S.-China relations are seen against a background of absolute Chinese hostility. Seven case studies constitute the bulk of the book, including two on Taiwan.

Teaching Approach. The approach is narrative, and the unit is written in a journalistic-descriptive style. The book uses five highly fictionalized case studies of how individuals react to the government.

Unit Evaluation. Were it not for the wide distribution potential of this unit, it would not have been included—it ranks among the worst available classroom materials. It is difficult to take seriously the stated intent of the authors ("The book . . . is not a propaganda book. It is not designed to make anyone hate China or love China," p. 3) when almost every paragraph contains value-laden terminology. Among the many examples: during the Great Leap Forward, the Chinese people "were supposed to eat, work, die, and be buried in their own 'anthill' "(p. 11); the Communists have "Looped the Party line over the once wide-open, sin-and-opium Shanghai, squeezing out *some* of its notorious wickedness," p. 9 (emphasis ours); "the entire upper and middle classes were savagely brought into line with a dogma based on the teaching of Marx-Lenin-Mao" (p. 21).

The traditional stereotypes of Chinese as wily, patient, and so on are reinforced by some particularly hostile descriptions. According to the unit, Chinese for centuries didn't tell the correct size of their families, hoping to keep sons off the military registers. "These days, by contrast, the peasants are more likely to report births promptly and deaths tardily, because cotton and rice rations are based on family size" (p. 13). In a case study outlining the dilemma of a farmer who is "supposed" to share four of his up-to-now-hidden piglets with the commune, the unit states, "A man of the soil who can't outsmart a government planner is a pretty poor character" (p. 28), and goes on to (silently) chuckle about how he bribed others to help him hide them. What is the student supposed to make of this? The "Think it Over" question at the end of this case study asks: "Although we do not recognize Red China, would it be wise for the State Department to invite

Chinese observers over here to examine our successful farming practices?" (p. 30).

The only positive language in the book is reserved for the readings on Taiwan, depicted as a happy and prosperous place which is in danger of being betrayed by its friends.

The unit is so stereotyped and value-laden that even those who are cynical about progress on the mainland today and the new American policy toward the People's Republic would find it embarrassingly propagandistic. The unit should never appear in a classroom.

Outstanding Contributions. None

Contents. Map—Communist China and Taiwan; Introduction—The Door Begins to Open; The Land—Physical Setting; The People—Cultural Setting; The Institutions—Political Setting. Case Studies: The Land—A Future in the West? Eight Little Pigs—Should the Farmer Tell? The People—Pride and Hunger: A Dilemma for Chang; A Teen-Ager Rebels by Government Order. The Institutions—Two Communist Giants Swap Insults in Public; Reforming the Thoughts of a 'Capitalist Dog'; Taiwan: Prosperous but Facing Uncertain Future. Reference Data on Communist China and Taiwan. Books for Further Reading

China, Korea, and Japan
Ardath W. Burks
Macmillan Company, 1970, 168 pp.
Price: $2.96

This is one unit in the Culture Regions of the World series edited by Seymour Fersh, professor of education at Fairleigh Dickenson University.

Author's Professional Background. Ardath W. Burks is professor of political science and Director of International Programs at Rutgers University. Consultants for the unit were Robert B. Hill, Jr., geographer, University of Rochester, and Dun J. Li, historian, Paterson State College.

Scope and Emphasis. This unit employs the "culture region" approach. Each chapter first indicates points of commonality between the several regions of East Asia and then treats each area separately. Three chapters of the book are devoted entirely to China.

The author's concepts, organization, and terminology resemble the style developed by professors John Fairbank and Edwin Reischauer in their college text *East Asia: The Great Tradition* (Boston: Houghton Mifflin, 1965).

Teaching Approach. The unit is written in historical-narrative style, and is in effect an elementary junior college text. The author introduces a great number of facts and figures, and as a result the explanation of several topics (e.g., the writing system) tends to be confusing.

The unit includes sixteen maps and forty-six photographs which are used with mixed results. No pronunciation guide is offered for the many references to Chinese (as well as Korean and Japanese) terms. No questions or other teaching aids are provided at the ends of chapters.

Unit Evaluation. The culture-hopping approach has both strengths and limitations, but is generally used to good effect in this unit. There is, however, a frequent lack of clarity resulting from stretched comparisons and contrasts, and a sense of never getting "settled" into a particular culture.

The author often assumes an unwarranted degree of knowledge among students; many important and technical concepts are introduced without explanation (examples are "loess," "feudal," and "modernization"). Often, a basic concept is first introduced in a dubious generality, and is only later employed with an adequate explanation. For example, we are first presented with the stereotype that Chinese tradition was totally Confucian (p. 40), but this is corrected later through an excellent presentation of the various traditions which contributed to Chinese culture (p. 49). The result may be that the handy "tag" identifications— which perpetuate stereotypes—remain in the mind of the student.

As might be expected in a unit which emphasizes culture, the modern period is skimmed only briefly. Although the book does provide short biographical sketches of Sun Yat-sen, Chiang Kai-shek, and Mao Tse-tung, one would gather that there was relatively little to be upset about in China during their early careers. The important social and political movements of the time—particularly the May Fourth Movement and the Warlord Period—are completely avoided.

Information on the People's Republic of China is even more scanty, and strangely chosen. Little attention is paid to the social basis or continuing aims of the new government. Although not hostile, and free of many stereotypes, the unit is often condescending. A passage which concludes the book is representative:

> There is, in the history of the ageless Chinese [a phrase used much too often, and a stereotype in itself] a tradition of responsible, moral leadership as strong as the habit of domination. The hope of the rest of East Asia and of the world is that mainland Chinese can somehow be helped to cultivate the former tradition [p. 160].

This is a statement of what the author thinks the Chinese government should do and does not contribute to an understanding of what the revolution actually means for the Chinese people in their own historical and cultural context. Again, our instinct for salvation, Western style, is showing.

Outstanding Contributions. The author generally achieves a careful balance between cultural, geographical, and historical considerations. The unit, suitable for an advanced level, is well written and full of information. Its cross-cultural approach is useful in dealing with the points of commonality and difference in Asian cultures as few other books do. In his chapter on China in conflict, the author does an admirable job of sorting out and weighing the various factors of Western expansionism and Chinese decline.

Contents. Introduction; Prologue; Land and Climate; Peoples; Languages; Old China; China: "The Middle Kingdom"; Old Japan; Traditional Philosophy and Religion; Traditional Arts; China in Conflict; The Rise and Fall of Imperial Japan; Modern Government; Population and Resources; Economic Planning; Epilogue; For Additional Reading; Index

East Asian Culture
Ethel E. Ewing
Rand McNally, 1967 (3d ed.), 133 pp.
Price: $1.40

Author's Professional Background. Ethel E. Ewing is a professor of anthropology at California State College at Long Beach; her approach is based on the theories of functional social anthropology.

Scope and Emphasis. Part 1 of a series entitled Our Widening World, this unit includes three chapters on China (85 pp.). Chapter 1 gives a useful view of the geographical, technological, political, social, and religious factors which first led to the formation of a unified Chinese society (about 200 B.C.). Chapter 2 jumps ahead to describe traditional Chinese society before the Western impact (circa 1700). Chapter 3 outlines the impact of the West on China and discusses two attempts to form a new society (Nationalist and Communist).

Each of the three chapters is divided into six parts, three dealing with geography, technology, and foreign relations. Geography is presented in an environmental framework; technology is stressed as the basis for China's social structure and the main factor in change; and incidents from foreign relations are carefully selected to show their influence on the society. The three remaining sections are concerned with social organization, integrating social factors, and culture.

The work de-emphasizes chronological history. Instead, it presents insights into the social and political patterns of Chinese civilization. Major emphasis is placed upon the interaction of environment and technology with the lives of the Chinese upper and lower classes. Historical changes within and between these two classes are traced throughout all three chapters. The influence of geography and technology on traditional Chinese society is well explained, particularly through short imaginary stories.

Teaching Approach. The unit's exposition ranges from fictional accounts to historical narrative. The imaginary episodes lay a foundation for general conclusions; the historical narrative fills in pertinent details on social development. The first two chapters capitalize on the inductive method and the comparative culture approach. The final parts of the book dealing with modern China employ a straight narrative format.

Features of the unit include about fifty photos and illustrations, eight maps, one diagram, and one chronology. The "Workshop" section includes questions, suggested projects, and words to identify.

Unit Evaluation. The unit's treatment of literature, art, and philosophy, particularly Buddhism, could usefully be supplemented with a more comprehensive work, for they are inadequately related to the major institutions of Chinese civilization.

The unit's handling of Communism would have been improved if the associated problems had been treated as social-historical questions. The Nationalists and Communists could have been depicted as dealing in divergent ways with the problems of the peasantry, with modernization in a large, bureaucratic, centralized agrarian society, and with the resistance to change in a traditional society. Instead, the author ignores the nationalistic aspects of Chinese Communism which many scholars view as equal to, if not more important than, the Russian influence. By presenting the confrontation between the Nationalists and Communists in rather black and white terms, the unit oversimplifies modern Chinese history. Its coverage of traditional China is more open-minded than that of modern China, and enables the student to see and discuss conflicting issues and problems.

Outstanding Contributions. Each chapter uses several short imaginary stories to introduce central concepts through concrete examples. A story of a porcelain factory is particularly well done, both in its historical reconstruction and its capacity to indicate the larger problems of technology and science as well as the problems of government control over business, communication, transportation, and labor.

Contents. Introduction; The Rise of the Chinese Empire; China 1700—Portrait of a Traditional Culture; China's Reaction to the West; Korea: An Ancient Small Nation; Japan: An Empire of Islands; Workshop: East Asian Culture; Index and Pronouncing Vocabulary

• *Social Change: The Case of Rural China*
Prepared by Sociological Resources for the Social Studies
Sociologist designer: Ezra Vogel. Coauthor: Philip West.
Teacher designers: David Grossman, Suzanne Davenport, John C. Williams
Allyn & Bacon, 1971, 84 pp.

Price: $8.20 (list) for set of 10, including one instructor's guide. The unit is part of the Episodes in Social Inquiry series.

Authors' Professional Background. Ezra Vogel of Harvard University and Philip West of Indiana University are both well-known sociologists in the China field; Professor Vogel is the author of several major studies on China and Japan.

Scope and Emphasis. This unit introduces the process of social change—broadly as a sociological concept and more narrowly in terms of the changes which took place in rural China between 1948 and approximately 1966. The first lesson examines the general concept of social change, introducing the "rules" under which it operates. The second sketches the historical background of pre-1949 China. The remaining six chapters deal with changes in today's rural China in land distribution, the family, village health and technology, and the communes.

There are no readings on urban China; social change is examined only in the countryside. Since few original source materials exist on rural China, most of the materials used in the "episode" were either written or adapted by the authors. Books and documents summarized are clearly identified in the footnotes.

The authors have largely achieved their goal of making the presentations factual and the interpretations objective. Although source materials by Communist writers are included, and there is implicit empathy with the Chinese model for social change, no explicit political stand is taken. The authors repeatedly stress that students should see what *is*, not what ought to be; empathy need not mean sympathy. From there, a line of inquiry and evaluation can develop, and the student is given a rare opportunity of exercising his own judgment.

Teaching Approach. In addition to two broad content objectives (analysis of social change and how this process occurred in rural China), the unit has two attitudinal objectives. First, the student is presented with controversial issues about which he is asked to form opinions. Second, the unit seeks to instill a "readiness on the part of the student to develop and integrate his own system of values by considering policies and practices very different from those in the U.S."

The inquiry method is used to implement these objectives and to present the materials. The unit is particularly noteworthy for its attempt to vary this teaching approach. The instructor's guide, a necessary and effective complement to the unit, suggests teaching procedures for each lesson. In addition, the episode contains twenty-two illustrations and photographs.

Current scholarly interpretations of Chinese history and politics prevail, and, while the unit is authoritative and scholarly, it is well written and easily understood by upper-level high school students. The unit constantly asks both teacher and student to fairly evaluate the material and topic under discussion.

Unit Evaluation. The unit is substantively and methodologically outstanding. It effectively combines an academic discipline (sociology) with area study (China), and, by employing the suggested teaching approach, should contribute to a most positive learning experience. This episode was the first work written expressly to remedy the serious faults in units then available for the classroom (1966), and has stood up very well as a model. The unit was thoroughly classroom tested.

The authors are realistic and objective about contemporary rural China. As a unit dealing with change, however, it might have contained more of a basis for comparison. Although the student reads about the new, there are no readings on "old" China except what the authors introduce through synopsized readings. The unit claims to be current through "about 1968," but it clearly was written before the start of the Cultural Revolution (1966), and the impact of this important social and political movement on the countryside is not dealt with. The teacher therefore may wish to supplement the unit with other readings.

Some teachers may find the concepts and materials too controversial in the sense that they clearly represent what China is today to the Chinese. But this is openly stated, and readings are carefully introduced. For example:

> The story on land reform is written by a writer sympathetic with the Communist approach to land reform. While you read the story you might think how others in the situation, or how outsiders with different views, would have written the story.

The unit, while subject to minor scholarly criticisms, goes a long way toward creating in the student a desire to find out precisely what social reality is in terms of China. With the help of a well-informed teacher (additional background is almost a necessity), the student can come to an empathetic consideration of things Chinese.

Outstanding Contributions. Through the unit's excellent historical and contemporary reconstructions and its use of varied educational techniques, the authors have gone a long way in remedying the standard set of stereotypes existing in most units available to the teacher. An empathetic understanding of rural China today is created through the imaginative presentation of what social reality *is* for the Chinese, not what some author would have us think it is.

Contents. Introduction; Some Generalizations on Social Change; Social Change; A Case Study of Social Change: Rural China and the Civil War; Land Reform: The Hurricane; The Family: Women, Youth; Village Health and Technology: Grandma Takes Charge; Health in China Today; The Communes

The Story of China
Miriam Greenblatt and Don-chean Chu
McCormick-Mathers, 1968, 156 pp.
Price: $2.44

Authors' Professional Background. Don-chean Chu is professor of comparative education, Indiana University of Pennsylvania. No identification is given for Miriam Greenblatt.

Scope and Emphasis. The unit introduces China's five-thousand-year history as its first "long march," and each section parades facts rather than concepts before the reader. The dynastic histories are compressed into the first twenty pages. The next section relates China's geography to its living patterns and provides much useful information in the process. The chapter on civilization is perhaps the best in the book, since it has a single theme, that is, the things that unified China (Confucianism, family system, writing, government). However, China is presented as a more or less static society which was "disrupted" when the Communists came to power (the second "long march"). The impression that today's China is somehow alien to the Chinese—although such traditional patterns as "nothing is wasted" and "all work is done by human labor" remain—is reinforced in the final section which deals with foreign policy. It depicts China as having taken action "against" Tibet, and having launched an unprovoked "surprise attack" against India. The unit leaves us with: "[The] Chinese are building communism at home. They will spread it through the underdeveloped nations of the world."

Teaching Approach. The text is in a simple narrative style designed for reading levels 6 and 7. The authors relate their topical discussions to common themes (the "long march" of history, the Communists' "long march," and the future "long march" of spreading Communism), and use fictitious third-person stories to illustrate social concepts such as class distinctions in old China, life on a farm, life in Peking today, and so on. The authors try in this way to make a huge body of material more concrete, but these fictitious reconstructions are sometimes stilted and occasionally misleading. The examples also fail to go beyond the ethnocentric bias of Western culture, and apparently were not intended to help us see China in her own terms (e.g., the unit emphasizes advancement of the individual as a key to modernization, and whether or not this is impeded apparently is the criterion for judging a society). The unit includes fifty-nine photos and illustrations with captions, and thirteen maps and charts. The phonetic spelling is given for Chinese names. At the end of each chapter is a section for review which includes word studies, true-false questions, identifications, issues for discussion, and so on. A glossary contains the words and terms referred to in the text.

Unit Evaluation. Although the approach is intentionally simple, the conclusions tend to be simplistic. The China of old is depicted as a steady-state society ruled by Confucianism, supported by mass labor, and decorated with (impressive) artistic achievements. Little attempt is made to understand today's changing China. Most of the China described in the book is that of the latter 1940s:

The country has few railroads or highways.
There is little gasoline for trucks and almost no cargo planes.

As a result, the best way to move food in China is by water [p. 38].

The Yellow River is described as breaking through its dikes "in one spot or another" about "every second year"; there is no word of the impressive achievements in flood control. The description of life in China today is climaxed by a parallel to Orwell's *1984* which ends with:

The Chinese government does not have two-way television screens. But it does have millions of people like Mrs. Chien Feng-hsu [the neighborhood spy and eternal busybody].

Remnants of the international Communist conspiracy theory remain in the text. More subtly, the pictures of People's China tend to be dour, with unsmiling people and age-old laborers. The pictures illustrating Nationalist China show mechanization and smiling faces. A paragraph on the state of agriculture on Taiwan (p. 124) could be equally true of reports from the People's Republic of China today, but this is overlooked.

Outstanding Contributions. The authors effectively explain the major innovations and contributions of the Chinese throughout their history. The unit's approach to those things which unify China, notably in the section on civilization, is perhaps the best aspect of the book.

Contents. The Long March; 1. Life in Old China (The Oldest Living Civilization; Family Life in Old China); 2. The Home of the Chinese People (China's Three Regions; China's Waterways; Villages and Cities); 3. The Arts of Civilization (Writing and Ruling; The Two Thousand Year Government; Chinese Art; Inventions and Constructions); 4. The Passing of Old China (Coming of the Europeans; Decline of the Manchus; The Republican Revolution; The Communist Triumph); 5. Under the Red Star (Life in China's Countryside; Life in China's Cities; Using Natural Resources; The Government of Communist China; Educating People in Communism); 6. Formosa and the Nationalists (A Government in Exile; The Good Earth; the Nationalist Government Today); 7. China and the Road Ahead (Filling the Rice Bowls; Entering the World of Machines; Keeping the Revolution Going; China and Other Nations)

Today's World in Focus: China
Earl Swisher
Ginn and Company, 1973 (Rev. Ed.), 122 pp.
Price: $2.53 list

Author's Professional Background. Earl Swisher is Professor Emeritus at the University of Colorado.

Scope and Emphasis. The eleven chapters of the unit fall into three categories: traditional China, with a focus on geography, people, places, and dynasties; the Chinese Revolution: 1911–49; and Communist and Nationalist China since 1949. The first half of the book is devoted to pre-Communist China and the second half to contemporary China.

Chapter 1 imaginatively evokes a feeling for the Chinese land and people; chapter 3 discusses the cities of China, a less-known yet fascinating subject; and chapters 4 and 5 describe the historical background of the Chinese Revolution and the social basis of the struggles between the Nationalists and Communists.

As a whole, however, the unit emphasizes the dramatic and the quirks of history often at the expense of making fundamental points.

Teaching Approach. The unit's presentation is essentially expository. There are no questions, exercises, or lesson hints to aid either teacher or student in discussing relevant issues. Liberally distributed throughout the unit, however, are well-reproduced visual aids. Brief vignettes of Chinese writing, proverbs, and cookery, a small glossary, and an unannotated bibliography are also included.

Unit Evaluation. Although the unit is advertised as a revised edition, a new cover, a rather pompous introduction, and a brief mention of President Nixon's visit to China are the only apparent changes from the unit reviewed in the first edition of this guide.

The unit vividly and sympathetically describes traditional China, and there is much to recommend it for a basic acquaintance with the land, people, and institutions of that era. Its discussion of the present day, however, is often unbalanced, and does not seem to take advantage of the last several years of China scholarship. Examples abound. Although Communist guerrillas received aid from Russia, the unit stretches the help to saying the Red Army was "led" by the Russians. It is at least questionable if not untrue that "overseas Chinese are used by Peking to influence or control local politics" (p. 110), and doubtful indeed that "China has already occupied or won over Tibet, North Vietnam, Laos and parts of India. Its objective is clearly to absorb all 'neutral' nations of Southeast and South Asia into the Communist bloc.... The Red Army is then prepared to 'liberate' the rest of Asia" (p. 109). The author's distortions also carry over to the domestic side: "the breakdown (Cultural Revolution) proved to be a much greater and more catastrophic disaster than the collapse of the Great Leap Forward more than a decade before" (p. 116).

Thus, beginning with chapter 8, the unit becomes more sensational in tone, sometimes ridiculing the People's Republic without adding to our understanding of what actually was happening or why. The positive tone of the unit is reserved for Taiwan, depicted as a showcase for "Free Asia," and an economic miracle. In the cultural sense, the author tells us, "Taiwan is the only 'real' China left in the world."

Outstanding Contributions. The author is gifted at giving an excellent feeling for traditional China, but the unit cannot be recommended for the study of contemporary society.

Contents. Editor's Introduction; Preface; The Setting: The Land and the People; The Chinese Past; Chinese Cities; The Chinese Revolution; The Communist Victory in China; The Government; China's Struggle to Become a Modern Nation; Taiwan: The Republic of China; Communist China and the World; China's Future; Written Chinese Characters; Printed Characters in a Chinese Newspaper; Useful Words and Phrases; Chinese Proverbs; Chinese Cookery; Glossary; Hints about Chinese Place Names; Bibliography

● *Through Chinese Eyes*
   Volume 1: *Revolution: A Nation Stands Up*
   Volume 2: *Transformation: Building a New Society*
Peter J. Seybolt, Editor
Praeger Books, 1974, Vol. 1: 136 pp.; Vol. 2: 158 pp.

Price: $2.75 per volume (paper); lesson plan books sold separately.

These two volumes are part of the "Praeger World Cultures" series under the general editorship of Leon E. Clark.

Author's Professional Background. Peter J. Seybolt is associate professor of history at the University of Vermont and a specialist on China's educational system. The lesson plans for each volume were written by Leon E. Clark and Jack Strauss. Professor Clark, a former high school teacher, now is on the faculty of the University of Massachusetts; Mr. Strauss teaches at Roger Ludlowe High School in Fairfield, Connecticut.

Scope and Emphasis. The first volume begins with the story of the Communist rise to power, presenting the rural revolution through several eyewitness accounts, and following selections focus on the changes brought about in the lives of women and the new educational system. A series of readings dealing with revolutionary literature and art—taken from contemporary Chinese fiction—conclude the volume.

Volume 2 begins by contrasting the teachings of Confucius with Maoist ideology. The main theme connecting the rest of the readings is the change in everyday life that this transformation of values seeks to bring about. Selections compare pre- and post-revolutionary politics, religion, and social organization. Also covered are topics of current popular interest (acupuncture, environment), several different views on U.S.–China relations, and a postscript on the experience of Chinese-Americans.

Teaching Approach. The stated purpose of the unit is to *show* and not *explain* China. Thus, "it does not offer 'expert' analysis by outside observers but, rather, attempts to recreate the reality of everyday life as experienced by the Chinese people." This is done by the presentation of some forty readings from original source materials. The lesson plan booklets which accompany the text group readings for use in a single class session. The introduction to the lesson plan describes how the teacher can utilize the units for inquiry and value clarification. Suitable for reading at the upper grade levels.

Unit Evaluation. This is an extremely well done collection of readings illustrating the cultural values of the new China as seen from the perspective of classes rarely "heard" from in curriculum units—peasants, women, children, and workers. In so doing, Peter Seybolt has presented a sympathetic and representative portrayal of the underlying social values of today's China, thereby living up to the unit's goal of letting us see the Chinese Revolution through Chinese eyes.

The readings are well tied together, with the editor's introductions placing each selection in its proper historical and social context. The readings often reflect the Chinese sense of moralism, sounding occasionally rigid. Yet the stories fascinate, and the society becomes more dynamic and tangible.

The books do have their limitations—inherent in the inquiry and value clarification approach—and would be more useful if used in combination with a standard history of China such as those mentioned at the end of this chapter, with a unit that helps set the historical and political context more broadly, or with a good film or audio-visual set. Yet the advantages of these units, with their excellent lesson plans, outweigh minor criticism; not only are they suitable for classes dealing exclusively with China, but also may be used thematically in conjunction with other studies—industrialization, peasant conditions, women's rights, or multi-ethnic problems.

Outstanding Contributions. Through Chinese Eyes is a welcome relief from the many impersonal and cold-war biased accounts of the aims and goals of the People's Republic of China. The book is an excellent guide, not only to modern China but to the variety of available historical materials and their use. The author has succeeded in broadening our perspective by presenting a Chinese view of China; for those looking for guidelines to understanding China today, there is no better start.

Contents. Volume 1: Lin-Hsien County—From Poverty to Prosperity; Lin-hsien County—A Recollection of the Past; Stone Wall Village Turns Over; "It's Terrible" or "It's Fine"; The Long March; The Pauper's Co-op; The Traditional Family Ethic; Maoist Ethics; Meng Hsiang-ying Stands Up; Lessons for Women; The Status of Women; The Home Life of a Saleswoman; Education at the Wen-hsing Street Primary School; New Forms of Higher Education; Teaching and Learning from the Peasants;

Romance in the New China; "How I Became a Writer"; Traditional and Modern Art and Poetry

Volume 2: The Confucian Heritage; The Scholar Who Passed the Examination; The Leakage System; The People's Democratic Dictatorship; Leadership and Democracy—The Model Official; Dissent in the People's Republic; Religion in Traditional China; Religion in China Today; Maoism as Religion; The Red Guards; Barefoot Doctors; Acupuncture; The World's Largest Population; Population, Pollution, and Industrial Development; The Iron Man of Taching; Industrial Management and Trade Unions; Instructions for the Chinese Army; Conventional Forces and Nuclear Weapons—Is China a Threat?; China and the United States; Postscript; America Through Chinese Eyes

3. ADDITIONAL BOOKS FOR CLASSROOM USE

Listed below are several books which readily adapt themselves to classroom use and are recommended as supplementary material:

China: Man in His World
James Forrester, with Gary Birchall, John Parr, and Robert Williamson
Bobbs-Merrill, 1972, 64 pp.
Price: $0.50 Paper

This highly recommended booklet falls just short of the strict definition of a classroom unit. Although written especially for elementary and junior high level, it would make a valuable adjunct for any class—its presentation, point of view, and excellent use of basic information adapt readily to many different teaching approaches and materials. The booklet is a potpouri of information sections, illustrations on language, history, philosophy, geography, traditional wealth/population ratios, signs and banners. Simple, yet thematically effective through the use of the case studies (e.g., the imagined reactions of family members being moved to a commune during the Great Leap Forward), the booklet includes good exercises and excellent use of the inquiry method. Some factual errors and occasional stereotyped illustrations (the last illustration is a rather negative cartoon of China's teeming masses in a leaking ship of state being lorded over by the

Communist leadership), dampen only slightly the overall effectiveness of this booklet.

China: Selected Readings on the Middle Kingdom
Leon Hellerman and Alan L. Stein, eds.
Washington Square Books, 1971, 332 pp.
Price: $1.25 Paper

Readings from a variety of sources including historical documents, scholarly analysis, journalistic reports, poems, and stories covering the whole range of Chinese history and culture. It tries to present different views on controversial subjects (e.g., U.S.–China relations). The book can be used in total or be adapted part-by-part.

A Chinese View of China
John Gittings
New York: Pantheon Books, 1973, 216 pp.
Price: $1.95 Paper

Like Peter Seybolt (*Through Chinese Eyes*), Gittings, a professor of Chinese history at Oxford has taken excerpts from Chinese sources to examine how the Chinese themselves view past and current events. Gittings focuses on the pre-1949 period, using contemporary and historical writings (Sun Yat-sen, Lu Hsun, Mao Tse-tung) to show how the past is interpreted to serve the present. Also included is a useful section of facts, figures, and suggestions for further reading.

Communist China: Communal Progress and Individual Freedom
American Education Publications
The Education Center, 1968, 63 pp.
Price: $0.45 Paper

This excellent booklet, which can easily be used as a unit, raises questions about the social and cultural relativity of values. It does so by examining the impact of the Chinese Revolution both in terms of its concrete achievements and its relationship to larger questions of personal values. The author also encourages students to relate their own values to those of American and Chinese society.

● *Modern China: The Making of a New Society from 1839 to the Present*
Orville Schell and Joseph Esherick
Vintage Books, 1972, 143 pp.
Price: $1.50 Paper

An excellent short history of modern China emphasizing the period prior to 1949, although the chapter on the People's Republic is concise and interesting. The text is lucid and frequently interspersed with substantial quotations from original sources and is enhanced by good photographs. The book views peasant uprisings as key ingredients in the evolution of China, concluding that revolution, especially the Communist one, has been beneficial to the people of China. Suitable for 11th and 12th grades, and a very good background survey for teachers.

We the Chinese: Voices from China
Neale and Dierdre Hunter
Praeger Books, 1973, 292 pp.
Price: $2.95 Paper

Especially compiled and written for high school readers, this book, by two Australian teachers, contains original materials of many sorts: speeches, poetry, songs, radio broadcasts, as well as books and periodicals.

5. Audiovisual Materials

1. INTRODUCTION

The effective use of audiovisual materials is especially helpful for building cross-cultural understanding. The written message, often esoteric, obtuse, or condescending, is not always the best way of communicating information. Since audiovisual materials can convey a feeling of actually sharing an experience, they can play a unique role in enriching perceptions through the imaginative presentation of reality.

Furthermore, for the nonspecialist trying to grapple with a complex subject, audiovisual materials rarely create the psychological difficulties that can arise in tackling the "big-name" expertise contained in books and scholarly articles. It is usually easier to question and discuss what one sees and hears than to explain or contradict the "authoritative" written word. Films and other audiovisual materials can help immensely in developing the spirit of inquiry so necessary in classroom discussion and learning.

A considerable quantity of audiovisual materials on China is available. This guide does not list all of these materials, but focuses mainly on films and filmstrips, while including some tapes. Because Americans only recently have been allowed to visit the People's Republic, most footage comes from foreign sources, unless otherwise noted.

Unfortunately, the quantity of materials available is not often paralleled by quality. Many of the films and filmstrips reviewed here are based largely on the creative editing of old material. Even though new material has been appearing in the last several years, many of the films—with some notable exceptions such as Irv Drasnin's *Shanghai*—are of the travelogue variety, noting the readily observable while adding commentary that is only impressionistic and reflects little depth of background. Thus, the assessment in the first edition of this guide still holds: there are few films that combine journalistic competence with creative insight and that get beyond the forms and culture-bound categories of analysis to the moral, social, and human substance beneath.

The reason for this, of course, is still the limited direct access of Western film-makers to the People's Republic. Moreover, the Chinese repeatedly express concern about the "accuracy" and sympathetic understanding reflected in any foreigner's portrayal— the negative example which Chinese authorities made of the 1973 film by the Italian director Antonioni is a special case in point.

Films made in the People's Republic of China are now becoming increasingly available in the United States, and are listed in Part 3 of this book along with other available materials. Thus, there is now more opportunity for Americans to see how the Chinese wish to interpret their own society, including its politics, economy, culture and sports.

In selecting materials and writing evaluations for this section, we recognized that the criterion of "objectivity" is itself vulnerable to political bias or ideological inclination. We attempted, however, to select materials that appear reasonably to meet the test of "objectivity" with regard to the principal historical and cultural facts. Others were included precisely *because* of their controversial nature—and sometimes even poor quality—in the belief that they can serve as points of departure for debate or discussion. By the very nature of the medium, of course, films are but one "eye" on a country and, ideally, the skillful educator uses a wide variety, supplementing them with written materials.

In preparing these reviews, we drew on the talents of many persons, including Stephen Andors, Louise Bennett, Daniel Lovelace, Paul Liston, and Shelley Metzenbaum.

Materials especially recommended are marked with a •.

2. FILMS

The film section is divided into the following categories:
A. China Before 1949
B. China After 1949
C. Hong Kong, Taiwan, and Overseas Chinese
D. Traditional Chinese Culture

All the films listed here may be obtained from the designated distributors, but in many cases are also available from other outlets (state universities, for example). Prices listed were those in effect as of January 1975; the current upsurge of interest in China might cause the prices of some films to rise. Rental terms vary from distributor to distributor, and penalties for late return, term extensions, mailing arrangements, and so on, differ. Most distributors suggest placing orders well in advance (at least three weeks), and will send films parcel post, special delivery, to ensure arrival by the scheduled date.

This guide includes films designed as instructional materials available through January 1975. For subsequent updating, and for a guide to films specifically available in certain regions of the United States, consult the resource centers listed in chapter 8.

Numerous films dealing with, or set in, China are also produced as popular entertainment for overseas Chinese communities and are not reviewed here. A wide variety of these Chinese feature films, many with English subtitles, is available from the Mercury Audio-Visual Center, 1207 33d Avenue, San Francisco, California 94122, (415) 566-1236. None of these films are from the People's Republic of China.

A. CHINA BEFORE 1949

The Ancient Chinese
16 mm, 24 minutes, color, 1974
Distributor: International Film Foundation, Inc.
                475 Fifth Avenue, Room 916
                New York, New York 10017
                (212) 685-4998
Cost: (Sale) $360.00
                (Rental) $36.00
Subject: Early Chinese Civilization
Audience: Senior high and adult

Fourth in a series on early civilization, this film covers the origins and legends of the Shang, Chou, Han, T'ang, and Sung dynasties and glimpses of events in the lives of Confucius, Huang Ti, Marco Polo, and the Mongol conquerors Ghenghis and Kublai Khan. Blending animation based on ancient Chinese motifs with photography of China today and works of art photographed at museums and private collections, the film, made by Julian Bryan, is intended to create an overall sense of the history and continuity of traditional Chinese civilization. Unfortunately, the collection of great art works is flashed on the screen almost at random, seemingly with little connection to the historical narration, thereby making the effect uneven. The most interesting aspect is a marvelous sequence balancing scenes of silkmaking in the People's Republic with paintings illustrating ancient techniques, conveying the continuity of this traditional craft.

China: The Revolution Revisited
16 mm, 82 minutes, black and white, 1972
Distributor: Films Incorporated
               1144 Wilmette Avenue
               Wilmette, Illinois 60091
               (312) 256-4730
Cost: (Sale) $445.00
               (Rental) $40.00
Subject: Modern Chinese history from the Boxer Rebellion to the Nixon Visit
Audience: General

An updated version of Theodore H. White's *China: The Roots of Madness*, this film is one of the better studies available of the origins and development of the Chinese Revolution and is a provocative commentary on modern China's attitudes toward the West. Through the use of extensive and significant historical film footage, it covers the dual strands of internal decay and foreign intervention and the rise of nationalism. It also shows China's consequent rejection of her Confucian heritage as well as of Western influence. Still taking the view that the roots of the People's Republic are found in instability and war, and that "madness" characterizes the present regime, Theodore White narrates the film, which also includes cameos and commentaries by other "old China hands" such as Pearl Buck. Although the image of the People's Republic may be misleading, the film is useful for its historical content.

It is also available from the distributor as a three part series entitled *China: A Century of Revolution.*

Part 1. *Agonies of Nationalism, 1800–1927*
             16 mm, 23 minutes, black and white
             (Sale) $145.00
             (Rental) $18.00
Part 2. *Enemies Within and Without, 1927–1944*
             16 mm, 25 minutes, black and white
             (Sale) $155.00
             (Rental) $18.00

Part 3. *Communist Triumph and Consolidation, 1945–1971*
16 mm, 20 minutes, black and white
(Sale) $130.00
(Rental) $15.00

● *City of Cathay*
16 mm, 25 minutes, color, 1961
Distributor: Chinese Information Service
              159 Lexington Avenue
              New York, New York 10016
              (212) 725-4950
Cost: (Sale) $240.00
              (Rental) Free
Subject: Seventeenth-century painting depicting daily life
Audience: General
    A *City of Cathay* is a Chinese scroll thirty-seven feet long,
originally painted in the eleventh century. This film, with an
accompaniment of traditional Chinese folk songs and other
music, slowly travels the distance of the scroll, and takes a
lingering look at the many and varied aspects of Chinese society
and daily life in Kai Feng (capital of Sung China) portrayed on
the scroll. A most interesting film which, because of the kaleido-
scopic content of the painting, provides an excellent introduction
to Chinese history.

The Fall of China
16 mm, 26 minutes, black and white, 1962
Distributor: Contemporary Films–McGraw Hill
              Princeton Road
              Hightstown, New Jersey 08530
              (609) 448-1700
Cost: (Sale) $135.00
              (Rental) $11.00
Subject: The Civil War in China (1945–49)
Audience: General
    This documentary film is narrated by Walter Cronkite, and
historical footage is interspersed with opinions by Mme Chiang
Kai-shek, General Albert Wedemeyer, Major General David G.

Films   77

Barr, and Pearl Buck. Historical background is furnished for each of these opinions. The role of the United States in the Civil War is traced, and the Communist victory is attributed to the military mistakes of the Nationalists and the ruthlessness of the Communists. Only good for its historical film footage.

● *Peking Remembered*
16 mm, 40 minutes, color, 1967
Distributor: MacMillan-Audio Brandon
              34 MacQuestern Parkway South
              Mount Vernon, New York 10550
              (914) 664-5051
Cost: (Sale) $450.00
              (Rental) $30.00
Subject: Life in Peking prior to 1911
Audience: General

Using a combination of still and motion photography, the film gives the viewer a good "feel" of life among the upper classes in Peking during the fading years of the nineteenth century. Shots of the Summer Palace, eunuchs and concubines, pigeons with flutes tied to their backs, jugglers and street peddlers all contribute to the film's portrayal of what was a removed and untypical aspect of Chinese life. There is a particularly good study of the personality of the Empress Tzu Hsi which uses her reign as a symbol of China's failure to reform its traditions and come to grips with the new challenges. Although the color cinematography has a rather fuzzy sepia cast, the film is generally a fine effort.

● *From War to Revolution*
16 mm, 20 minutes, black and white, 1970
Series: Revolution in China
Distributor: Time-Life Films
              100 Eisenhower Drive
              Paramus, New Jersey 07652
              (201) 843-4545
Cost: (Sale) $125.00
              (Rental) $12.00
Subject: China's political history, 1900–49
Audience: General

This British Broadcasting Corporation film is an excellent survey of the political history of modern China. It begins with the early 1900s—the revolution of Sun Yat-sen and the birth of the Nationalist party—and then covers the off-and-on-again alliance between the Communists and Nationalists in the 1920s and 1930s, as they strive for some sort of national unity in response to the Japanese invasion. The film has rare footage of the peasant mobilization drives and the Communists' Long March (1934). It concludes with scenes of the Civil War and the victory of Mao's revolution in 1949. This is an interesting, intelligent, and well-balanced film particularly suited for audiences with little knowledge of China.

The Good Earth
16 mm, 42 minutes, black and white, 1952
Distributor: Films Incorporated
                      1144 Wilmette Avenue
                      Wilmette, Illinois 60091
                      (312) 256-4730
Cost: (Sale) $245.00
                      (Rental) $28.00
Subject: The life of the peasants in the 1930s
Audience: General
    The film is condensed from the feature-length film *The Good Earth* (1937) adapted from Pearl Buck's novel, and depicts the family, customs, and problems of China in the 1930s. The harshness of peasant life and the traditional Chinese view of women as inferior to men and objects of economic value are vividly portrayed. However, Western actors playing the parts of Chinese peasants detract somewhat from the film's impact.

Mao Tse-tung
16 mm, 27 minutes, black and white, 1964
Distributor: Contemporary Films–McGraw Hill
                      Princeton Road
                      Hightstown, New Jersey 08520
                      (609) 448-1700
Cost: (Sale) $170.00
                      (Rental) $14.00

Subject: Biography of Mao Tse-tung
Audience: General
   This film covers Chinese history since 1912, with Mao Tse-tung as its central figure. Aspects of Mao's personality are described, and the film traces the portions of his life involved with the Communists' struggle for victory. Some interesting old footage is used. The film concludes that Mao and China are a direct military and ideological threat to the United States. May be useful as a supplement to a written biography of Mao. Interesting as history; questionable as to interpretation.

Mao vs. Chiang: Battle for China
16 mm, 30 minutes, black and white, 1964
Distributor: Films Incorporated
               1144 Wilmette Avenue
               Wilmette, Illinois 60091
               (312) 256-4730
Cost: (Sale) $155.00
               (Rental) $18.00
Subject: History of the Chinese Civil War
Audience: General
   Created by extensive editing of interesting documentary footage, this film takes a sharply anti-Communist view of the Chinese Civil War (1945–49). It traces the roots of the conflict, describes the recent history of China, and develops the personalities and roles of Mao Tse-tung and Chiang Kai-shek in the protracted Civil War.

A Town by the Yangtse
16 mm, 10 minutes, color, 1971
Distributor: Pictura Films Distribution Corporation
               43 West 16th Street
               New York, New York 10011
               (212) 691-1730
Cost: (Sale) $150.00
               (Rental) $10.00
Subject: A time standstill portrait of pre-1949 China
Audience: General

The film presents a rather poetic picture of the medieval town of Changsu as it appeared before 1949. The village is on the shore of the Yangtse River, and daily life includes farming, fishing, boatbuilding, peddling, and housewifely chores. Scenes of ancestral tombs, temples, and an underlying theme of "returning home to die" add to a picture of China as untouched by the onrush of revolutionary change. A fond glimpse of a way of life now passed into history. Produced and narrated by Wan-Go Weng in the 1950s.

War in China
16 mm, 26 minutes, black and white, 1959
Distributor: Contemporary Films–McGraw Hill
               Princeton Road
               Hightstown, New Jersey 08520
               (609) 448-1700
Cost: (Sale) $135.00
               (Rental) $11.00
Subject: The Japanese invasion of China, 1937
Audience: General
    Walter Cronkite narrates this film, which uses old newsreels to graphically illustrate the poverty, death, and destruction which resulted from the Japanese invasion of China in 1937. The role of the Nationalist government and its army in the resistance is emphasized with little mention of the Communists. The film does not adequately deal with the politics of the time it seeks to portray, but is interesting as an example of cold war news reporting.

B. CHINA AFTER 1949

Assignment: Red China
16 mm, 25 minutes, color, 1973
Distributor: Avon Productions, Inc.
               200 West 57th Street
               New York, New York 10019
               (212) LT 1-4460
Cost: Free on loan basis to schools, clubs, social
               organizations
Subject: Life in China today

Films   *81*

Audience: General, especially for those with no background

This is an unusual film. John Duprey, Senior Photographer for the New York *Daily News*, narrates a series of still photographs he took on a visit to China in 1973. Specialists would bridle at the simple explanations, the folksy narrative, and the offhand and sometimes gratuitous statements. Yet, for many audiences, this film is engaging, lively, and down-to-earth, giving an overview of the progress made since 1949 in housing, education, health care, nutrition, and so on—along with the problems that still remain. Although there is no attempt to explain the complexities of Chinese society, it succeeds as an unpretentious introduction.

Behind the Great Wall of China
16 mm, 70 minutes, color, 1954
Distributor: Film Images
              17 West 60th Street
              New York, New York 10023
              (212) 279-6653
Cost: (Sale) $850.00
              (Rental) $60.00 classroom only
              $90.00 admission audiences
Subject: Economic and social changes in China during the
              early 1950s
Audience: General

Although this film was made before the completion of agricultural collectivization and the elimination of private industry, it is still an excellent depiction of the enormous changes that have swept the People's Republic of China. By contrasting the traditional patterns of economic and social life with emerging developments, the film portrays the contradictory forces that are at work in Chinese society and illustrates how the new is replacing the old. Emphasis is on the calm and peaceful nature of the transition, however, with little mention of the turmoil which sometimes accompanies the political campaigns.

China
35 mm, 16 mm, 65 minutes, color, 1963
Distributor: Impact Films

144 Bleecker Street
New York, New York 10012
(212) 674-3375
Cost: (Sale) $745.00
(Rental) $145.00 or 50 percent of the proceeds of
admission, whichever is greater. For classes of no
more than 50, a 30 percent discount is available.
Subject: Life in China prior to the Cultural Revolution
Audience: General

The film was made by Felix Greene, a British citizen living in the United States. At the time of its appearance, the film was highly controversial in the U.S. because it was a warm, sympathetic account of the new China as seen during Greene's travels. It concentrates on life in factories and communes and among the more Westernized segments of the population in Shanghai. China is presented as a proud and dynamic nation making progress toward modernization and self-respect. The photography is excellent, with superb color. Considerable Chinese government footage is used. In light of recent developments, the film is no longer shocking to an American audience, and adds up as a somewhat dated documentary—especially in view of Greene's new series of films (See: *One Man's China*, p. 103).

China
Six films in an untitled series by Jens Bjerre
16 mm, 13 minutes each, color, 1973
Distributor: Pictura Films Distribution Company
43 West 16th Street
New York, New York 10011
(212) 691-1730
Cost: (Sale) $175.00 each
(Rental) $20.00 each
Subject: An overview of life in China
Individual films in the series include:
At Home in China: The Modern Family
How families have bridged the gap between
tradition and the requirements of the present
social system
Barefoot Doctors of China

Education of "barefoot doctors" and their relationship with the people they treat
Cities of China
Peking, Shanghai, and Canton
Growing Up in China
A look at primary and secondary schools
Industrial China
Close-up view of industry and the workers
Life in a Chinese Commune
Life in a large commune near a big city, and a more primitive one in a remote rural area

Audience: Elementary; possibly junior high

The entire series works very well as an introduction to China for the younger student. Remarkably free of political comment even though many scenes may tempt such remarks. The films are technically well done and their shortness as well as excellent editing will hold the attention of even the youngest. Visually colorful and lively, the best of the series are *Barefoot Doctors, At Home in China,* and *Growing Up in China.*

China: The Awakening Giant
16 mm, 17 minutes, color, 1966
Distributor: Contemporary Films–McGraw Hill
               Princeton Road
               Hightstown, New Jersey 08520
               (609) 448-1700
Cost: (Sale) $225.00
               (Rental) $15.00
Subject: China's agricultural and industrial development
Audience: General

Stressing the role of the frontier in China's future, the film shows China in the process of great political, economic, and social change, and emphasizes her efforts in agriculture and industry. Excellent geographical background is provided through maps and commentary, making the film especially suited as an introduction to the subject of Chinese modernization.

China: The Big Question
16 mm, 16 minutes, color, 1968

84   Audiovisual Materials

Distributor: AV-ED Films
              7934 Santa Monica Boulevard
              Hollywood, California 90046
              (213) 654-9550
Cost: (Sale) $170.00
              (Rental) $10.00
Subject: Political control in China
Audience: General

According to the study sheet which accompanies this film, the "big question" is: What does the future hold for these children born in hate, taught that all individuals must think and act alike? What does the future hold for us? The film probes its answer through a critical look at the massive effort in China to create a society of absolute equality by means of political control. After mentioning the great improvement in the general living conditions of the people (albeit at the cost of freedom), the film focuses on the control exercised by the Communist party and its intensive and all-pervasive propaganda machinery. Emphasis is placed on the elements of blind obedience to the state and on the hatred that is learned toward the United States. Not recommended.

China: Cities in Transition
Super 8 mm, 16 mm, 18 minutes, color, 1969
Series: Red China
Distributor: Doubleday Multimedia
              1371 Reynolds Avenue
              Santa Ana, California 92705
              (714) 540-5550
Cost: (Sale) $150.50 super 8 mm
              $240.50 16 mm
              (Rental) $22.00 16 mm only
Subject: Urban life in Shanghai
Audience: General

This film conveys something of the flavor of life in Shanghai, China's largest city. It was taken in the late 1960s by a Japanese camera crew, and the result is a colorful yet superficial study. Much is made of the contrast between "old" and "new" Shanghai, with clean but spartan housing projects juxtaposed against some of the city's remaining prerevolutionary slums. Some very good shots of people in the streets and parks, waterfront traffic, department stores, and various forms of public entertainment highlight the film, and the commentary is adequate; but Chinese words and names are consistently mispronounced. The last few minutes consist of a montage of scenes from Peking and environs (T'ien An Men Square, the Forbidden City, the Great Wall) and give the impression of having been tacked on as an afterthought.

● *China: Commune*
16 mm, 35 minutes, color, 1974
Distributor: Westinghouse Learning Corporation
               100 Park Avenue
               New York, New York 10017
               (212) 983-5077
Cost: (Sale) $350.00
               (Rental) $35.00
Subject: A closeup look in to the life of the people and institutions of a Chinese commune
Audience: General

Produced as a television documentary for Westinghouse Broadcasting Company by Peggy Printz and Paul Steinle, a husband and wife journalistic team, "Commune" is a view of Kwang Li commune in Kwangtung Province, 55 miles west of Canton. In addition to showing the daily lives of the peasants, the film depicts commune administration, schools, the market, department stores, factory work, fishing, local entertainment and medical facilities. Members of two families are singled out to show their role within the commune, and the film blends a view of daily tasks with the political ideology and organization behind it.

While effectively conveying the generations-old tasks of rural life, the film is less successful in explaining the new motivation and organization now underlying them—the work brigades and teams, work points, and the general operation of the commune system. The photography is excellent (particularly of the geographic setting), and, overall, the film provides a good comprehensive view of life on a Chinese commune.

● *China: An End to Isolation?*
16 mm, 25 minutes, color, 1970

Distributor: ACI Films, Inc.
               35 West 45th Street
               New York, New York 10036
               (212) 582-1918
Cost: (Sale) $300.00
               (Rental) Inquire from distributor
Subject: Contemporary Chinese society and politics
Audience: General

Surveys kindergartens, department stores, apartment blocks, factories, communes, fish farms, schools, and streets of Peking and Shanghai. The Yangtse River bridge at Nanking is presented as a symbol of China's commitment to self-reliance. A visit to the Canton Trade Fair provides an introduction to a discussion of China's foreign trade patterns. A trip to Mao's birthplace at Shao Shan is followed by an excellent explanation of the origins and goals of the Cultural Revolution. Other topics given good treatment are reforms in the educational system and the drive to reduce the dichotomy existing between town and countryside. By and large one of the more successful films on the P.R.C. The color cinematography is good; the dialogue is objective and asks useful questions.

China: Feeding One-Quarter of the Human Race
16 mm, 16 minutes, color, 1967
Distributor: Contemporary Films–McGraw Hill
               Princeton Road
               Hightstown, New Jersey 08520
               (609) 448-1700
Cost: (Sale) $215.00
               (Rental) $15.00
Subject: Food and population problems in China
Audience: General, particularly junior and senior high

By examples from various regions of China, the film shows the great variety in patterns of Chinese agriculture. It focuses on improvements in land utilization and agricultural techniques introduced since 1949. Noting the potential for agricultural development which lies in the virgin lands of Western China, the film ends on a cautious note of optimism about the future of China's food-population ratio. Good maps and an intelligent commentary add to the instructional value of the film.

China: A Hole in the Bamboo Curtain
16 mm, 28 minutes, color, 1973
Distributor: Carousel Films, Inc.
1501 Broadway, Suite 1503
New York, New York 10036
(212) 279-6734
Cost: (Sale) $350.00
(Rental) Apply to distributor
Subject: A tourist view of today's China
Audience: General

Two television newsmen from New Orleans made this film as they accompanied a Congressional delegation to China in 1973. It is a detailed account of their visit to Shenyang, Peking, Shanghai, and Kwangchow (Canton), focusing on what they saw of the people, their lifestyles, their schools, factories, and other institutions. The delegation visited with a rice farmer in his commune home and a factory worker in his high-rise apartment. There was a visit to the Great Wall, to the Forbidden City, and to a hospital to observe surgery performed with acupuncture anaesthesia. This is the China exhibited on the "standard tour" and the producers manage it objectively, informatively, and with a sensitive touch.

China: The Industrial Revolution
16 mm, 16 minutes, color, 1967
Distributor: Contemporary Films–McGraw Hill
Princeton Road
Hightstown, New Jersey 08520
(609) 448-1700
Cost: (Sale) $215.00
(Rental) $15.00
Subject: Industry in China
Audience: General

Beginning with a map showing the geographic distribution and quantity of China's raw materials, the film goes on to show the tremendous progress made in heavy industry (through the usual shots of hot, molten steel) and local industry (such as basic implements, weaving, and so on) in support of agricultural mechanization. The film sees the large labor supply as the most abundant resource in China's development strategy. Although this film is generally a good introduction to the subject, there is little mention of the relationship between politics and modernization—a link especially important to Chinese leaders.

China: Life on the Land
Super 8 mm, 16 mm, 15 minutes, color, 1969
Series: Red China
Distributor: Doubleday Multimedia
             1371 Reynolds Avenue
             Santa Ana, California 92705
             (714) 540-5550
Cost: (Sale) $131.50 super 8 mm
             $195.50 16 mm
             (Rental) $20.00 16 mm only
Subject: The agricultural economy of China
Audience: Junior and senior high
    This film offers a brief and somewhat superficial introduction to agricultural production techniques in contemporary China as seen by a Japanese camera crew in 1968. There is some good footage of agricultural production teams in action, students and People's Liberation Army contingents on volunteer labor missions, drills of the People's Militia, and rural life in general. But the commentary is occasionally marred by gross distortions such as "starvation for the Chinese is a normal state of affairs." Although there is some brief coverage of mechanized farming in the Shanghai area, the general impression conveyed is that of the continuing backwardness of China's agricultural sector.

China: Modernization through Human Power
Super 8 mm, 16 mm, 16 minutes, color, 1969
Series: Red China
Distributor: Doubleday Multimedia
             1371 Reynolds Aveue
             Santa Ana, California 92705
             (714) 540-5550

Cost: (Sale) $146.50 super 8 mm
                   $230.50 16 mm
                   (Rental) $22.00
Subject: Industrialization of the People's Republic of China
Audience: Junior and senior high, college

This is the best in the Red China series filmed by a Japanese camera crew in China during the last stages of the Cultural Revolution. It performs a valuable service by focusing on the role of the urban labor force in China's expanding industrialization. The life of the Chinese worker as producer, consumer, and citizen is seen in the cities of Shanghai and Wuhan. Topics covered include: factory conditions, housing facilities, schools, day care centers, food markets, medical care, and militia drills (with which the film ends, leaving a rather military emphasis on human power). The film also includes a good discussion of the role of women and of living conditions—salaries, rents, food costs, school and medical fees, and so on. The photography is excellent, and, on the whole, the commentary is well balanced.

China: The Old and the New
16 mm, 16 minutes, color, 1966
Distributor: Contemporary Films–McGraw Hill
                 Princeton Road
                 Hightstown, New Jersey 08520
                 (609) 448-1700
Cost: (Sale) $215.00
                   (Rental) $15.00
Subject: Economic and social change in China
Audience: General

By contrasting urban and rural China and the differences in generations within families, the film examines changes in language, religion, education, status of women, music, art, medicine, transportation, health, and housing since 1949. Stress is on change amid continuity (which social patterns of traditional China remain, and which are the Communists changing?), with an emphasis on the new patterns of life such as communal living. The photography is good and the commentary intelligent.

China: An Open Door
16 mm, 55 minutes, color, 1973

Distributor: Oxford Films
                 1136 North Las Palmas Avenue
                 Los Angeles, California 90038
                 (213) 461-9231
Cost: (Sale) $720.00 complete set
                 (Rental) $90.00 complete set
Subject: History, culture, and politics
                 Part 1: *An Awakening Giant* 20 minutes
                 (Sale) $260.00
                 (Rental) $30.00
                 Part 2. *The Past is Prologue* 20 minutes
                 (Sale) $260.00
                 (Rental) $30.00
                 Part 3: *Today and Tomorrow* 15 minutes
                 (Sale) $200.00
                 (Rental) $30.00
Audience: Senior high and adult

Produced by Sam Summerlin and filmed by journalist John
Roderick during President Nixon's visit to China in 1972, the film
attempts to present modern China through its history, culture,
modern politics, and current leaders. Unfortunately, the film
gives simplistic and categorical interpretations of major events in
Chinese history that are still highly debatable, and is marred by
frequent and irresponsible use of words like "brutal," "forced,"
and so on. A statement such as "compromise runs in the blood of
most Chinese" (used to describe negotiating skills) tends to take
on the aspect of a racial slur. Not recommended.

China: A Portrait of the Land
16 mm, 18 minutes, color/black and white, 1967
Distributor: Encyclopaedia Britannica
                 1822 Pickwick Avenue
                 Glenview, Illinois 60025
                 (312) 321-7311
Cost: (Sale) $225.00 color
                 $130.00 black and white
                 (Rental) $11.00 color
Subject: Geography and population of China
Audience: General

The film focuses on the regional differences in China in terms
of population density, climate, geography, and economic devel-

opment. Dividing the country into five major areas (North China, South China, Tibet, Manchuria, and Inner Mongolia), the film emphasizes the potential for population expansion and economic development of the vast territories of Western and Northern China. The photography is excellent and the commentary intelligent.

China: The Social Revolution
16 mm, 17 minutes, color, 1967
Distributor: Contemporary Films–McGraw Hill
                      Princeton Road
                      Hightstown, New Jersey 08520
                      (609) 448-1700
Cost: (Sale) $225.00
                      (Rental) $15.00
Subject: Changes in the pattern of Chinese society
Audience: General
   The film focuses on China's use of political indoctrination and control to narrow the traditional gaps and antagonisms between formerly disparate social strata such as the upper classes and peasants, officials and common people, and intellectuals and workers. The film also discusses the changing roles of women and religion. It is a well-balanced presentation which makes an excellent introduction to discussion of how and why the Chinese are attempting to induce social change.

● *China and the World*
16 mm, 20 minutes, black and white, 1970
Series: Revolution in China
Distributor: Time-Life Films
                      100 Eisenhower Drive
                      Paramus, New Jersey 07652
                      (201) 843-4545
Cost: (Sale) $125.00
                      (Rental) $12.00
Subject: China's foreign policy, 1917–67
Audience: General, particularly junior and senior high
   In answer to the question, Why is China the rogue elephant of

92   Audiovisual Materials

world politics? the film begins with a description of China's geography and then presents a concise history of her humiliation by foreign powers during the nineteenth century. Excellent newsreel footage is used to depict in detail the Republican era (1911–37), the Japanese War, the Communist victory in 1949, China's involvement in Korea, and the conflict between China and the U.S. over the status of Taiwan. There are also intelligent presentations of the deterioration of Sino-Soviet relations, the China-India boundary dispute, and China's relations with Third World countries. This film was originally produced by the British Broadcasting Corporation and is particularly suited for audiences with little knowledge of China.

China's Chair
16 mm, 28 minutes, color, 1971
Distributor: Contemporary Films–McGraw Hill
               Princeton Road
               Hightstown, New Jersey 08520
               (609) 448-4700
Cost: (Sale) $260.00
               (Rental) $20.00
Subject: Representation of the People's Republic of China
               in the United Nations
Audience: General

This is a straightforward history of the relationship between the United Nations and the People's Republic of China before her entry into the world body in 1971. Since it was produced by the film division of the UN, which prohibits editorial comment, the closest the film comes to subjective analysis is an interview with Chester Ronning, a former Canadian ambassador to Peking. Except for the comments by Mr. Ronning, the film consists of historical documentary footage from the Second World War, the Chinese Civil War, the Korean War, the 1954 Geneva Conference, and the various discussions of the Chinese representation issue in the UN Security Council and General Assembly.

China's Industrial Revolution
16 mm, 15 minutes, color/black and white, 1967

Distributor: Encyclopaedia Britannica
                1822 Pickwick Avenue
                Glenview, Illinois 60025
                (312) 321-7311
Cost: (Sale) $220.00 color
                $115.00 black and white
                (Rental) $11.00
Subject: Industrialization in China from 1949 to 1966
Audience: General, particularly junior and senior high
   The film depicts China's pattern of industrialization after 1949.
The need to balance development in both the industrial and
agricultural sectors is the general theme of the film. It shows
China as increasingly self-sufficient and self-reliant as a result of
her ability to build up her machine industry while gradually
solving the problem of maintaining sufficient agricultural output.
The role played by substantial aid from the Soviet Union during
the 1950s is emphasized, and there is a short commentary on
China's foreign policy. An intelligent presentation.

China's Villages in Change
16 mm, 20 minutes, color/black and white, 1967
Distributor: Encyclopaedia Britannica
                1822 Pickwick Avenue
                Glenview, Illinois 60025
                (312) 321-7311
Cost: (Sale) $290.00 color
                $150.00 black and white
                (Rental) $13.50
Subject: Chinese agriculture and rural life
Audience: General
   The film deals with China's problems in agriculture and the
peasant economy. By focusing on three different villages in widely
separated parts of the country, the film presents instructive
contrasts in economic standards, living conditions, and patterns
of social behavior. A very useful film for stimulating discussion on
Chinese agriculture and rural life and what must be done to
achieve "progress."

The China Story: One-Fourth of Humanity
16 mm, 74 minutes, color, 1968

Distributor: Impact Films
144 Bleecker Street
New York, New York 10012
(212) 674-3375
Cost: (Sale) $800.00
(Rental) $145.00
Subject: Panorama of Chinese Communist history
Audience: General

This film is a feature-length color documentary by the late American journalist Edgar Snow and contains some rare footage from Snow's private collection. It surveys the Chinese Revolution from the Long March to the Great Proletarian Cultural Revolution, and includes interviews with Mao Tse-tung and Chou En-lai. Snow was a close friend of some of China's top leaders, and the film is a visually pleasing and sympathetic account of the new China.

● *China Today*
16 mm, 29 minutes, color, 1972
Distributor: Films Incorporated
1144 Wilmette Avenue
Wilmette, Illinois 60091
(312) 256-4730
Cost: (Sale) $355.00
(Rental) $25.00
Subject: Social and political life in China today
Audience: General

China Today is one of the better documentaries available on the People's Republic of China. Produced, written and narrated in 1972 by Joe Schlesinger for the Canadian Broadcasting Corporation, the film is highly recommended for its intelligent, objective commentary and smooth continuity. It finds the Chinese people "hard at work, orderly, tranquil, and transformed" as it moves between topics and cities in an orderly and highly instructive way. The result is a feeling of "wholeness" seldom achieved in films about contemporary China.

There are interesting views of life in and around Peking, Shanghai ("irrepressibly lively"), and Tientsin which focus on factories, housing projects, a commune, transportation, children, the role of women in the work force, schools and universities, the supply of consumer goods and food, and eating facilities. The film

Films   *95*

conveys a sense of how Mao's ideas (self-reliance, personal involvement, dignity of manual labor) are applied to daily life, and how politics not only dominates work but can inspire it. The ending, a display of fireworks, comes naturally as a celebration of the achievements of China that are so vividly presented in the film. A condensed version, *Mao's China*, is also available from the distributor, but is less effective.

China under Communism
16 mm, 22 minutes, color/black and white, 1962
Distributor: Encyclopaedia Britannica
                  1822 Pickwick Avenue
                  Glenview, Illinois 60025
                  (312) 321-7311
Cost: (Sale) $290.00 color
                  $150.00 black and white
                  (Rental) $13.50
Subject: China's problems in economic development
Audience: Senior high

This film deals with economic conditions in China during the Great Leap Forward (1958–59) as told by refugees in Hong Kong. This, of course, leads to a highly distorted picture of the campaign, focusing only on the mistakes and failures of this period, and on the human cost of the progress made in technology and industry. Because the policies of the Great Leap Forward were soon abandoned as admitted failure, their description in the film as consistent Chinese policy makes it seriously outdated.

The Chinese-Soviet Relationship
16 mm, 28 minutes, black and white, 1964
Series: The Meaning of Communism
Distributor: Sterling Films
                  600 Grand Avenue
                  Richfield, New Jersey 07657
                  (201) 943-8200
Cost: (Sale) $150.00
                  (Rental) $12.50
Subject: The Sino-Soviet split
Audience: Senior high and college

This film presents a discussion between professors A. Doak Barnett and Marshall Schulman on the nature and development of the ideological split between China and the Soviet Union. The major points of dispute, and also those of agreement, are outlined in this film, which can serve as background for further discussion of Sino-Soviet relations. However, it lacks liveliness and is now dated.

Communist China
16 mm, 23 minutes, black and white, 1965
Distributor: Contemporary Films–McGraw Hill
                Princeton Road
                Hightstown, New Jersey 08520
                (609) 448-1700
Cost: (Sale) $140.00
                (Rental) $10.00
Subject: Problems of change and development in China
Audience: General
This film focuses chiefly on China's population problem, and the prospects for the future. It discusses the traditional "conservatism" of the peasants, and outlines the Communists' efforts to induce social change among them. Giving a slightly pessimistic view of the future, the film then propounds the thesis that flood control, water conservation, education, and land reform will—given enough time—allow the problems of food production and population growth to be solved.

• *The Forbidden City*
16 mm, 43 minutes, color, 1973
Distributor: NBC Educational Enterprises
                30 Rockefeller Plaza
                New York, New York 10020
                (212) 247-8300
Cost: (Sale) $435.00
                (Rental) $21.00
Subject: The Imperial Palace in Peking and the role of art
                in China today
Audience: General
  "Forbidden City" was produced by Lucy Jarvis, and shown

nationally on television. It recalls a part of the history of China when emperors ruled in isolated splendor while many of the Chinese people lived in hopeless misery. The viewer is given a tour of the compound of palaces in the center of Peking which house the treasurers of the emperors, and is reminded that these rulers were protected from foreigners by the Great Wall and from their own people by walls and moats. Today, the Ku Kung (Forbidden City) is open to all the Chinese people, and is undergoing constant restoration.

Ms. Jarvis shows us the palace treasures through the eyes of three generations of a Chinese family—a grandfather, his son, and the son's family—who come to visit the Forbidden City. The film departs from her other two works on world art treasures ("The Louvre" and "The Kremlin") in that it ensures a view largely in accord with Chinese Communist interpretation of history.

Visually beautiful, the film can be recommended as an excellent presentation of China's past and present, and for providing an opportunity to hear how the Chinese themselves consider the place of art in their society.

Inside Red China
16 mm, 54 minutes, black and white, 1957 (sound track updated 1965)
Distributor: Audio-Brandon Films
                34 MacQuesten Parkway South
                Mt. Vernon, New York 10550
                (914) 664-5051
Cost: (Sale) $250.00
                (Rental) $22.50
Subject: Overview of China's economy and politics
Audience: General

Inside Red China was made by Robert Cohen, an American who accompanied a group of U.S. students who, despite the U.S. travel ban, went to China on a "friendship tour" in 1957. This record of his forty-five-day, seven-thousand-mile tour covers a wide variety of subjects. China's progress in agriculture and industry, at a time when Russian aid was still available and welcome, is emphasized. It also depicts communication and transport facilities, sampan life, student life, and mass demonstrations. Although dated, the film is a fairly interesting and sympathetic travelogue.

Inside Red China
16 mm, 51 minutes, color/black and white, 1967
Distributor: Carousel Films
              1501 Broadway
              New York, New York 10036
              (212) 524-4126
Cost: (Sale) $550.00 color
              $275.00 black and white
              (Rental) Apply to distributor
Subject: China since the Great Leap Forward (1958)
Audience: General

In this film, produced by CBS news from foreign film clips, scenes of industrial growth and the communes are contrasted with the generally low technological level, the labor-intensive economy, and the inadequate transport system. Especially interesting are the views of the clean and efficient Chinese railroads, and the faces of youth. The film ends with a somewhat superficial discussion on the causes and development of the Red Guard and the Cultural Revolution.

Life in China: Agricultural Worker in the Commune
16 mm, 28 minutes, black and white, 1971
Distributor: Film Distribution Supervisor
              Department of Photography and Cinema
              Ohio State University
              156 West 19th Avenue
              Columbus, Ohio 43210
              (614) 422-2223
Cost: (Sale) $120.00
              (Rental) $7.50
Subject: Commune structure and the place of the individual
              within it
Audience: General

Part of the Life in China series filmed by Australian educator Myra Roper during her trips to China between 1958 and 1969, and one of a projected series of seven films attempting to understand the Chinese within the context of their own society, "Agricultural Worker in the Commune" is a sympathetic portrayal of the social and administrative structure of one commune whose output has continually increased. Uneven transition and other effects of muddled editing tend to detract from the film and cause it to seem longer than its running time. (For other films in the series, see "Mill Worker's Family" and "Industry.")

Life in China: Industry
16 mm, 28 minutes, black and white, 1972
Distributor: Film Distribution Supervisor
              Department of Photography and Cinema
              Ohio State University
              156 West 19th Avenue
              Columbus, Ohio 43210
              (614) 422-2223
Cost: (Sale) $135.00
              (Rental) $8.00
Subject: Light and heavy industry in China
Audience: General

Light and heavy industry along with the life of the industrial worker is the subject of this film, using footage taken in 1958–62 by the Australian educator Myra Roper. The iron and steel mills of Wuhan are depicted as representative of heavy industry, and a fertilizer plant, ceramics factory, textile mill, and a commune tea factory are examples of light industry. The living conditions of the average worker are shown. Graphically, the film is of uneven quality, and the editing has only made it worse. A cursory script further detracts from the film, making it ineffective in general. (Others in the series are: "Mill Worker's Family" and "Agricultural Worker in the Commune.")

Life in China: Mill Worker's Family
16 mm, 17 minutes, black and white, 1971
Distributor: Film Distribution Supervisor
              Department of Photography and Cinema
              Ohio State University
              156 West 19th Avenue
              Columbus, Ohio, 43210

Cost:　　　　(614) 422-2223
　　　　　　　(Sale) $120.00
　　　　　　　(Rental) $7.50
Subject:　　 Everyday life of an industrial worker in Peking
Audience:　 General

Filmed by the Australian educator and traveler Myra Roper, this is the least pretentious and most straightforward film in the series covering life in China today (actually, the 1958–62 period— see "Agricultural Worker in the Commune" and "Industry.") The film portrays the everyday life of a mill worker and his wife who work on the same factory team. Working conditions, a communal kitchen, nursery and kindergarten activities, apartment housing, factory medical facilities, street markets, and leisure hours are all shown. The photography is excellent; however, Miss Roper, a sympathetic observer, tends to overgeneralize about some aspects of Chinese life.

Life in North China
16 mm, 18 minutes, color, 1971
Distributor:　 Films Incorporated
　　　　　　　 1144 Wilmette Avenue
　　　　　　　 Wilmette, Illinois 60091
　　　　　　　 (312) 256-4730
Cost:　　　　 (Sale) $230.00
　　　　　　　 (Rental) $19.00
Subject:　　　Life in China during the Cultural Revolution
Audience:　　 Junior and senior high

This is an edited version of the ninety-minute film, *Report from China*. The original film was effective in explaining the Chinese attempt to "integrate" the revolution—bridging the gaps between management and labor, intellectuals and common people, city and countryside, and so on. Unfortunately, the shortened version lacks creative editing and is reduced to a simple travelogue— showing the usual scenes of farms, factories, and mass rallies with little concern for the spirit and outlook of the Chinese people. An inaccurate statement ("the individuals own the land, but work it on a collective basis") and some new and incongruous background music add to the sense of disappointment. However, the cinematography is excellent, and the film serves as a good first glance at an interesting part of China.

● *Misunderstanding China*
16 mm, 50 minutes, color, 1972
Distributor: CBS Educational and Publishing Group
                383 Madison Avenue
                New York, New York 10017
                (212) 688-9100 (ext. 795)
Cost: (Sale) $575.00
                (Rental) $50.00 plus airmail shipping
Subject: American perceptions and misperceptions of China
Audience: General

An excellent historical presentation of how Americans have viewed China, relying upon clips from old films, illustrations from comic books and texts, and other sources that generally presented China to Americans as either quaint or ruthless, elegant or impoverished, and of course always inscrutable. The film uses considerable newsreel footage taken during China's war with Japan and builds to a candid and often harsh description of the weakness and collapse of the Nationalist armies and the success of Mao's revolution. Produced by Irv Drasnin and narrated by CBS news correspondent Charles Kurralt, this film is highly recommended as an excellent lesson in cultural values and stereotyping. *Misunderstanding China* also would complement several of the better units reviewed in chapter 4.

● *The New China*
16 mm, 20 minutes, black and white, 1970
Series: Revolution in China
Distributor: Time-Life Films
                100 Eisenhower Drive
                Paramus, New Jersey 07562
                (201) 843-4545
Cost: (Sale) $125.00
                (Rental) $12.00
Subject: Social, political and economic organization in
                China
Audience: General

This is the third in a series of three films produced for television by the British Broadcasting Corporation. (See *China and the World* and *From War to Revolution*.) It focuses on social, political, and economic reorganization in China since 1949 and presents intelligent commentary on land distribution, the organization of communes and industry, mechanization, education, the role of women, political indoctrination, and the causes of the Cultural Revolution. This well-done film is particularly suited for audiences with little knowledge of China.

Norman Bethune
16 mm, 60 minutes, black and white, 1965
Distributor: Contemporary Films–McGraw Hill
             Princeton Road
             Hightstown, New Jersey 08520
             (609) 448-1700
Cost: (Sale) $350.00
             (Rental) $30.00
Subject: The life of Dr. Norman Bethune and his role in the Chinese Revolution.
Audience: General, with some knowledge of China helpful
   This film, particularly effective artistically, traces the life and political evolution of the Canadian surgeon Dr. Norman Bethune. It shows his early life as a bon vivant doctor, his dedication to the cause of Republican Spain, and ends with a portrayal of his medical work with Mao's forces during the Chinese Revolution. Since Bethune's life is now portrayed as a model of dedication and service to the Chinese people, this film provides insight into the content of revolutionary doctrine.

One Man's China
Seven films, 16 mm, 25 minutes each, color, 1972
Distributor: Time-Life Films
             100 Eisenhower Drive
             Paramus, New Jersey 07652
             (201) 843-4545
Cost: (Sale) $1800.00 series
             $300.00 each film
             (Rental) $210.00 series
             $35.00 each film
Subject: Various aspects of China today
Films in the series include:
- *Eight or Nine in the Morning*. A look at changes in education as the basis for building the new society.
- *The People's Commune*. Ways in which China, where the

majority of its 800 million people work the land, is reaching self-sufficiency in agriculture.

One Nation, Many People. The diversity and life-style of the national minorities.

The People's Army. In addition to a fighting force, the People's Liberation Army is involved in politics, engineering, and agriculture.

Self-reliance. China's progress in decentralizing industry and fostering local, small-scale technical enterprise.

A Great Treasure House. The revolution in Chinese medicine, including the blending of the modern and traditional (e.g., acupuncture) means for treatment.

- *Friendship First, Competition Second.* Chinese sports, including acrobatics, gymnastics, and Wushu.

Audience: General

The British journalist Felix Greene, a frequent traveler to China over the past two decades, produced this series of films in cooperation with Chinese authorities during his 1972 visit. *One Man's China* originally was intended to be a single film, but Greene began to feel that China's developmental experience was "so totally different from anything that is happening elsewhere in the world that it cannot be captured in a single (even long) film." Thus, he produced this series of excellent documentaries which present China in a favorable and sympathetic light. The photography is uniformly spectacular—even breathtaking at times. In spite of some tendency toward oversimplification and generalization, the series can be recommended as lively, visually pleasing, and a solidly informative portrayal of what the Chinese are accomplishing.

Red China
16 mm, 54 minutes, black and white, 1962
Distributor: Contemporary Films–McGraw Hill
                Princeton Road
                Hightstown, New Jersey 08520
                (609) 448-1700
Cost: (Sale) $300.00
                (Rental) $25.00
Subject: Survey of China during the Great Leap Forward
Audience: General

The film was taken by a Swiss journalist during the height of the Great Leap Forward (1958) and focuses on street life, construction projects, political rallies, and aspects of commune life during this intensive economic drive. The film does not examine any of the political and ideological values underlying the effort, thereby limiting its effectiveness. In addition, the overall impression left with the viewer is one of China as a country of drab conformity and forced labor.

● *Red China*
16 mm, 35 minutes, color, 1971
Distributor: Time-Life Films
               100 Eisenhower Drive
               Paramus, New Jersey 07652
               (201) 843-4545
Cost: (Sale) $425.00
               (Rental) $45.00
Subject: China after the Cultural Revolution
Audience: General

Produced and filmed by the British Broadcasting Corporation, "Red China" surveys the state of Chinese society, economics, and politics through visits to sites in Canton such as a sewing machine factory, the Hsin Hua People's Commune, the East is Red Food Market, the Peasant Movement Institute, and the Trade Fair. Perhaps the film's most valuable contribution lies in its demonstration of what was then seen as certain results of the Cultural Revolution: the intensity of the "cult of Mao Tse-tung" (later repudiated), the "half-work, half-study" system of education (since modified), the "barefoot doctors," and the emphasis upon "spiritual remolding" by manual labor. Edited from a fifty-minute presentation, this version is less effective, yet, it is one of the better available films on China dealing with the Cultural Revolution period.

Red China: Peking and the Commune
16 mm, 22 minutes, color, 1968
Distributor: Universal Education and Visual Arts
               100 Universal City Plaza
               Universal City, California 91608
               (213) 985-4321

Cost:	(Sale) $286.00
	(Rental) $29.00
Subject:	City life in Peking and the surrounding communes before the Cultural Revolution
Audience:	General, but especially younger audiences

This film was made in 1965 and 1966 by the Australian educator and traveler Myra Roper. It is a sympathetic survey of Chinese life in relatively prosperous areas of North China around Peking. The living conditions of a husband and wife team of skilled urban workers are seen, and the film then focuses on a rural commune where it covers food supply and eating facilities, schools, and market places. Ubiquitous children are a favorite target of Miss Roper's camera. The photography is excellent and the final sequence of a National Day celebration in Peking is spectacular.

Red China: Year of the Gun
16 mm, 50 minutes, color, 1966

Distributor:	Contemporary Films–McGraw Hill
	Princeton Road
	Hightstown, New Jersey 08520
	(609) 448-1700
Cost:	(Sale) $610.00
	(Rental) $25.00
Subject:	Foreign policy and domestic development
Audience:	General

Chinese actions in Korea, Tibet, India, and Vietnam are portrayed in this film produced in 1966 by ABC-TV to convey an image of the P.R.C. as a political/military momolith menacing the world. Inaccurate and outdated, the film is not recommended.

Red China Diary with Morley Safer
16 mm, 54 minutes, color/black and white, 1968

Distributor:	B.F.A. Educational Media
	2211 Michigan Avenue
	Santa Monica, California 90404
	(213) 829-2901
Cost:	(Sale) $575.00 color
	$275.00 black and white

(Rental) $40.00 color
Subject: China's Great Proletarian Cultural Revolution
Audience: General
In 1968, four years before Americans began to visit People's China, Morley Safer, a CBS news correspondent of British nationality, traveled to five major cities (Peking, Sian, Yenan, Shanghai, Canton), where in his film he interviews students, workers, and peasants and attempts to elicit their judgments about what the "thought of Mao Tse-tung" means to them in everyday life. Scenes of school and factory groups holding their own theatrical productions and study groups, although giving the effect of being staged, point to the adulation campaign for Chairman Mao at that time, as well as giving a vivid impression of Chinese fears of revisionism and imperialism. The color photography and music are excellent, and the commentary generally intelligent.

● *The Red Sons*
16 mm, 52 minutes, color, 1971
Distributor: Contemporary Films–McGraw HIll
                     Princeton Road
                     Hightstown, New Jersey 08520
                     (609) 448-1700
Cost: (Sale) $595.00
                     (Rental) $30.00
Subject: China during the Cultural Revolution
Audience: General, with prior knowledge about China helpful
In 1968, fifty-seven Australian and New Zealand university students took a one-month tour of China. This film is a record of their journey to Canton, Shanghai, Tsinan, Peking, Wuhan, and Changsha. Through the interpretive skills of Australian China specialist Stephen Fitzgerald, it builds upon personal interviews with people on the street and talks with Red Guard university students on such topics as their daily life, changes caused by the Cultural Revolution, Chinese knowledge of the West, and the meaning of studying Chairman Mao's works. Interpretations of the Cultural Revolution are presented in interviews with the late Anna Louise Strong (an American writer who lived in China for the last thirty years of her life) and expatriate American doctor George Hatem, director of the Research Institute of Dermatol-

ogy and Venereal Diseases in Peking. The film conveys a unique sense of "being there" through the personal encounters and impromptu interviews, hindered only slightly by some technical imperfections. A four-page study guide is included.

● *Report from China*
16 mm, 35 mm, 90 minutes, color, 1968
Distributor: Film Images/Radim Films
                17 West 60th Street
                New York, New York 10023
                (212) 279-6653
Cost: (Sale) $995.00
                (Rental) $120.00 or 50 percent of proceeds for pay-
                ing audience
                $60.00 classroom rate
Subject: Everyday life in China during the Cultural Revolu-
                tion
Audience: General

Report from China documents China's revolutionary society in terms of the nonviolent aspects of the Cultural Revolution. Filmed in 1967 in North China by a talented Japanese crew, it is concerned with the spirit and outlook of the Chinese people. The film takes a close and objective look at communes, factories, workers' collectives, rural villages, cities, and so on, and illustrates daily life and work. It is most effective in presenting China's attempt to "integrate" the revolution—to bridge the gaps between management and labor, intellectuals and common people, city and countryside. The film teaches without being didactic and is sympathetic without being naïve. It is, however, a particular view, and the scenes shown are but one part of China and one aspect of the Cultural Revolution. The cinematography is superb, often highly artistic. The narrative, a straight translation of the original Japanese commentary, is excellent. Because the film deserves to be seen, it is unfortunate that the rental rate for schools is abnormally high.

The Rise of China
16 mm, 30 minutes, black and white, 1966
Distributor: NET Service
                Audio-Visual Center

Indiana University
Bloomington, Indiana 47401
(812) 337-2853
Cost: (Rental) $6.75
Subject: Chinese foreign policy
Audience: General
This film interprets Chinese foreign policy through a series of interviews with specialists on China and with national leaders of various countries. It examines China's policy toward Vietnam, Taiwan, and Korea, the question of Chinese nuclear weapons, and the Sino-Indian border controversy. The overall picture that emerges is one of China as a careful and intelligent nation which nevertheless can and will use national power in pursuit of her goals. China's overall military posture is seen as essentially defensive, even though her foreign policy rhetoric encourages revolutionary outbreaks in Third World states.

● *Shanghai: The New China*
16 mm, 33 minutes, color, 1974
Distributor: BFA Educational Media
              2211 Michigan Avenue
              Santa Monica, California 90404
              (213) 829-2901
Cost: (Sale) $450.00
              (Rental) $35.00
Subject: Life in Shanghai today
Audience: General
This is a remarkable film that succeeds both visually and substantively in giving the viewer a deeper understanding of today's China. Irv Drasnin, a CBS documentary film producer with an academic background on China (see, e.g., his *Misunderstanding China*), spent eight weeks in Shanghai in 1973. The result is an intelligent account of several aspects of life in the world's largest city.

Unlike some of the superficial travelogues on the P.R.C. which have appeared recently, Mr. Drasnin's film develops several well-chosen themes, tracing some of them through the lives of a number of residents. Perhaps the best segments are the interviews—with a dock worker who compares pre- and post-revolutionary conditions in a colorful style; with students at Futan

University (Shanghai's largest); and with city officials who lead Shanghai's Revolutionary Committee. In editing the many hours of film to the one-hour television special, and now to this half-hour production, in-depth coverage of some themes had to be sacrificed (for example, modern industry such as shipbuilding). Overall, however, this is a superb film, and a "must" for increasing understanding about the People's Republic.

The complete film (50 minutes) is available for purchase only ($575.00) from CBS Educational and Publishing Group, 383 Madison Avenue, New York, New York 10017.

Sunday in Peking
16 mm, 19 minutes, color, 1956
Distributor: American Society of Eastern Arts
              2640 College Avenue
              Berkeley, California 94704
              (415) 433-1791
Cost: (Rental) $11.00
Subject: Life in Peking
Audience: General

This is a Parisian's impression of a Sunday in China's capital. It contains the usual scenes of the Forbidden City, the Summer Palace, and a parade in T'ien An Men Square, but the film is most worthwhile for its portrayal of the activities of ordinary Chinese at work and play: shopkeepers, vendors in street markets, acrobats, children at the zoo, lovers in the park. The one major weakness is the musical sound track, which contains some incongruous passages. The film will also disappoint those interested in serious political or social analysis. But these are not the concerns of the film's creators, and it is a delightful study which, unlike many others, treats the Chinese as full-fledged members of the human race. The cinematography is superb, and the narrative subtle and witty.

Two Faces of China
16 mm, 50 minutes, color, 1966
Distributor: Pictura Films
              43 West 16th Street
              New York, New York 10011

	(212) 691-1730
Cost:	(Sale) $500.00
	(Rental) $50.00 high school
	$60.00 college
Subject:	Persistence of the traditional in China today
Audience:	General

Two Faces of China was filmed for BBC-TV in 1966 by the French cameraman Rene Burri. Developing the theme that "no people can be separated from their history," this artistically and substantively rewarding film focuses on aspects of historical continuity in Chinese society today. It includes scenes of everyday life in cities and in the countryside, as well as commentary on education, language, religion, medicine and public health, art, and so on. The footage of rural China is particularly outstanding, and there are rare scenes of nomadic tribes in Inner Mongolia.

The emphasis is on the traditional, trying to show that in many fields (e.g., religion, medicine, agriculture, and even industry) there is no real conflict between the old and the new. The character of the Chinese people is interpreted as being concerned largely with self-preservation ("they are able to shout the slogans of today, yet retain individual loyalties"). Past and present, change and continuity are skillfully interwoven, often leading to the impression that very little has changed in the new China; few of the changes made by the Communists are shown. Although this impression by itself would be misleading, the film is most valuable in providing a balance to films showing only how things are different in the People's Republic.

A Village in China Today
16 mm, 17 minutes, color, 1966

Distributor:	Contemporary Films–McGraw Hill
	Princeton Road
	Hightstown, New Jersey 08520
	(609) 448-1700
Cost:	(Sale) $210.00
	(Rental) $15.00
Subject:	Rural life in China
Audience:	General

A survey of life in a Chinese village, stressing the changes that have occurred in local industry, education, medicine, agriculture, commerce, sports, and leisure. Interesting photography, combined with an intelligent presentation of the accomplishments of the Chinese government and a listing of some problems yet to be faced, contribute to the merit of the film. This could make a good comparison with a more traditional picture, such as *A Town by the Yangtse.*

C. Hong Kong, Taiwan, and Overseas Chinese

Born Chinese
16 mm, 57 minutes, black and white, 1967
Distributor: Time-Life Films
               100 Eisenhower Drive
               Paramus, New Jersey 07652
               (212) 691-2930
Cost: (Sale) $300.00
               (Rental) $40.00
Subject: Life in Hong Kong for a middle-class Chinese family
Audience: General

Produced by BBC-TV, this film offers some valuable insights into the psychology and values of prerevolutionary Chinese society and culture. Through the activities of the Lung family, some basic characteristics of one Chinese subcultural group are effectively demonstrated. The film includes an excellent discussion of the fundamentals of the Chinese written and spoken language, and of the strong physical and regional differences inherent in the general term "Chinese." The film also deals with the economic structure and accomplishments of the Chinese business community in Hong Kong, with emphasis upon the "family" organization of a Chinese entrepreneur. The most important contribution is the portrayal of the Chinese as proud heirs to a vital non-Western civilization who are fully capable of competing successfully with the West and determining their own future.

The Chinese American
  The Early Immigrants
  The Twentieth Century
16 mm, 20 minutes each, color, 1973
Distributor: Handel Film Corporation
               8730 Sunset Boulevard
               West Hollywood, California 90069

```
                (213) 657-8990
Cost:           (Sale) $270.00 each
                (Rental) $27.00 each
Subject:        History of Chinese in the United States
Audience:       General
```

Narrated by Sam Chu Lin, a newscaster of Chinese descent, the films depict the history of the Chinese in the United States, and their contributions to its growth. The first film, "The Early Immigrants," tells of the first Chinese to come to America, their role in the gold rush, the building of the transcontinental railroad, their persecution and eventual racist exclusion. The second deals with the development of Chinatown in San Francisco following the earthquake of 1906, introduces important personalities, follows President Nixon's trip to China, and ends with a discussion of the unusual position and problems of Chinese-Americans. A film summary and discussion sheet (error-filled) accompany the films.

Since the subject of Americans of Chinese descent is such an important one, and yet so widely ignored, it is unfortunate that these films are rather superficial and lack focus. "The Early Immigrants" is the better of the two, yet both have stereotypes and present an over-generalized view. An important subject not yet realized on film.

Industrial Development of Free China
16 mm, 40 minutes, color, 1967
```
Distributor:    Chinese Information Service
                159 Lexington Avenue
                New York, New York 10016
                (212) 725-4950
Cost:           (Sale) $168.00
                (Rental) Free
Subject:        Industrial and economic development on Taiwan
Audience:       General
```

This official film presents the impressive industrial growth on Taiwan, and attributes it to the free enterprise development strategy of the Nationalist Chinese government.

● *The Third China*
16 mm, 16 minutes, color/black and white, 1969

Distributor: Carousel Films
                1501 Broadway
                New York, New York 10036
                (212) 524-4126
Cost: (Sale) $195.00 color
                $100.00 black and white
                (Rental) contact distributor for information
Subject: Overseas Chinese in Southeast Asia
Audience: General

The "Third China" is neither Communist nor Nationalist but the hybrid world of the overseas Chinese. This film, produced for CBS's "60 Minutes" and narrated by Harry Reasoner, is an excellent portrayal of the twenty million Chinese who live in the countries of Southeast Asia—particularly Singapore, Thailand, Indonesia, Hong Kong, and Malaysia. It deals primarily with unresolved personal dilemmas: Should one be loyal to the adopted country? To the traditional culture? To the new China? The film concludes that except for the unique case of Singapore, the overseas Chinese, both by choice and by pressure, have not been assimilated into their adopted countries. This is well depicted in scenes which contrast the lingering respect for traditional culture (funeral practices, acupuncture, remittances mailed to the mainland, and so on) with the bitter resentment of the local populations caused by racial and religious forces and fueled by envy of Chinese economic achievements.

An objective and intelligent presentation which contributes effectively to an understanding of Who are the Chinese?

D. CHINESE TRADITIONAL CULTURE

The Beautiful Bait
16 mm, 25 minutes, color, 1963
Distributor: Chinese Information Service
                159 Lexington Avenue
                New York, New York 10016
                (212) 725-4950
Cost: (Sale) $240.00
                (Rental) Free
Subject: Chinese opera
Audience: General

A condensed version of the traditional Chinese opera *Tiao Ch'an*, telling the story of a beautiful concubine and political

114   Audiovisual Materials

intrigue in the latter Han Dynasty. The performers are students of the Foo Hsing Opera School in Taipei.

Buddhism in China
16 mm, 30 minutes, color, 1974
Distributor: Pictura Films Distribution Corporation
                43 West 16th Street
                New York, New York 10011
                (212) 691-1730
Cost: (Sale) $400.00
                (Rental) $40.00
Subject: Development of Buddhism in China
Audience: Advanced senior high and above, with some background in the basic tenets of Buddhism.

The development of Buddhism in China is surveyed from its introduction to its subsequent spread and transformation. Basic ideas of Chinese Buddhism and their influence on the character and life of the people are discussed. In addition to "live" scenes, animation, art works, and maps are used to develop the theme. However, the complicated narration is too concerned with irrelevant and unexplained facts, and we are given endless names of emperors and monks and references to "being" and "non-being". The priceless art objects escape us as well, hidden by the animation and lost in the nature scenes. Knowledge of the philosophical concepts of Buddhism is essential for viewing this film.

Buddhism, Man and Nature
16 mm, 13 minutes, color, 1968
Distributor: American Society of Eastern Arts
                2640 College Avenue
                Berkeley, California 94704
                (415) 433-1791
Cost: (Rental) $9.00 nonmembers
                $6.00 members
Subject: Buddhist world view
Audience: Adults

Although not specifically related to China, this film describes and explains the Buddhist world view, which had considerable influence in China during the first eight centuries A.D. It includes some Chinese paintings and a word about the Chinese adaptation of the philosophy, implicitly demonstrating that China's cultural tradition was not monolithic Confucianism. The film is an artistic achievement.

Chinese Bronzes of Ancient Times
16 mm, 20 minutes, color, 1971
Distributor: Pictura Films Distribution Corporation
                43 West 16th Street
                New York, New York 10011
                (212) 691-1730
Cost: (Sale) $250.00
                (Rental) $20.00
Subject: Development of Chinese bronze ceremonial vessels from the Shang through the Ch'in dynasties
Audience: General, but particularly college art classes
    This is a pictorial history of the development of Chinese bronze ceremonial vessels through the Shang, Chou, Ch'u and Ch'in dynasties (ca. 1760 B. C.-200 B.C.). A rather sophisticated film, perhaps most suited for college art students or others with a serious interest in the topic, it was produced and narrated by artist Wan-Go Weng in the 1950s and has both excellent photography and clear narration.

Chinese Brush Strokes
16 mm, 17 minutes, color, 1961
Distributor: (Sale) Martin Moyer Productions
                900 Federal Avenue East
                Seattle, Washington 98102
                (206) 322-9308
                (Rental) Film Rental Library
                Syracuse University
                1455 East Colvin Street
                Syracuse, New York 13210
                (315) 479-6631
Cost: (Sale) $205.00
                (Rental) $8.50
Subject: Chinese writing

Audience: Senior high and college

Fay Chong, artist and teacher of calligraphic art, traces the history of Chinese writing from its early pictographic form to the present style, and illustrates the use of the brush and ink. A final sequence points out the application of calligraphy in modern art. A good introduction to Chinese writing.

Chinese Ceramics through the Ages

Chinese Painting through the Ages

Chinese Sculpture through the Ages
16 mm, 20 minutes each, color, 1971
Distributor: Pictura Films Distribution Corporation
                43 West 16th Street
                New York, New York 10011
                (212) 691-1730
Cost: (Sale) $250.00 per print
                (Rental) $20.00 per print
Subject: Historical survey of China's major potters, paint-
                ers, and sculptors
Audience: General; some knowledge of Chinese art and cul-
                ture recommended

This series, produced by the Chinese-American artist Wan-Go Weng, presents a general historical survey of traditional China's major potters, painters, and sculptors and discusses leading styles and techniques. The narration abounds in factual detail and sophisticated terminology which those unfamiliar with Chinese art and culture might find bewildering; the instructional value of these films therefore would be enhanced by introductory remarks which explain the terms used and provide some general artistic and cultural background. The films nevertheless can be a stimulating visual introduction to these Chinese art media.

Chinese Firecrackers
16 mm, 10 minutes, color, 1971
Distributor: Pictura Films Distribution Corporation
                43 West 16th Street
                New York, New York 10011

(212) 691-1703
Cost: (Sale) $150.00
            (Rental) $10.00
Subject: History and production of firecrackers
Audience: General

Produced and narrated by artist Wan-Go Weng in the 1950s and recently revised, this film explains the history of Chinese firecrackers and how they are made—using methods and tools which probably date back to the Sung dynasty.

Chinese Ink and Water Colors
16 mm, 18 minutes, color, 1961
Distributor: (Sale) Martin Moyer Productions
            900 Federal Avenue East
            Seattle, Washington 98102
            (206) 322-9308
            (Rental) Film Rental Library
            Syracuse University
            1455 East Colvin Street
            Syracuse, New York 13210
            (315) 479-6631
Cost: (Sale) $220.00
            (Rental) $9.00
Subject: Chinese art
Audience: Junior high, senior high, and college

An artist and teacher of calligraphic art demonstrates the use of Chinese ink, mounted rice paper, Chinese brushes, and water colors by painting a picture with a combination of Oriental and Western techniques and materials. Although useful for a general discussion of Chinese art, the film is especially valuable for the art instructor.

Chinese Jade Carving
16 mm, 10 minutes, color, 1971
Distributor: Pictura Films Distribution Corporation
            43 West 16th Street
            New York, New York 10011
            (212) 691-1730
Cost: (Sale) $150.00
            (Rental) $10.00

Subject: Traditional techniques of Chinese jade carving
Audience: General
   Produced and narrated by artist Wan-Go Weng in the 1950s
and recently revised, the film demonstrates the techniques of the
traditional Chinese artisan and explains the special virtues that
the Chinese ascribed to jade. The demonstrator, Kung-fu Ma, is a
fourth-generation member of a famous jade-carving family; the
types of tools he uses have undergone little change during the past
two thousand years. Brilliant photographs of jade objects illustrate the range and variety of this art.

Chinese Music and Musical Instruments
16 mm, 28 minutes, color, 1969
Distributor: Chinese Information Service
               159 Lexington Avenue
               New York, New York 10016
               (212) 725-4950
Cost: (Sale) $240.00
               (Rental) Free
Subject: Chinese musical instruments
Audience: General
   This film introduces the instruments used in Chinese classical
music throughout the ages and demonstrates their use both
individually and in ensemble. The film can be useful both for a
simple classroom discussion of Chinese music and for more
formal ethnomusicology classes.

Chinese Shadow Play
16 mm, 10 minutes, color, 1971
Distributor: Pictura Films Distribution Corporation
               43 West 16th Street
               New York, New York 10011
               (212) 691-1730
Cost: (Sale) $150.00
               (Rental) $10.00
Subject: A Chinese fairy tale
Audience: General
   Produced by artist Wan-Go Weng in the 1950s and recently
revised, the film presents a shortened version of one of the most
popular Chinese fairy tales, "The White Snake Lady." The

performance is conducted behind an illuminated screen, demonstrating one of the folk arts of China. After the performance, the audience is taken backstage to see the puppets and their manipulators as well as the props and musical instruments.

Confucianism
16 mm, 30 minutes, black and white, 1956
Distributor: University of California Extension
            Media Center
            Berkeley, California 94720
            (415) 642-0460
Cost: (Rental) $10.00
Subject: Life of Confucius
Audience: High school and college
    Through paintings and other artistic renderings, the life of Confucius is portrayed. Through the description of his life and the use of his sayings, the film presents Confucius as teacher and statesman, and explains how Confucianism grew out of one man's search for order amidst the chaos that was China in the sixth century B.C. A romanticized version of the Confucian legacy which reinforces stereotypes.

Heritage of Chinese Opera
16 mm, 28 minutes, color, 1973
Distributor: Chinese Information Service
            159 Lexington Avenue
            New York, New York 10016
            (212) 725-4950
Cost: (Rental) Free
Subject: Explanation of Chinese opera
Audience: General
    A splendid introduction to traditional Chinese theater as performed by the Nationalist Chinese Opera Troupe of Taiwan. After a brief glimpse of several different forms of Chinese theater, the film looks more closely at the art form that only Westerners know as Chinese "opera." Focusing on the early training of the performers, as well as the meaning of the movements, make-up and costumes, the film provides excellent background for an understanding of this traditional performing art.

Masterpieces of Chinese Art at the National Palace Museum
16 mm, 28 minutes, color, 1973
Distributor: Chinese Information Service
               159 Lexington Avenue
               New York, New York 10016
               (212) 725-4950
Cost: (Sale) $240.00
               (Rental) Free
Subject: Fifty works of Chinese art introducing the subject
Audience: Art students

When the Nationalists fled the mainland in 1949, they took with them vast art treasures, now housed in the National Palace Museum in Taipei. The fifty selected masterpieces in this film include bronzes from the Shang Dynasty, jade artifacts, porcelain wares, carved lacquer, and calligraphy. The film concludes with a detailed examination of three famous Chinese paintings: "Early Snow on the River," by Chao Kan of the Five Dynasties, "Travellers on a Mountain Path," by Fan Kuan, and "Early Spring," by Kuo Ksi, both of the Northern Sung Dynasty.

Although the film provides a good in-depth introduction to Chinese art, it is rather specialized and should be seen only by those with a serious interest in the subject. There are some technical flaws in the film as well.

A Night at the Peking Opera
16 mm, 20 minutes, color, 1959
Distributor: Film Images/Radim Films
               17 West 60th Street
               New York, New York 10023
               (212) 279-6653
Cost: (Sale) $275.00
               (Rental) $25.00
Subject: Excerpts from three classical Chinese operas
Audience: General

After a brief explanation of some of the conventions of Chinese opera, the film presents three excerpts from traditional performances. The choice of stories gives a real flavor of traditional Chinese opera, and makes the film understandable to the observer unfamiliar with this unique art form as well as to the connoisseur.

Oriental Brush Work
16 mm, 16 minutes, color, 1956
Distributor: Encyclopaedia Britannica
             1822 Pickwick Avenue
             Glenview, Illinois 60025
             (312) 321-7311
Cost: (Sale) $220.00
             (Rental) $11.00
Subject: Techniques of oriental art
Audience: General

The Chinese artist Tyrus Wang demonstrates Chinese techniques, and Japanese artist Chiura Obata demonstrates the Japanese style of using the brush. The film includes comment on the Oriental contribution to art, and features masterpieces from the Freer Gallery of Art in Washington, D.C.

Painting the Chinese Landscape
16 mm, 10 minutes, color, 1971
Distributor: Pictura Films Distribution Corporation
             43 West 16th Street
             New York, New York 10011
             (212) 691-1730
Cost: (Sale) $150.00
             (Rental) $10.00
Subject: Traditional technique and philosophy of painting
             the Chinese landscape
Audience: General

Produced and narrated by artist Wan-Go Weng in the 1950s and recently revised, the film illustrates the four principal steps in painting Chinese landscapes and explains the philosophy underlying the art. Specific techniques are explained and then demonstrated as the artist works on various stages of his painting. In the concluding sequence, four paintings representing the seasons show how the traditional Chinese view of man's harmony with nature influenced the landscape painter. Beautiful photography and intelligent narration.

The Religions of Man: *Confucianism*
                              Buddhism, Parts 1, 2, 3

16 mm, 30 minutes each, black and white, 1958
Distributor: Audio-Visual Center
               University of Indiana
               Bloomington, Indiana 47401
               (812) 337-2853
Cost: (Rental) $6.75 each
Subject: *Confucianism.* Deals with Confucius as both teacher
               and statesman, and provides an introduction
               to basic Confucian ideas and practices.
               Buddhism, Part 1. Describes the origins of Bud-
               dhism in terms of the personal experience of Gau-
               tama Buddha, "the man who woke up."
               Buddhism, Part 2. Discusses the "Eightfold Path"
               central to the Buddhist approach to life.
               Buddhism, Part 3. Surveys Buddhism as a mission-
               ary movement, explaining the differences between
               the Hinayana and Mahayana schools.
Audience: Senior high and college
  Although produced in 1958 by National Educational Television,
the films have not lost their great value, thanks to the superb
organization and delivery of Professor Houston Smith's lectures.
However, the high level of sophistication makes the films inappropriate for students below senior high school or college.

Report on Acupuncture
16 mm, 28 minutes, color, 1973
Distributor: Macmillan Films, Inc.
               34 MacQuestern Parkway South
               Mount Vernon, New York 10550
               (914) 664-4277
Cost: (Sale) $360.00
               (Rental) $25.00
Subject: The techniques of acupuncture and moxibustion
Audience: General
  Filmed at the China Medical College in Taiwan, "Report on
Acupuncture" explores in sophisticated language and concepts
traditional Chinese medical practices. Although the narrative
may seem somewhat dull, the film is highly informative in
describing both the actual process and the concepts behind the
use of traditional Chinese medicine.

Story of Chinese Art
16 mm, 22 minutes, color, 1971
Distributor: Pictura Films Distribution Corporation
                43 West 16th Street
                New York, New York 10011
                (212) 691-1730
Cost: (Sale) $250.00
                (Rental) $20.00
Subject: Art
Audience: General
    An excellent survey of Chinese art from its unknown begin-
nings to modern times. The influence of Central Asia, India, and
Europe on Chinese culture, as well as the reciprocal influence of
China on her Asian neighbors, the Middle East, and the West, are
illustrated. The use of superb works of art, together with
animated maps and graphs, makes this film a valuable introduc-
tion to the study of Chinese art. The film was produced by artist
Wan-Go Weng in the 1950s and recently revised.

T'ai Chi Ch'uan
16 mm, 8 minutes, black and white, 1969
Distributor: Tom Davenport Films
                Pearlstone
                Delaplane, Virginia 22025
                (703) 592-3701
Cost: (Sale) $80.00
                (Rental) $15.00
Subject: The Chinese art of T'ai Chi Ch'uan
Audience: General
    Filmed on the seacoast of Taiwan with no sound track other
than the rush of the surf and the occasional intrusion of chimes
and clapsticks, this is an artistic tour de force and an extremely
effective introduction to one of China's oldest traditional arts: the
dance/exercise known as T'ai Chi Ch'uan. The subtle movements
of the exercise are performed by T'ai Chi Ch'uan master, Nan
Huai-ching. The total effect is nearly hypnotic, and illustrates,
without the interference of language, the classical Chinese
attitude toward man's relationship with the universe.

3. FILMSTRIPS AND MULTIMEDIA

A. CHINA BEFORE 1949

Ancient China
Filmstrip, 40 frames, color, no sound, teacher's guide, 1967
Distributor: Denoyer-Geppart AV
               5235 Ravenswood Avenue
               Chicago, Illinois 60640
               (312) 561-9200
Cost: $7.50
Subject: Ancient China
Audience: Junior and senior high

This filmstrip surveys the key elements of China's past, her agricultural patterns, trade, commerce, and intellectual traditions. A fairly successful attempt is made to cover those characteristics which are still relevant to an understanding of modern China. A good catalyst for further study and discussion of the relationship of ancient to modern China.

● *China in Perspective: Roots of Civilization*
Two filmstrips, 226 frames, color/black and white, sound, discussion guide, 1970
Distributor: Guidance Associates
               757 Third Avenue
               New York, New York 10017
               (212) 754-3700
Cost: $41.50 with LP records
               $46.50 with cassettes
Subject: Traditional China
Audience: Junior and senior high

Strip 1 deals with traditional Chinese society, politics, and economics. There is a particularly good survey of the major accomplishments of premodern China and the roots of Chinese ethnocentrism. The second strip covers the modern period of China's history, from roughly the Opium War to the founding of the Chinese People's Republic in 1949. The analysis of the Chinese Revolution is generally objective and extremely well done.

Overall, the pictures are well chosen and the narration intelligent and insightful, although Chinese words and names are

Filmstrips and Multimedia   *125*

mispronounced throughout. The script includes a number of commentaries from such specialists as A. Doak Barnett, Pearl Buck, and John King Fairbank. The discussion guide is excellent.

Rise of Chinese Civilization
Filmstrip, 48 frames, 20 minutes, color, no sound, teacher's guide, 1963
Distributor: Encyclopaedia Britannica
             1822 Pickwick Avenue
             Glenview, Illinois 60025
             (312) 321-7311
Cost: $6.00
Subject: Early history of Chinese civilization
Audience: Junior and senior high
   This filmstrip is a rather standard exploration of China's cultural history from the time of the semilegendary Shang and Chou dynasties through unification by the Ch'in emperor (221 B.C.). The cultural and political legacies of the Han and later dynasties are also reviewed. Good for exploring a particular period of Chinese history.

B. CHINA AFTER 1949

● *Art in Communist China*
Three slide sets, color, taped commentary, written text, 1972
Distributor: The East Asian Center
             University of Rochester
             Rochester, New York 14627
             (716) 275-2121
Cost: Set 1. $50.00, 80 color slides, 30-minute taped commentary
             Set 2. $50.00, 80 color slides, 38-minute taped commentary
             Set 3. $20.00, 29 color slides, 10-minute taped commentary
Subject: Set 1. *Art and Ideology in Communist China*
             Set 2. *Painting in Communist China*
             Set 3. *Revolutionary Art: The Modern Chinese Woodblock Print*
Audience: Advanced senior high, junior college, college
   These color slide sets with accompanying taped commentary

were prepared by Ralph C. Crozier, professor of Chinese history at the University of Rochester, and represent the only audiovisual presentation of the whole range of the arts and their political function in the People's Republic. Set 1 shows development of the Chinese party policy toward the arts from 1949 through the Cultural Revolution. Set 2 deals with tension between traditional Chinese style and modern Western styles, as well as the policy of using art to serve politics. The final set shows the origin of this art of social protest in the 1930s and its development in the People's Republic. Each set contains slides, tape or cassette, printed list of slide titles, written text of commentary, and suggestions for further reading. The series is well done, and is useful in history and social science courses on China as well as in art courses.

● *China*
Five filmstrips, 2 transparencies, sound, 10 booklets, 19 activity sheets, teacher's guide, 1973
Distributor: A. J. Nystrom and Company
3333 Elson Avenue
Chicago, Illinois 60618
(517) 688-3056
Cost: $125.00 with cassettes
Available at extra cost: relief map ($52.00) and a relief globe ($30.00)
Subject: Events that led to the victory of the Communists, and the subsequent impact on Chinese society
Individual titles include:
Birth and Rebirth
Moving Mountains
Dare to Struggle
A Better Way of Life
Two Views on China
Audience: Junior and senior high
Despite the rather high price, this unit can be recommended as the best multimedia kit available on the People's Republic of China. Attractively packaged, it employs a wide range of teaching techniques (including unusual art illustrations) to explain China's geography, history, and current social and economic development. The text and narration are unusually accurate, and the accompanying readings are suitable for a wide range of age

Filmstrips and Multimedia   127

groups. The filmstrip *Two Views on China* is excellent for generating provocative classroom discussion about the role of values in attempting to understand other cultures.

Although some of the pictures are out of context (especially those dealing with the 1949 Communist victory) and a stereotyped Chinese accent is used by one of the narrators, the package is one of the best on China to date.

China
Series: The School Times
Two filmstrips, 42 frames each, color, sound, teacher's guide, 1971
Distributor: Teaching Resources Films
                Station Plaza
                Bedford Hills, New York 10506
                (914) 241-1350
Cost: $25.00 with LP record
Subject: Philosophical roots of China's past and the goals
                and achievements of the P.R.C.
                Individual titles include:
                Understanding China
                China Today
Audience: Junior and senior high
Traditional Chinese behavior is analyzed in filmstrip 1 through an examination of the teachings of Confucius and the dynastic history of the Chinese people. The second analyzes the many improvements in the life of the people today and concludes that a highly structured regimentation has been necessary to achieve this. A teacher's guide includes topics for discussion and a selection of articles by *New York Times* journalists Tillman Durdin, James Reston, and Seymour and Audrey Topping. Overall, a balanced and well photographed presentation.

China: The Door Reopens
Two filmstrips, 87 frames each, color, sound, teacher's guide, 1973
Distributor: Social Studies School Service
                10,000 Culver Boulevard
                Culver City, California 90230
                (213) 839-2436
Cost: $35.00 with LP record

$37.00 with cassettes
Subject: People, history, and lifestyle
Audience: Senior high and above
This Associated Press "Special Report" is divided into two sections: the first puts China in historical and cultural perspective and the second covers the 1972 Nixon visit and includes a description and assessment of the social structure. The narration includes the voices and views of Pearl Buck, Marshall Green, John Roderick, and Ross Terrill, who comment on various aspects of social and political life. Although Terrill is obviously sympathetic, most of the other commentators tend to use the old cliches; for example, Pearl Buck on the role of women in China: "Chinese women were very strong because they learned how to manage a man—and I notice they do that here, too, if they are sensible" (p. 113). These and some other parts of the narration are of little value as instructional material on China and tend to detract from the cohesiveness of the general program. An adequate teacher's guide includes questions, supplementary activities, vocabulary, and a bibliography.

China: Revolution in Progress
Two filmstrips, 45 frames each, color, sound, teacher's guide, 1972
Distributor: Multi-Media Productions
                P.O. Box 5097
                Stanford, California 94305
                (415) 968-1061
Cost: $14.95 with LP record
                $16.95 with cassette
Subject: China's continuing revolution
Audience: Junior and senior high
What are the problems China faces as it builds itself up industrially, agriculturally, and ideologically? How was China changed by the Communist revolution, and what was the Cultural Revolution? What is Mao's place in China today? Inadequate treatment of these questions gives one little conclusive information. The first filmstrip, a discussion of the history of the revolution and the resulting changes in education, the army, medicine, agriculture and industry, lacks continuity and tends to leave the viewer with an assortment of unrelated facts. The second, somewhat better, conveys a reasonable understanding of

the concept of revolution in China today. An inadequate teacher's guide and poor sound/picture coordination contribute to an overall negative evaluation.

China: Twenty Years of Revolution
Five filmstrips, 75–87 frames each, color, sound, teacher's guide, supplementary essays, 1969

Distributor: Encyclopaedia Britannica
              1822 Pickwick Avenue
              Glenview, Illinois 60025
              (312) 321-7311

Cost: $13.00 per unit (strip and 33⅓ RPM record)
              $14.95 per unit (strip and cassette)
              $58.50 (five strips and five records)
              $67.28 (five strips and five cassettes)

Subject: The quality of life in the "New China"
              Individual titles include:
              China: The Revolution and the People
              China: The Revolution and the Arts
              China: The Revolution and the Schools
              China: The Revolution and the Land
              China: The Revolution in Industry

Audience: Junior and senior high

The five units cover the bases of post-1949 Chinese politics, economics, and society, including material on urban and rural ways of life, the arts, political participation, education, and agricultural and industrial development. The unifying theme is the impact of the Chinese Revolution upon the daily life of the Chinese people. Although only passing reference is made to the revolution's influence on foreign policy, and Chinese words and names are occasionally mispronounced, the series is well organized and cohesive. The selection of color photographs is excellent throughout, and the caliber of the sound effects and narration is generally first-rate. The narration sheets accompanying each unit include useful "questions and topics for discussion," and the supplementary essays by Professor Franz Schurman of the University of California, Berkeley, provide additional valuable information for the instructor.

● *China in the Modern World*
Four filmstrips, 296 frames, color, sound, teacher's notes, 1972
Distributor: Educational Audio Visual, Inc.
                Pleasantville, New York 10570
                (914) 769-6332
Cost: $60.00 with LP records
                $68.00 with cassettes
Subject: China's political history, customs, and culture
                Individual titles include:
                The End of Imperial China
                The Struggle for Power
                The Growth of Chinese Communism
                The People's Republic of China Today
Audience: Junior and senior high
This filmstrip package deals with China's political history, customs and culture. Beginning with the 18th century, it shows traditional ways of life, events that led to the downfall of Manchu rule and thereby the dynastic cycles, and the history of the Nationalist (KMT) and Communist movements by examining the leaders who were instrumental in the formation of today's China: Sun Yat-sen, Chiang Kai-shek, and Mao Tse-tung, among others. Aspects of traditional and modern Chinese life are effectively interwoven throughout.

The selection of photographs is excellent, the narration objective, and the musical background superb. Incorporation of stimulating key discussion questions encourages the teacher to interrupt the program for classroom discussion. Because of its effective use of stories, poems, plays, songs, quotations, and slogans from original sources (both modern and traditional), this is one of the better available filmstrip series.

China Joins the World
Filmstrip, 65 frames, black and white, sound, teacher's guide, map, 1972
Distributor: Social Studies School Service
                10,000 Culver Boulevard
                Culver City, California 90230
                (213) 839-2436
Cost: $9.00 with LP record

$10.00 with cassette
Subject: China's foreign policy
Audience: Junior and senior high
This *New York Times* sound filmstrip examines China's new role in world affairs. Provocative questions on how China has emerged from its isolated position of the past and what the Sino-Soviet relationship implies for U.S.-China relations are discussed, along with the life-style of the "average" Chinese citizen. A concise teacher's guide suggests good teaching strategies and offers a useful bibliography. Natural breaks in the script allow the teacher to interrupt for student discussion. The filmstrip is enlivened by political cartoons as well as good photography, and the narration and text are objective and challenging.

China Now
Four filmstrips, 231 frames, sound, teacher's guide, wall map, 4 source books, 1973
Distributor: EMC Corporation
              180 East 6th Street
              St. Paul, Minnesota 55101
              (612) 227-7366
Cost: $84.00 complete kit (record or cassettes)
Subject: Chinese society today
              Individual titles include:
              The Long March to Unity
              The Human Side
              Meeting the People's Needs
              Ideas in Action
Audience: Junior and senior high
The set presents some aspects of the People's Republic that are more characteristic of the period immediately following the Cultural Revolution than China now—emphasis is on the role of the military, mass demonstrations, and the "cult of Mao." Scenes of family life, education, the role of women, recreation, cultural activities, medicine, and housing dispel many of the commonly held stereotypes of China, especially that of a "faceless" robotlike mass. Efforts toward modernization of agriculture and industrial progress are well depicted in the filmstrip *Meeting the People's Needs*, however, *Ideas in Action* does not systematically itemize

and demonstrate in action the major ideas, values, and goals of the P.R.C.

The set is technically good, enhanced by an excellent wall map showing the political divisions of China, a helpful teacher's guide, and four sourcebooks, but the filmstrips and the narration often lack a clear and organized sequence and rationale.

China Today
Three slide sets (carousel mounted), 266 slides, color, study guides, 1974

Distributor: Audio-Visual Department
Harper and Row, Publishers
10 East 53d Street
New York, New York 10022
(212) 593-7000

Cost: $115.00 Unit 1
$78.00 Unit 2
$78.00 Unit 3

Subject: Unit 1: *Life in Contemporary China*
Unit 2: *Molding the Mind of a Nation*
Unit 3: *The Family*

Audience: Junior and senior high

The first unit attempts to introduce China through a cross-cultural approach, the second deals with the basic structural and attitudinal differences in Chinese and American society, and the third provides information about the Chinese family today and its relation to the social system. Included in the study guides are slide descriptions, questions for testing comprehension, as well as suggestions for classroom activities and a bibliography of supplementary materials.

A well-produced, widely available basic slide set on the People's Republic of China would offer the teacher a flexibility not provided by films and filmstrips. This one, however, does not live up to that potential. Some of the slides tend to be trite and of poor quality (especially Unit 1) and the text has some questionable interpretation: "Perhaps if you have never known freedom, you do not miss it" (Unit 2). The author of Unit 3 seems to measure China by what she feels is an important yardstick—the lack of closet space.

Filmstrips and Multimedia

China Today: As Seen through the Eyes of a Typical Chinese Family
Six filmstrips, 395 frames, color, sound, teacher's guide, 1973
Distributor: Spoken Arts, Inc.
                310 North Avenue
                New Rochelle, New York 10801
                (914) 636-5482
Cost: $120.00
Subject: An introduction to China
                Individual titles include:
                China's Yesterdays
                China's Communes
                Flood Control and Transportation
                Culture and Sports
                The Revolution
                City Life
Audience: Elementary through junior high

Using the voices of a young girl, a young woman, and an old man, the series provides an overview of China. Written and photographed by Audrey Topping, who spent much of her youth in China and revisited in 1972–73, the filmstrips also use news clips, paintings, and maps. The teacher's manual provides excellent and provocative questions for discussion and includes helpful reading suggestions. A good stimulus for in-depth exploration.

China's New Look
Ten filmstrips, 58 frames each, color, sound, teacher's guide, 1972
Distributor: Social Studies School Service
                10,000 Culver Boulevard
                Culver City, California 90320
                (213) 839-2436
Cost: $129.00 (with 5 LP records)
                $134.00 (with 5 cassettes)
Subject: Goals and achievements of the P.R.C.
                Individual titles include:
                Educational Goals
                Peasantry: A Way of Life
                Life Styles in the Cities
                Cultural Heritage
                Geographic Diversity

Agricultural Challenges
Progress Through Industry
City Scenes and Sights
Peking and the Forbidden City
Years of Revolution

Audience: Junior and senior high

A broad background picture of life in China today, with a constant eye on the changes since the revolution, this filmstrip program was produced by the *New York Times*. Excellent photographs depict China's cultural heritage, its revolutionary movements, its people and institutions, its industrial and agricultural challenges, and urban and rural life. However, captions which do not always match the pictures and the use of complex vocabulary detract from the value of the material as an introductory unit on China.

Communist China: Asia's First Superpower
Filmstrip, 66 frames, black and white, sound, discussion guide, 1972

Distributor: Current Affairs Films
               24 Danbury Road
               Wilton, Connecticut 06897
               (203) 762-0301
Cost: $20.00 with LP record
               $22.00 with cassette
Subject: China as a superpower
Audience: Junior and senior high

With the aid of a two-page discussion guide, this filmstrip tries to assess China's potential for superpower status. It concludes that because of external pressures (USSR, U.S.) on China, and her internal instability (simplistically recounted as "red" vs. "expert"), only Japan can achieve this status in Asia today.

The strip portrays the struggle between Mao's "ideological hardliners" and the "realists," represented by Chou En-lai (seen as a "tough, cultured Communist"). Visually, this struggle is depicted by two aged, stereotyped Chinese; one is handing out "Little Red Books" to a peasant wailing at his empty rice bowl, and the other ladling out rice to a smiling peasant with a full bowl (frame 36). China's progress is noted with the comment that "the Chinese today share more equally in the country's wealth—or, as some say, in her poverty" (frame 45). A "final confrontation with the West" shows Mao on top of the world leading a gang of ruffians (including a black man with a club, an Arab with a "Little Red Book," and a Vietnamese with a sickle) (frame 54).

Although current enough to include pictures of the People's Republic of China delegation in the UN and Nixon's announcement of his planned visit to Peking, the filmstrip is a remnant of cold war images and rhetoric.

Contemporary China
Six filmstrips, 45 frames each, color, sound, teacher's guide, 1973
Distributor: Doubleday Multimedia
               1371 Reynolds Avenue
               Santa Ana, California 92705
               (714) 540-5550
Cost: $96.00 with LP record or cassette
Subject: Life in contemporary China
               Individual titles include:
               Cities of China
               Rural China
               Contemporary Culture
               Education and Health
               Monuments of the Past
               Agriculture, Industry, Transportation
Audience: Junior high (grades 6–9)

If one were to take a general tour of China in the early 1970s, the slides and impressions taken home might very well accord with what is seen in this series of filmstrips. The viewer is given the overall "standard tour," showing agriculture, education, art, recreation, theater, industry, and medicine. The strips also include the filmmaker's interviews with workers, farmers, and students.

Although the photographs are good, a weak teacher's guide, mispronounciation of common Chinese words, and only fair audio quality detract from the effectiveness of the program.

Discovering Today's China
Two filmstrips, 88 frames each, color, sound, teacher's guide, 4 paperbacks, map, 1973
Distributor: EMC Corporation
              180 East Sixth Street

Cost: St. Paul, Minnesota 55101
(612) 227-7366

Cost: $49.50 complete set (teacher's guide, paperbacks, map available separately)

Subject: Changes in the culture and environment of China
Individual titles include:
Challenge and Change
Building a New Society
Books (by Norman Webster) include:
The Stubborn Land
City Life, City People
Posters and Pedicarts
Youth on the March

Audience: Elementary and junior high

China's communes and rural life, urban life, politics, economy, and education are treated in this multimedia kit, which includes four books written by Norman Webster, former Peking correspondent of the Toronto *Globe and Mail*. This has potential as an excellent teaching unit, but the value-laden tone of the commentary and the jumpy and uneven presentation of the photos spoil it. An unexplained statement like,"Their (the Chinese) lives are controlled and regulated in a way that we, a free people, would never accept," does little to instruct us on the values the Chinese are teaching and how these values are applied in Chinese society.

Inside The People's Republic of China
Six filmstrips, 48 frames each, color, sound, 6 student guides, 1972

Distributor: Eye Gate House
146-01 Archer Avenue
Jamaica, New York 11435
(212) 291-9100

Cost: $63.50 with LP records
$64.00 with cassettes

Subject: Background for understanding modern China
Individual titles include:
The People of China
Work of the People of China
Trade and Transportation in China
Education and Communication in China
Health Services in China
Communes in China

Audience: Junior and senior high

This set of six filmstrips provides a general background for the evolving situation in China today. It depicts how people live, compares modern and traditional institutions, and discusses the effect of political and economic policies on the lives of China's citizens. Although the publishers do not send out the packages for review (a 15-frame synopsis is provided), the strips seem to give the viewer a good substantive grasp of the subjects covered.

Life in the People's Republic of China
Six filmstrips, 55 frames each, color, sound, student's guides, 1973
Distributor: Eye Gate House
               146-01 Archer Avenue
               Jamaica, New York 11435
               (212) 291-9100
Cost: $64.00 with cassettes
Subject: Urban and rural life in China
Audience: Junior and senior high

In this set one sees life in the major cities of Peking, Shanghai, and Kwangchow (Canton), as well as different areas of rural China. While only a surface view of the subjects covered, they are treated with a compassion lacking in many other units. A unique contribution is a discussion of China's film and television industries. Intelligent individualized learning guides for the student (6 included) are coordinated with the presentation.

Living in China Today
Four filmstrips, 70–75 frames each, color, sound, teacher's guides, 1967. Original scripts, photos, and sound provided by Felix Greene.
Distributor: Society for Visual Education
               1345 Diversey Parkway
               Chicago, Illinois 60614
               (312) 525-1500
Cost: $11.00 each filmstrip, plus record and study guide
               $32.50 4 filmstrips, 2 LP records ($36.50 with
               cassettes), 4 study guides
Subject: Life in contemporary China

Audience: Junior and senior high

This introduction to life in contempoary China stresses change, modernization, youth, and the new status of women. Old is balanced against new in agriculture and industry, public health, village and urban life. Scenes of city life, natural resources, transportation systems, and so on, all add to a picture of positive change and growth. The section on political education emphasizes the political indoctrination and the role of the Communist party. The photography is outstanding.

Mao, China, Revolution
Two filmstrips, 186 frames, color, sound, teacher's guide, 1972
Distributor: Westinghouse Learning Press
               100 Park Avenue
               New York, New York 10017
               (212) 983-2894
Cost: $39.00 with LP records or cassettes
Subject: Background for the Communist revolution and the
               Cultural Revolution
Audience: Junior and senior high

This filmstrip focuses on the beginnings of communism in China, the emergence of Mao, the causes of the 1949 revolution, and the reasons for the Cultural Revolution. Many weaknesses throughout the unit severely limit its effectiveness. Chinese words are consistently mispronounced, some photos are cut off at the top or are not representative of the period or event being described, and the musical background is less than adequate. Moreover, the discussion of the impact of the West on Chinese society is limited, the discussion of the origins of the Chinese Revolution inadequate, and the explanation of American involvement in China's civil war is superficial. The "Cult of Mao" and the Great Proletarian Cultural Revolution are dealt with in a simplistic and misleading way, and there is no discussion of China's foreign policy other than a photo of the explosion of a nuclear device. Not recommended.

Perception/Misperception: China/U.S.A.
Four sound filmstrips, one silent filmstrip, 87 frames each, color, teacher's guide, student booklets, set of role cards, 1975

Distributor:	School Services Department
	Schloat Productions
	150 White Plains Road
	Tarrytown, New York 10591
	(914) 631-8300
Cost:	$175.00 (complete set)
Subject:	The U.S.–China relationship
	Individual titles include:
	Images of Others
	Exploring Perceptions
	Through the Cultural Looking Glass
	The Historical Legacy
	Current Images
Audience:	Junior and senior high

This inquiry-oriented mini-course, produced in cooperation with the Center for War/Peace Studies, focuses on how and why perceptions and misconceptions occur. Tracing American images of China and Chinese images of the U.S. from the early nineteenth century to the present, the unit examines the U.S.–China relationship in light of the numerous elements of stereotyping, prejudice, and ethnocentrism. Specifically designed for the classroom, this is a thought-provoking and revealing study of the cultural differences between the United States and China.

Revolution: China and Mexico
Two filmstrips, 211 frames, color, booklet of readings, 1971
Distributor:	Current Affairs Films
	24 Danbury Road
	Wilton, Connecticut 06897
	(203) 762-0301
Cost:	$39.00 with LP record
	$43.00 with cassette
Subject:	Comparative revolutions
Audience:	Senior high

The intent of these filmstrips, produced by the World Law Fund, and the accompanying source booklet is to offer a model for studying seven identified aspects of comparative revolutions. The filmstrips are admirable in that they place the Chinese Communist Revolution in the context of the overall disintegration of Chinese society. They point to the progress made under the

Kuomintang rule of the 1930s, but are not shy about discussing the reasons for Chiang Kai-shek's ultimate failures. The success of the Communists is also fairly treated. Although Chinese names are consistently mispronounced, the strips give us a good overview of the revolution in China from 1911 to 1966. The accompanying readings are rather sophisticated but are well chosen and vivid. In addition, a teacher's guide suggests questions and activities. Intent to show the "basic forces at work in any revolution" is never quite demonstrated in the case of China, but overall the package deserves a high rating for giving the student a good feeling for the deeper forces of change which form the process of revolution.

The Shape of Modern China
Three filmstrips, 95–107 frames, color, sound, teacher's guide, 1972

Distributor: Time-Life Educational Materials
              c/o "China"
              Box 834
              Radio City Station
              New York, New York 10019
              (800) 621-8200 (toll free)
Cost: $45.00 with LP records
              $47.50 with cassettes
Subject: Geography, history and foreign relations
              Individual titles include:
              Within the Great Wall
              The World Mao Made
              The Continuing Revolution
Audience: Senior high

These sophisticated filmstrips present a comprehensive picture of China's development in the past several decades. The first focuses on the geography of China and the efforts of the people to transform the landscape; the second traces China's political history since the 1920s; and, the third, "The Continuing Revolution," deals with the revolutionary efforts continually underway to rebuild Chinese society. Foreign policy is also covered.

Included in the set is an incisive teacher's guide with suggestions for student discussion. The photography and narration are excellent, and the filmstrips can be recommended as a stimulus for more extensive reading and classroom discussion.

C. HONG KONG, TAIWAN, AND OVERSEAS CHINESE

The Changs Celebrate the New Year
Series: Six Families in the U.S.
Filmstrip, 62 frames, color, sound, teacher's guide, 1971
Distributor: Encyclopaedia Britannica Educational Corporation
              1822 Pickwick Avenue
              Glenview, Illinois 60025
              (312) 321-7311
Cost: $13.00 with LP record
              $14.95 with cassette
Subject: Life of a Chinese family in a large city
Audience: Elementary and junior high
Through the activities of the Chang family we are given a glimpse of how Chinese born in America blend their Oriental background with everyday life in an American city. Although the Changs do not live in "Chinatown," they frequently spend time there, and in their home preserve and teach their children many traditional customs. Yet, daily life for the Changs is typical of that of many other urban Americans in work, play, school, and religion. Recommended for the younger student as a good introduction to Chinese traditional culture, but care should be taken not to let this one view of a Chinese-American family create a stereotype for all.

Hong Kong
Filmstrip, 71 frames, color, no sound, captions, teacher's guide, 1969
Series: Asian World
Distributor: BEE Cross-Media
              36 Dogwood Glen
              Rochester, New York 14625
              (716) 381-5554
Cost: $8.50
Subject: Social life and economic activity in Hong Kong
Audience: Elementary and junior high
This filmstrip provides a simple yet effective study of social life and economic activity in Hong Kong. Special attention is paid to the life of the sampan people and the refugees from the People's

Republic. A variety of industrial enterprises is surveyed, and although the importance of Hong Kong's commercial activity is well documented, there is no coverage of the city's important role as a financial center. The best materials are those which focus on the daily lives of the Hong Kong Chinese in their shops, schools, and crowded apartments, and in the processing of foodstuffs such as ginger root. A teacher's guide which accompanies the filmstrip is adequate, with paragraph-length explanations for each frame. The frames are clear and their color is good. Although the filmstrip was produced in 1969, it is likely that the photographs were actually taken in the late 1950s.

Hong Kong—Crossroads of the East
Filmstrip, 48 frames, color, no sound, teacher's guide, 1963
Distributor: Encyclopaedia Britannica
              1822 Pickwick Avenue
              Glenview, Illinois 60025
              (312) 321-7311
Cost: $6.00
Subject: Hong Kong
Audience: Junior and senior high
  The agricultural economy of the British Crown Colony of Hong Kong is explored, and the life of the people on sampans briefly glimpsed. The filmstrip does not cover Hong Kong's commercial activity. The study guide is adequate, and the pictures generally of excellent quality, although the unit is now clearly dated.

Taiwan: The Republic of China
Filmstrip, 55 frames, color, no sound, brief captions, short narration guide, 1969
Series: Asian World
Distributor: BEE Cross-Media
              36 Dogwood Glen
              Rochester, New York 14625
              (716) 381-5554
Cost: $7.00
Subject: Everyday life on the island of Taiwan
Audience: Elementary and junior high
  Although somewhat out of date, this filmstrip offers a useful

cursory introduction to everyday life on the island of Taiwan. Most of the photographs deal with agricultural production, religious ceremonies, and cultural activities. Conspicuously absent is any material dealing with the island's rapid industrial development in the past decade, and except for a scene of the Nationalistic Chinese Legislative Yuan in session, no political information of substance is included. Although the filmstrip was produced in 1969, the photographs might have been taken in the late 1950s.

Taiwan Today
Four filmstrips, 35 frames each, color, sound, study guide, 1972
Distributor: Aims Instructional Media Services
               P.O. Box 1010
               Hollywood, California 90028
               (213) 467-1171
Cost: $42.50 (with 2 LP records)
Subject: *Taiwan—General Background*—parts 1 and 2
               Taiwan—Cultural Traditions and Cultural Strains
               —parts 1 and 2
Audience: Senior high and college
    These excellent filmstrips (photographs taken in 1966–68) provide intelligent and objective background information about the people of Taiwan, their cultural traditions, and the existing economic and political conditions. One of the better audio-visual materials available on the subject, the set is a good introduction to the study of Taiwan and the blend of traditional and modern Chinese culture which prevails there.

D. CHINESE TRADITIONAL CULTURE

Chinese Poetry
Two filmstrips, 191 frames, color, sound, teacher's guide, 1973
Distributor: Social Studies School Service
               10,000 Culver Boulevard
               Culver City, California 90230
               (213) 839-2436
Cost: $40.00 (with LP records)
               $46.00 (with cassettes)
Subject: Poetry and folk songs from the time of Confucius
               to the present.

Audience: Junior and senior high

The purpose of these filmstrips is to "acquaint the American student with examples of Chinese poetry as a background for looking at the Chinese people, their history, culture, philosophy, and literature." The unit includes:

Part 1 (91 frames):   Themes and styles of ancient Chinese poetry with folk songs dating from 1000 B.C. through the T'ang period (900 A.D.)

Part 2 (100 frames):   Cultural history of China in the nineteenth century, poets of the twentieth century, and modern communist folk songs.

An excellent teacher's guide presents the poems in their entirety with interpretive notes, explains the types and themes of Chinese poetry, and includes comprehensive questions and a glossary of terms used in the narration. There is also a time line of developments in Chinese literature.

An unusual subject for a filmstrip, it is very well covered. Moreover, the material is so well organized that even the teacher unfamiliar with the subject but willing to study the text can present it effectively.

4. OTHER MATERIALS

A. PHOTOGRAPHS

The following are sources for photographs on China which are available for reproduction. (Prices for individual photographs may be obtained from the distributors.)

Black Star Company
450 Park Avenue South
New York, New York 10016
(212) 679-3288

Eastfoto-Sovfoto Agency
25 West 43rd Street
New York, New York 10036
(212) 279-8846

Magnum Photo
15 West 46th Street
New York, New York 10036
(212) 541-7570

Other Materials

Shostal Associates, Inc.
60 East 42nd Street
New York, New York 10017
(212) 687-0696

US–China Friendship Association
41 Union Square West
New York, New York 10003
(212) 255-4727

B. AUDIO-TAPES

Much of the material on audio-tapes is a rendition of the views
and analyses contained in books and monographs written by the
scholar or journalist. Tapes, however, add the element of personal voice contact, and can offer a lively interchange of ideas and
interpretation between people.
    The following audio-tapes are recommended:

John K. Fairbank: *China Talks*
Distributor: Harper and Row, Publishers
                10 East 53rd Street
                New York, New York 10022
                (212) 593-7000
Cost: (Sale) $60.00 the complete set
Subject: A collection of six one-hour lectures by Professor
                Fairbank
                Individual cassettes include:
                The Confucian Social Order
                China and the Barbarians
                Traders, Missionaries, and Diplomats
                The Revolutionary Process
                The People's Republic
                A Perspective on Ourselves
Audience: General; for adults who seek a solid background
                for understanding China.

China Conversations
Produced by Arlene Posner for the National Committee on U.S.-
China Relations
Distributor: Broadcasting Foundation of America

	52 Vanderbilt Avenue
	New York, New York 10017
	(212) MU4-2505
Cost:	(Rental) 14-day free loan (plus postage), reel-to-reel only
Distributor:	Social Studies School Service
	10,000 Culver Boulevard
	Culver City, California 90230
	(213) 839-2436
Cost:	(Sale) 1–9, $7.95 each; 10 or more, $7.00 each, cassettes only
Subject:	Series of one-half-hour taped interviews with China specialists and recent visitors on a variety of current issues. Provides authoritative information on China and U.S.–China relations by scholars, journalists, and others. Reading lists accompany the tapes.
	List of individual topics available from the distributors.
Audience:	Schools, libraries, radio stations, community groups.

Conversations from Wingspread

Distributor:	The Johnson Foundation
	Racine, Wisconsin 53401
	(414) 639-3211
Cost:	(Rental) $1.60 each
Subject:	Half-hour panel discussion programs on various topics, including 9 on the People's Republic:
	U.S.–China Cultural Exchanges (2 parts)
	Education in China
	China After the Cultural Revolution
	Science in China
	A Visit to China
	Health Care in the People's Republic of China
	The United States and China
	China
	A Profile of Madame Mao
Audience:	General, including library, schools. Tapes may not be used for broadcast or paid admission.

Other Materials

C. VIDEO-TAPES

Red Flag Canal
Distributor: Media Materials Distribution Service
                55 Elk Street, Room 101
                Albany, New York 12210
Cost: No charge for New York State use
                $35.00 out of state
                Blank tape must be supplied by all users

The New York State Education Department has produced a 30-minute video-tape cassette of the Chinese documentary film of the same title (see chapter 9, section 3). Narrated by Jack Chen, a long-time resident of China and a former consultant to the New York State Education Department, the film depicts the changes in the lives of peasants resulting from the building of an irrigation canal in North Central China and stresses one of China's fundamental values: the people can overcome all obstacles through their own physical labor and cooperation with one another.

6. Books

1. INTRODUCTION

The wealth of published material on China now available places a heavy burden on those attempting to inform themselves, or to inform others, about China and U.S.-China relations. This section is designed to assist the nonspecialist in selecting books from among a wide range of topics and viewpoints. Special effort has been made to include volumes that are the best of their type and are generally available for purchase; in the case where both a cloth and paper edition are available, the less expensive edition is listed. As this is an introduction, and not a catalog, many excellent works necessarily have been omitted, as have most specialized scholarly studies.

Most books listed in the guide contain their own bibliographies, and the reader is advised to refer to them for additional suggestions. For many of the reviews of the new books included in this edition, we have relied on the work of a former colleague, Robert Goldberg, who compiled an excellent bibliography to supplement the first edition of this guide (see Robert Goldberg, *Recent Materials on China and U.S.-China Relations: An Annotated Bibliography*, Service Center Papers for Asian Studies, no. 8, 1974).

Books and periodicals listed below can, for the most part, be ordered from local bookstores. Items not locally stocked can be ordered directly from the publisher (see Appendix 1 for addresses).

A distinction has been made in selecting the titles for the sections "Firsthand Impressions" and "State and Society." Obviously, many firsthand accounts reflect the authors' views on the current state of society in the People's Republic, but for the most part, these books by travelers to China—appearing more widely since Americans have begun to visit the P.R.C.—reflect a generalist's view and the tourist nature of the visit. Books written by scholars and other specialists on China, whether or not the author has had an opportunity to visit the People's Republic, appear in section 8.

The annotated bibliography is divided as follows:

2. Reference and Source Books
3. History and General Background
4. Culture and the Arts
5. Biographies, Writings, and Modern Literature
6. The Communist Rise to Power
7. Firsthand Impressions
8. State and Society
9. Economic Studies
10. Military Studies
11. Taiwan
12. China in World Politics
13. United States–China Relations
14. Chinese in America
   Materials especially recommended are marked with a •.

2. REFERENCE AND SOURCE BOOKS

• *An Illustrated Atlas of China*
[No author listed]
New York: Rand McNally and Company, 1972
80 pp. $4.95
This atlas, based on one compiled and distributed by the Central Intelligence Agency in 1971, is an excellent introduction to China's geography. More than a collection of maps, it contains information of economic and historical interest, including charts and descriptions of population, railways, natural resources, roads and inland waterways, administrative regions, and so on. The most up-to-date quick-reference atlas available.

Biographical Dictionary of Republican China

Vol. 1, Ai-Ch'u	483 pp.	$22.50 (1967)
Vol. 2, Dalai-Mai	481 pp.	$22.50 (1968)
Vol. 3, Mao-Wu	471 pp.	$25.00 (1970)
Vol. 4, Yang-Yun	431 pp.	$35.00 (1971)

Howard L. Boorman, ed.
New York: Columbia University Press
   This four-volume series contains some six hundred biographical articles on prominent Chinese of the Republic period (1911–49). The essays, contributed by both Chinese and Western scholars, are of varying but generally high quality, and include entries on most Chinese figures currently in the news. A full

bibliography of the sources used forms the major portion of the fourth volume.

Essential Works of Chinese Communism
Winberg Chai, ed.
New York: Bantam Books, 1972
560 pp. $1.45 Paper
   Primarily for the nonspecialist, this collection of thirty-one basic documents spanning the past five decades provides a useful introduction to the study of Chinese Communism. The volume contains an introduction by the editor outlining the history of Communism in China and explanatory comments accompany each document. Many of the selections, e.g., the best-known writings of Mao Tse-tung, Liu Shao-ch'i, and Lin Piao, also appear in other works listed in this guide. Included are the constitutions of the People's Republic and of the Chinese Communist party, and various resolutions issued by the Central Committee of the party.

Asia's Lands and Peoples
George B. Cressey
New York: McGraw-Hill, 3d ed., 1963
622 pp. $14.50
   This standard geography of Asia contains about 130 pages on China, including an analysis of its prospects for economic development; it also has many interesting photographs of the diverse regions of China.

Sources of Chinese Tradition
Wm. Theodore de Bary, Wing-tsit Chan, and Burton Watson, eds.
New York: Columbia University Press, 1964
Vol. 1: 564 pp. $4.00 Paper
Vol. 2: 314 pp. $3.00 Paper
   Excerpts from Chinese literature, both classical and contemporary, are brought together in twenty-nine chapters ranging in subject matter from antiquity and the Confucian tradition (vol. 1) to modern nationalism and the theory and practice of Chinese

Communism (vol. 2). In an attempt to represent all dimensions of Chinese thought, the compilers have included articles on the social, political, philosophical, and religious heritage. A valuable collection for both the general reader and the serious student of Chinese history.

China: Man and His World
James Forrester, with Gary Birchall, John Parr, and Robert Williamson
Indianapolis: The Bobbs-Merrill Company, 1972
64 pp. $0.50 Paper
   The booklet is a potpouri of information sections, illustrations on language, history, philosophy, geography, traditional wealth/ population ratios, signs, and banners. Simple, yet thematically effective through the use of the case studies (e.g., the imagined reactions of family members being moved to a commune during the Great Leap Forward), the booklet includes some factual errors and occasional stereotyped illustrations which dampen only slightly its overall effectiveness. Its presentation, point of view, and excellent use of basic information make it a valuable adjunct for the classroom.

China in Maps
Harold Fullard
Chicago: Denoyer-Geppert, 1968
25 pp. $3.50 Paper
   In this handy atlas, each map, whether historical or physical, is accompanied by a descriptive text. The information on "China in the Modern World" is somewhat out of date, including the population figures. But the maps are good and cover a wide range of information on history, climate, topography, geology, agriculture, industry, demography, and communication networks.

A Chinese View of China
John Gittings
New York: Pantheon Books, 1973
216 pp. $1.95 Paper
   Gittings, a professor of Chinese history at Oxford University, has taken excerpts from Chinese sources to examine how the

Chinese themselves view past and current events. He focuses on the pre-1949 period, using contemporary and historical writings (Sun Yat-sen, Lu Hsun, Mao Tse-tung) to show how the past is interpreted to serve the present. Also included is a useful section of facts, figures, and suggestions for further reading which enhances the book's value to the teacher.

● *China: Selected Readings on the Middle Kingdom*
Leon Hellerman and Alan L. Stein
New York: Washington Square Press, 1971
332 pp. $1.25 Paper

This is the first source book written expressly for a high school audience and is excellent for studying the history, politics, society, poetry, and legends of China. It is divided into four parts: "Understanding China," "Traditional China," "China in Transition," and "Contemporary China." Each section contains a number of readings by leading Western and Asian authorities representing a diversity of viewpoints. Maps, political cartoons, and a good annotated bibliography are included. The book can be used in total or adapted part-by-part.

We the Chinese: Voices from China
Neale and Diedre Hunter
New York: Praeger Books, 1973
292 pp. $2.95 Paper

This book, compiled by two Australian teachers, is an anthology of twenty-three readings on the Chinese past and present from a variety of original materials: speeches, poetry, songs, radio broadcasts, as well as books and periodicals. The subjects discussed and examined are Chinese history, industrial and technical progress, education, life in the cities, and the Cultural Revolution. Especially compiled and written for the high school reader, the book is also well illustrated with photographs.

Biographic Dictionary of Chinese Communism
Donald W. Klein and Anne B. Clark
Cambridge, Mass: Harvard University Press, 1971
2 vols. 1,196 pp. $30.00

This major volume provides the most comprehensive picture of contemporary Chinese leadership and institutions yet available. It provides biographies of 433 of the most prominent and influential Chinese Communist figures, written in a highly readable style, and ninety-six comprehensive appendixes outlining Chinese governmental institutions and their staffs. The biographies contain all available information on the person's family, education, socioeconomic status, early revolutionary activity, and career since the Communists came to power in 1949. Indispensable for the scholar and a valuable resource for the layman.

Modern China: The Making of a New Society from 1839 to the Present
Orville Schell and Joseph Esherick
New York: Vintage Books, 1972
143 pp. $1.50 Paper

An excellent short history of modern China emphasizing the period prior to 1949, but the chapter on the People's Republic is concise and interesting. The text is very readable and is frequently interspersed with substantial quotations from original sources. The photographs are superb. The book views peasant uprisings as key ingredients in the evolution of China, concluding that revolution, especially the Communist one, has been beneficial to the people of China. It can be used either as a text for 11th and 12th grades or as additional reading for interested students. Highly recommended as background reading for teachers.

● *The China Reader*
Franz Schurmann and Orville Schell, eds.
New York: Vintage Books, 1967–74

Vol. 1 *Imperial China*	287 pp.	$2.40 Paper
Vol. 2 *Republican China*	369 pp.	$2.40 Paper
Vol. 3 *Communist China*	647 pp.	$2.95 Paper
Vol. 4 *People's China*	659 pp.	$3.95 Paper

In these four volumes, the editors have assembled excellent selections from a wide variety of primary and secondary sources. They include a wealth of descriptive material and a variety of viewpoints, linked together and analyzed in introductory comments. The fourth volume concentrates on the Cultural Revolution period and its aftermath. One of the best popular compilations of writing to have appeared thus far, the set is a valuable source of background material for anyone with a general interest in Chinese history and contemporary Asian affairs.

China's Changing Map: National and Regional Development, 1949-71
Theodore Shabad
New York: Praeger, 1972
370 pp. $5.95 Paper
This is the most comprehensive political and economic geography of China available. Part 1 surveys China as a whole: its physical geography, ethnic groups, and economic resources. Part 2 traces regional political, administrative, and economic changes. This book, completely revised since the earlier edition (1956), provides a coherent and detailed picture of the changes in China's economic development since 1949 and relates them to China's overall development strategy. Includes sixteen maps and fifty-seven tables.

3. HISTORY AND GENERAL BACKGROUND

● *China's Cultural Tradition: What and Whither?*
Derk Bodde
New York: Holt, Rinehart and Winston, 1957
90 pp. $2.00 Paper
In this classic pamphlet, a noted scholar deals with the distinctive characteristics of traditional Chinese institutions and thought. In a short space, he covers religions, views of nature, the family system, individualism and social mobility, the law, the army, and the emperor of the Confucian state. The work is enhanced by quotations from both primary and secondary sources. An outstanding introduction which can serve as a springboard for discussion and further reading on features of Chinese society.

● *Chinese Thought from Confucius to Mao Tse-tung*
Herrlee G. Creel
Chicago: University of Chicago Press, 1971
303 pp. $2.95 Paper
Chinese philosophy before the Christian era is emphasized in

this nontechnical summary of Chinese thought. Professor Creel also deals with Confucianism, the ideas of Mo-tsu and Mencius, Taoism, Legalism, and their variations and adaptations. As an introduction for the general reader, this book stands among the best.

A History of China
Wolfram Eberhard
Berkeley: University of California Press, 1969
367 pp. $3.45 Paper 3rd rev. edition
This excellent introduction to Chinese history traces the main currents of China's social and cultural development from prehistoric times to the present. It constitutes, in Professor Eberhard's words, a "new synthesis" of information about China's past, focusing on broad trends and cultural development rather than on historical events and personalities. Called "daring and iconoclastic" when first published in 1950, *A History of China* has become a standard work in the field.

● *Chinese Civilization: An Introduction*
Werner Eichhorn
New York: Praeger, 1969
360 pp. $3.50 Paper
Professor Eichhorn emphasizes the period from prehistoric times to the Mongol invasion of the late thirteenth century; later periods are covered more briefly. He describes the evolution of China's political and social organization and within this framework studies the rise of China's three major religions: Confucianism, Taoism, and Buddhism. Topics such as class conflict, the economy, the position of women, the imperial bureaucracy, law, education, technology, philosophy, art, literature, and music are also dealt with.

Although the author states in his foreword that the book is aimed at the nonspecialist, he makes such interesting use of cultural data—oracle bone texts, bronze inscriptions, anecdotes, legends, songs—that even the specialist will find much of value.

China's Gentry: Essays on Rural-Urban Relations
Fei Hsiao-tung. Rev. and ed. by Margaret Redfield, with Six Life

Histories of Chinese Gentry Families by Yung-teh Chow
Chicago: University of Chicago Press (Phoenix Books), 1953
290 pp. $2.45 Paper

Professor Fei, a noted anthropologist, originally wrote these six essays as newspaper articles on the social role of the scholar-gentry in imperial and modern China, the power structure in rural communities, and the relations between villages and towns. The fascinating case studies in the appendix demonstrate the effects of revolutionary change on six particular gentry families.

Daily Life in China on the Eve of the Mongol Invasion: 1250–1276
Jacques Gernet
Stanford: Stanford University Press, 1962
254 pp. $2.95 Paper

By focusing on a small fraction of Chinese history, and one city (Hangchow, the capital at that time), the author imparts the full flavor of life in thirteenth-century China. Gernet's account is a rich depiction of the daily life of traditional China, picturing not only the court structure and philosophic and family system normally described in histories, but also the physical layout of the city, the occupations of the common man as well as their use of leisure time, and the physical appearances of the people and their dwellings.

The Rise and Splendour of the Chinese Empire
Rene Grousset
Berkeley: University of California Press, 1963
342 pp. $2.45 Paper

A splendid survey of the history of China through the eighteenth century giving major emphasis to the earlier periods. Grousset's enthusiasm is infectious as he traces in a clear, lucid style China's cultural achievements and political process.

China's Three Thousand Years: The Story of a Great Civilization
Louis Heren, et. al.
New York: Collier Books, 1974
252 pp. $3.95 Paper

An incisive overview and interweaving of the major historical events and artistic achievements of over three thousand years of Chinese civilization. Sections by other contributors on the land and the people, modern history, and the People's Republic are interesting, but it is C. P. Fitzgerald's interweaving of China's history with her philosophy, religion, and art up to the nineteenth century that forms the bulk of the book and gives it its appealing literary quality. A good book for the general reader, it is enhanced by color illustrations and black and white photographs.

Under the Ancestors' Shadow: Kinship, Personality, and Social Mobility in China
Francis L. K. Hsu
Stanford: Stanford University Press, 1967
370 pp. $3.45 Paper
As the subtitle indicates, this book is a study of various anthropological aspects of life in traditional China. Professor Hsu presents a detailed, informative, and very readable analysis of the basic social institutions which made up traditional Chinese society.

An Introduction to Chinese Civilization
John T. Meskill, ed.
New York: D. C. Heath, 1973
700 pp. $6.95 Paper
This book consists of a brief history of China and ten essays on major aspects of Chinese civilization, such as anthropology, archaeology, art, economics, geography, politics, and literature. Although it is meant as a general survey for undergraduates, certain chapters are very useful background for anyone interested in a particular topic.

Ruling From Horseback: Manchu Politics in the Oboi Regency, 1661–1669
Robert B. Oxnam
Chicago: University of Chicago Press, 1975
250 pp. $12.50
According to an old Chinese proverb, "Though the empire can be conquered on horseback, it cannot be ruled from horseback." In this book, historian Robert B. Oxnam questions the old proverb. Meticulously using previously untapped primary source material he argues that "the Manchu system, Manchu officials, and

Manchu ideas held undisputed control over Ch'ing China" (1644–1912) in spite of the traditional Chinese claim that the Chinese always overcame their foreign conquerers by sinification. To further explain the Manchu-oriented authoritarianism, the author carefully examines the ruthless Oboi regency (1660s): the forces of sinification and Manchu dominance, the key decisions and episodes, and the factional clashes of the Manchus. Although highly specialized, an important and useful book for the study of the history of modern China and the general study of the problems of alien rule.

Daughter of Han: The Autobiography of a Chinese Working Woman
Ida Pruitt
Stanford: Stanford University Press, 1945
257 pp. $2.95 Paper
Ida Pruitt, daughter of missionary parents, has taken the life story of her friend Ning Lao and turned it into a warm, human document which portrays the life of the common man in China before the advent of the People's Republic. A rich storehouse of descriptions of traditional Chinese social customs and life-styles.

● *A History of East Asian Civilization*
Vol. 1, *East Asia: The Great Tradition*
Edwin O. Reischauer and John K. Fairbank
Boston: Houghton Mifflin, 1958
739 pp. $12.95
Vol. 2, *East Asia: The Modern Transformation*
John K. Fairbank, Edwin O. Reischauer, and Albert M. Craig
Boston: Houghton Mifflin, 1965
955 pp. $13.50
Developed from lectures given at Harvard by these three historians, this two-volume work is probably the most intelligent and comprehensive text on East Asian history yet produced in the United States. It is used both as a reference for the scholar and in introductory courses on Asian history. Volume 1 outlines the development of Chinese, Korean, and Japanese history up to the nineteenth century. The central theme of volume 2, which covers the period from the mid-nineteenth century to the present, is the

transformation of the traditional societies of China and Japan in response to the challenge of Western expansion. It contains an introductory chapter on early Western contacts with Asia beginning in the sixteenth century and chapters on colonialism and nationalism among China's neighbors in Southeast and Central Asia.

The Mind of China: The Culture, Customs, and Beliefs of Traditional China
Ben-Ami Scharfstein
New York: Basic Books, 1974
182 pp. $8.95

China has undergone a great, and no doubt unfinished, revolution. The enigma of whether this radical revolution can succeed in eliminating the old culture and its hold upon the Chinese people is the issue which underlies this scholarly study. The main focus of the book is on the intellectual and artistic culture of old China as seen through the eyes of rulers, artists, historians, cosmographers, and philosophers.

To Change China: Western Advisers in China, 1620–1960
Jonathan Spence
Boston: Little, Brown, 1969
335 pp. $2.65 Paper

From among the hundreds of "Western advisers" who have labored in China, Mr. Spence has chosen to write about sixteen whose careers spanned four centuries from the early 1600s to the mid-twentieth century. The author examines not only their personal contributions, but also the complex motives that brought men such as the Jesuit missionary Adam Schall, revolutionary organizer Mikhail Borodin, and the American general Joseph Stilwell to China. This readable book will be of value to anyone interested in the history of Western contact with China or concerned about the problems that arise when representatives of the West, confident that their civilization has much to offer, choose to labor in foreign lands.

Emperor of China: Self-Portrait of K'ang-hsi
Jonathan D. Spence
New York: Alfred A. Knopf, 1974
217 pp. $8.95

A careful analysis of the letters, edicts, commands, pardons and poems of K'ang-hsi (1661–1722) that reveal the inner life of this great, but enigmatic, Chinese emperor. The book is an engaging story which conveys to the reader a believable and human figure, and "depicts the events of a lifetime as they can be reborn by a few moments of mental concentration." A delightful and rich portrait of the man central to the history of this period, although that history itself is not the subject of this book.

● *Three Ways of Thought in Ancient China*
Arthur Waley
New York: Anchor Books, 1964
216 pp. $1.95 Paper

A clear, well-written study of Confucianism, Taoism, and Legalism, the three main components of the state orthodoxy in imperial China. Waley, generally recognized as the finest translator of Chinese literature into English, presents numerous extracts from the writing of spokesmen from each school of thought.

The Dragon Empress: Life and Times of Ts'u-hsi, Empress Dowager of China
Marina Warner
New York: Macmillan, 1972
271 pp. $12.95

From 1861 to 1908 China was ruled by the iron hand of a woman—the Empress Dowager Ts'u-hsi. She was opportunistic, ruthless, malicious, and xenophobic. During her reign, while she kept her court in corrupt and isolated splendor, China plunged into poverty and political and social disintegration (exacerbated by foreign invasions), which led to the collapse of the Ch'ing dynasty in 1911. An interesting biography, with lavish illustrations.

4. CULTURE AND THE ARTS

Arts of China: Buddhist Cave Temples
Arts of China: Neolithic Cultures to the T'ang Dynasties; New Discoveries
Terukazu Akiyama et. al.
Tokyo and Palo Alto: Kodansha, Limited, 1969
540 pp. $25.00 (each)

Archaeology of Ancient China
Chang Kuang-chih
New Haven: Yale University Press, 1968
320 pp. $3.95 Paper

Unearthing China's Past
Jan Fontein and Tung Wu
Greenwich, Connecticut: New York Graphic Society, 1973
238 pp. $8.95 Paper

• *The Art and Architecture of China*
Lawrence Sickman and Alexander Soper
Baltimore: Penguin Books, 1971
280 pp. $2.95 Paper

Collectively, these books represent an excellent overview of Western interpretations of different aspects of the Chinese artistic tradition. The Akiyama book, the most richly illustrated of those mentioned, serves both as a scholarly analysis and a visual introduction. Professor Chang is one of the few experts on Chinese archeology in this country, and he provides an introduction to both its scope and heritage. Jan Fontein put together a show of Chinese art objects and photographs for an exhibition in the Boston Museum of Fine Arts, and this book, which is essentially a catalog of that exhibition, gives a good photographic overview (solely in black and white) of the kinds of art objects found by archeologists in China. Finally, the Sickman and Soper work, although now somewhat dated, still stands as the best overall layman's guide to the subject.

● *China Today*
Jerome Alan Cohen and Joan Lebold Cohen
New York: Harry N. Abrams, 1975
400 pp. $25.00
This handsome book combines photographs of a recent trip to China with a compressed artistic history, using illustrations ranging from old bronzes and paintings to the handicrafts of today that exemplify this artistic tradition. To accompany the photographs and illustrations, Professor Cohen has written a lucid and insightful section on contemporary China and how, in the arts, today's China carries out the directive to "let the old serve the new." An excellent addition to any library.

Chinese Writing
Herrlee G. Creel
Washington, D.C.: American Council on Education, 1969
$0.50 Pamphlet
This little pamphlet was written for nonscholars by a fine scholar. On the first page Creel says, "Let's read Chinese" and thrusts a line of characters before the reader. Then, in fifteen enjoyable pages, he explains the characters and enables the reader to interpret them. A fast and pleasant way for anyone to discover that Chinese ideographs are an effective medium of written communication. A longer and also very effective introduction to Chinese written language is *The Chinese Language for Beginners* by Lee Cooper (Rutland, Vermont: Charles E. Tuttle, 1971).

The Horizon History of China
C. P. Fitzgerald
383 pp. $22.00 ($25.00 DeLuxe)

The Horizon Book of the Arts of China
Thomas Froncek, managing ed.
413 pp. $22.00 ($23.00 DeLuxe)
Boxed set of both volumes, $45.00
New York: American Heritage Publishing Company, 1969

These two books constitute one of the most visually rewarding surveys of the history and the arts of China yet published in English. The history volume combines photographs, paintings, charts, maps, poems, and prints with an excellent and well-balanced explanatory text. Each period—from the legendary Hsia Dynasty through the present—is described in terms of its political and social institutions.

The book on art, with its lovely black and white and color reproductions, is divided thematically rather than chronologically, devoting a chapter to each art form: jade, bronze, sculpture, calligraphy, painting, rubbings, woodcuts, ceramics, decorative arts, crafts, and architecture. Unlike the history book, which covers events in China since 1948, it does not mention the contemporary scene. The only reference to art in the People's Republic is one quotation from Mao Tse-tung about art "serving the people." Although these two volumes may be too expensive to be included in the average layman's library, they are a must for school collections on China.

Dianying, Electric Shadows: An Account of Films and the Film Audience in China.
Jay Leyda
Cambridge, Mass.: M.I.T. Press, 1972
515 pp. $12.50

A historical survey of the Chinese cinema from 1897 to 1966, focusing on the role of the film in Chinese society today. The book sees a creative tension between film as an expression of social vision and film as a vehicle for social message. A groundbreaking study.

China on Stage
Helen Wheeler Snow
New York: Random House, 1972
300 pp. $2.45

The first overall introduction to Chinese drama as it is presented in the People's Republic of China today. The author gives a sympathetic look at how the Chinese use the theater to portray and teach their model political and social behavior. The book also includes the texts of several Chinese plays.

● *The Arts of China*
Michael Sullivan
Berkeley: University of California Press, 1973
256 pp. $5.95 Paper
   Michael Sullivan's book is a revised and expanded edition of
his *A Short History of Chinese Art* (Berkeley, University of
California Press, 1967). Like that earlier work, it relates the
development of China's art to history and examines what the art
of the era can tell us about the social and political life of the
people. This good introduction for the layman as well as the
college art student incorporates the important archaeological
finds made in the People's Republic over the last several years.

5. BIOGRAPHIES, WRITINGS, AND MODERN LITERATURE

Anthology of Chinese Literature from Early Times to the Present
Cyril Birch & Donald Keene, eds.
New York: Grove Press, 1965 (vol. 1), 1972 (vol. 2)
Vol. 1 (Early Times to the 14th Century)   492 pp. $3.95
Vol. 2 (14th Century to the Present)   476 pp. $4.95
   Professor Birch's anthology contains poems, short stories,
essays, letters, and philosophical and historical writings, arranged
chronologically by dynasty, in readable translations. This is a
valuable supplementary text for teaching about ancient China.
The editor has also compiled and translated six short stories
originally published in 1620 dealing with murder, love, satire,
and everyday life in the Ming Dynasty (1368–1644). This book is
entitled *Stories from a Ming Collection* (New York: Evergreen
Books, 1965). An analytic discussion of China's literary tradition
may be found in Liu Wu-chi's *An Introduction to Chinese Literature* (Bloomington, Indiana: Indiana University Press, 1966). Liu
focuses on traditional literature and comments on prose, poetry,
drama, and the novel. The modern era is covered only through
the early twentieth-century works of Mao Tun and Lu Hsun.

Guide to Chinese Poetry and Drama
Roger B. Bailey
Boston: G. K. Hall, 1973
108 pp. $9.50

Guide to Chinese Prose
Jordan D. Paper
Boston: G. K. Hall, 1973
144 pp. $9.50

These two companion volumes are products of the Asian Literature Bibliography Series under the general editorship of the Asian Literature Program of the Asia Society. They fill a long-standing need of the nonspecialist, the student of Asian literature, and the librarian for carefully annotated bibliographies of the best in Chinese literature available in the English language.

● *Mao*
Jerome Ch'en
Englewood Cliffs, N.J.: Prentice-Hall, 1969
176 pp. $1.95 Paper
An excellent short volume on China's supreme leader compiled by a noted student of Mao. The book is divided into three sections: selections of Mao's own writings (many translated for this volume), views of Mao by his contemporaries, and evaluations of Mao's place in history by Western scholars. In his introduction, the author interprets the principal social and historical influences on Mao. A very readable work for high school students. See also the author's *Mao and the Chinese Revolution* (New York: Oxford University Press, 1967), which examines the entire revolution in relation to Mao's personal experience, and includes thirty-seven of Mao's poems.

Folktales from China
Wolfram Eberhard, ed.
New York: Pocket Books, 1973
275 pp. $1.25 Paper
The collection contains a selection of traditional Chinese fairy tales and folk tales, plus six recently translated stories from the People's Republic of China. Extensive historical notes and an index to motifs add a scholarly dimension for those interested. A delightful book.

● *Mao Tse-tung: An Anthology of His Writings*
Anne Fremantle, ed.
New York: New American Library, 1962
297 pp. $1.25 Paper
This small collection of Mao Tse-tung's political, military, and philosophical writings includes selections from "The Struggle in the Chingkang Mountains" (1928), "Strategic Problems in the Anti-Japanese Guerrilla War" (1938), "On Coalition Government" (1945), and "On the People's Democratic Dictatorship" (1949). The volume also contains brief explanatory notes and an introductory essay by the editor. For the general reader, the book is a useful guide to some of Mao's best-known works.

Chou En-lai: China's Gray Eminence
Kai-yu Hsu
Garden City, N.Y.: Doubleday, 1968
233 pp. $1.75 Paper
Like Martin Ebon's biography of Lin Piao (New York: Stein & Day, 1970), this book is useful primarily because so little other information about the man is generally available. The volume outlines the events of Premier Chou's life and, in the process, spans the history of the Chinese Communist party. Lack of hard data often makes it necessary for the author to rely on anecdotes and speculation, but he concludes that Chou En-lai is a natural administrator and diplomat—two propositions that go far toward explaining his value to, and survival among, the top leadership in China.

Twentieth Century Chinese Poetry
Kai-yu Hsu, ed. and trans.
Ithaca: Cornell University Press, 1963
471 pp. $3.45 Paper
Although the book contains an introductory discussion of Chinese poetry, this is an anthology rather than a scholarly analysis. It presents the works of nearly fifty important poets of the twentieth century—from Hu Shih, father of the Chinese "literary revolution," through Mao Tse-tung, father of the Chinese "political revolution." Brief biographies and analyses of

each poet are presented along with selections of their works. Recently written folk poems by unknown authors are also included.

Revolutionary Leaders of Modern China
Chün-tu Hsueh
New York: Oxford University Press, 1971
560 pp. $4.95 Paper
A valuable collection of eight original articles and twelve reprinted essays dealing with the top leaders of the three revolutions in modern Chinese history: the Taiping Rebellion, the Republican Revolution, and the Communist movement. The men described include Hung Hsiu-chuan, Sun Yat-sen, Huang Hsing, Sung Chiao-jen, Wang Ching-wei, Chen Tu-hsiu, Chen Po-ta, Liu Shao-chi, Chou En-lai, and Mao Tse-tung.

Straw Sandals: Chinese Short Stories, 1918–1933
Harold Isaacs, ed.
Cambridge, Mass.: MIT Press, 1974
444 pp. $10.00
A collection of 23 stories, a play, and a poem by Chinese writers selected to represent the radical literature produced in China between 1918 and 1933. It was assembled in Peking in 1934 by the editor with the advice and guidance of Lu Hsun, China's foremost literary figure of this century, and Mao Tun, leading novelist of the younger group that gathered around Lu Hsun in those tumultuous years. The book includes updated biographical notes on the writers, many of which were originally supplied by the writers themselves, and some notes by Mao Tun on underground literary magazines of the period. Isaacs, who lived in Shanghai and edited a journal there in the early 1930s, describes the historical setting in which this short-lived and violence-ridden literary movement tried to make its way.

● *Modern Chinese Stories*
W. J. F. Jenner
London: Oxford University Press, 1970
271 pp. $2.50 Paper

A collection of twenty stories by China's best writers of this century. Three are by Lu Hsün, China's preeminent twentieth-century literary figure, one is by Kuo Mo-jo, president of the Chinese Academy of Sciences, and two are stories of post-1949 China. The stories reflect much of the political and social ferment of their respective times, and are a valuable medium for understanding modern China.

Selected Stories of Lu Hsün
Lu Hsün
Peking: Foreign Languages Press, 1972
$1.75   Paper
   Thirteen stories by China's greatest twentieth-century author which depict life among ordinary Chinese in the early decades of this century.

Chinese Literature: An Anthology from the Earliest Times to the Present Day
William McNaughton, ed.
Rutland, Vermont: Charles E. Tuttle Company, 1974
836 pp. $15.00

Chinese Literature: Popular Fiction and Drama
H. C. Chang
Chicago: Aldine Publishing Company, 1973
466 pp. $8.95

The Orchid Bear
Kenneth Rexroth and Ling Chung
New York: McGraw Hill, 1972
150 pp. $6.95

   These three books, although different in scope and emphasis, represent comprehensive anthologies of China's literature. McNaughton's book is the most comprehensive, incorporating excerpts from folktales, short stories, dramas, and novels. Chang has made his an illustration of the art of the story teller and of how the conventions of the story teller's repertoire were incorporated into dramas and novels between the thirteenth and eighteenth centuries.

With the advent of the women's movement, it was natural that some publisher would bring out a representative offering of Chinese women's poetry in translation. The Rexroth and Ling volume covers the topic from the earliest court poetry of the courtesans, palace women, and Tao priestesses to work by contemporary Chinese women living in the East and West. Appendixes include notes on the poems, an introductory essay on Chinese women and literature, and a bibliography.

Chiang Kai-shek
Robert Payne
New York: Weybright and Talley, 1969
338 pp. $10.00
This generally criticial biography attempts to "divorce Chiang Kai-shek from the legend, to see him as he really was and not as his propagandists saw him." Mr. Payne, who lived in China from 1941 to 1945, focuses on the period from 1927 to 1948 when the generalissimo was at the height of his power; but the two concluding chapters on the little-studied topic of political life in Taiwan under Nationalist rule are of special interest. An interesting and readable narrative. (The best-known work attributed to Chiang, first published in English in 1947, is *China's Destiny and China's Economic Theory*, with notes and commentary by Philip Jaffe [New York: Roy Publishers, 1947].)

● *Chairman Mao Talks to the People: Talks and Letters, 1956–1971*
Stuart R. Schram, ed.
New York: Pantheon Books, 1974
352 pp. $10.00
Contributing to our knowledge of events in China from 1956–1971, this highly readable collection brings together in one book some of Mao Tse-tung's most important speeches, discussions, and writings about economic, political, and philosophical problems. Translated by John Chinnery and Tieyun, most of these materials appeared in tabloids and other periodicals of Red

Guard organizations during the Cultural Revolution. These documents were used as ideological weapons in the struggle to weed out revisionism as the various cultural revolution groups saw it. Topics discussed include: education, organizational principles, patterns of economic development, and foreign relations. Compiled primarily for the general reader, the work is also of value to the China scholar.

● *Mao Tse-tung: A Biography*
Stuart R. Schram
New York: Pelican Books, 1967
351 pp. $1.65 Paper

This carefully written biography of Mao Tse-tung begins with a sketch of his boyhood and student days. It concentrates, however, on the three decades from the establishment of the Communist party in the early 1920s to the Communist victory in 1949. Concluding chapters outline the period from 1949 to the Cultural Revolution. Schram identifies two basic themes, "revolutionary voluntarism" and "militant nationalism," which he suggests have dominated all of Mao's thought and work since the beginning of his career. For a documentary presentation and analysis of Mao's political thought see, by the same author, *The Political Thought of Mao Tse-tung* (New York: Praeger, 1969).

Sun Yat-sen: His Life and It's Meaning
Lyon Sharman
Stanford: Stanford University Press, 1968
520 pp. $3.45 Paper

First published in 1934, this book remains indispensable for an understanding of the father of the Chinese Revolution. Mrs. Sharman, who lived in China as a child, wrote to preserve the knowledge of a historic figure who had "lived so spectacularly in the world's eye." Toward this end, she sought to demolish the hero-legend which his successors erected in his name in order to legitimize their own rule. For a scholarly study of Sun's life and role in Chinese politcs through 1905, drawing upon Chinese, Japanese, and Western sources, see Harold Z. Schiffrin, *Sun Yat-sen and the Origins of the Chinese Revolution* (Berkeley: University of California Press, 1968).

6. THE COMMUNIST RISE TO POWER

The Scalpel, the Sword: The Story of Doctor Norman Bethune
Ted Allen and Sidney Gordon
New York: Monthly Review Press, 1973 (rev. ed.)
320 pp. $3.95 Paper

This book has sold more than a million copies since its first publication in 1952 and has appeared in 19 languages. Considered as a folk hero and model of selfless dedication to the Chinese Communist Revolution, Bethune was a prominent Canadian thoracic surgeon; he was also, in varying degrees, a painter, poet, soldier (Spanish Civil War), critic, teacher, medical writer, and theorist. He arrived in China shortly after the Japanese invasion of 1937, and informed Mao Tse-tung and the Communist leadership that 75 percent of the serious battle casualties would survive if operated on immediately. Mao commissioned Bethune to organize a mobile operating unit, bringing him to the center of the war of resistance against the Japanese in the interior of North China. There he worked for almost two years, eighteen hours a day, until he died of septicemia contracted when he cut himself performing an operation under great pressure. His extraordinary devotion is still pointed to today in Chinese films, comics, and revolutionary writing.

China Shakes the World
Jack Belden
New York: Monthly Review Press, 1970
524 pp. $3.95 Paper

First published in 1949, *China Shakes the World* recounts the story of the Chinese Revolution primarily in terms of its meaning for the Chinese people and the peasantry in particular. A war correspondent with many years' experience in China, Burma, and North Africa, Jack Belden returned to China in 1946 to cover the Civil War. The stories he gathered as he traveled in both Communist- and Nationalist-controlled areas suggest the reasons for the wide popular support for the Communist movement. This work has been considered one of the American classics on the Chinese Revolution.

Origins of the Chinese Revolution
Lucien Bianco

Stanford: Stanford University Press, 1971
223 pp. $8.50

Lucien Bianco is a French scholar of Chinese rural society whose book was first published in French in 1967. Rather than the standard historical-political account of the origins of the Chinese Communist movement, Bianco focuses on the dynamic social forces underlying this revolution. His emphasis is on social crises, relating rural discontent to the rise of the Communist movement; he deals less with the events themselves than with their social origins. His often controversial interpretations contribute to a lively and stimulating book which clearly lost nothing in translation.

Stalin's Failure in China: 1924–1927
Conrad Brandt
New York: W. W. Norton, 1958
226 pp. $1.95 Paper

This book traces the complexities of Stalin's involvement in China in the 1920s and his unsuccessful efforts to manipulate both the Kuomintang government and the Chinese Communist party. Brandt also examines Trotsky's arguments with Stalin over the China question, and young Mao's compromises and conflicts with the Stalin line. A scholarly book for anyone with a special interest in this period.

● *Twentieth Century China*
O. Edmund Clubb
New York: Columbia University Press, 1972
500 pp. $3.95 Paper

Written by a retired United States foreign service officer with some twenty years of experience in the Far East, this revised and updated edition of his political history of China covers the period from the decline and fall of the Manchu Dynasty through the Cultural Revolution. The book provides a general introduction to the people and processes that have dominated twentieth-century Chinese history, and contains a chronology of major events, maps, and a bibliography. An informative work for the general reader or student.

● *Communism Takes China: How the Revolution Went Red*
C. P. Fitzgerald
New York: McGraw-Hill, 1971
128 pp. $2.45 Paper
   Instead of the unsympathetic narrative one might expect from the title, C. P. Fitzgerald presents a balanced and concise history of the Chinese Communists' rise to power. Beginning with a brief overview of the difference between life in prerevolutionary and revolutionary China, Professor Fitzgerald then deals with "The Origin of the Chinese Revolution," "The Early Republic: The Warlord Period," "Nationalists and Communists," and the "Japanese Invasion and Communist Victory." The book is made especially interesting by the abundance of pictures, maps, charts, and political cartoons—a number of them in color.

The Long March to Power: A History of the Chinese Communist Party, 1921-72
James P. Harrison
New York: Praeger Publishers, 1973
647 pp. $6.95 Paper
   Professor Harrison develops his study in terms of one basic question: what, in face of all the obstacles, were the factors which led to the victory of the Communists in 1949? The result is as good—and thorough—a general overview as one can find.
   Those looking for additional perspectives on this historical period should not overlook several other recent studies. Michael Gasster, in his *China's Struggle to Modernize* (New York: Alfred A. Knopf, 1972), takes a general approach that combines intellectual, political, and cultural history in tracing the efforts of Chinese leaders to understand and adapt Western ideas to a Chinese setting. *A Short History of Chinese Communism* by Franklin Houn (Englewood Cliffs: Prentice Hall Inc., 1973, paper) covers the same ground as the Harrison volume in a more superficial manner, and includes a section on the Cultural Revolution and foreign policy. The current period is the focus of Harold Hinton's *An Introduction to Chinese Politics* (New York: Praeger Publishers, 1973, paper), which serves not only to introduce political developments in China but also to place them in the author's occasionally controversial theoretical framework.
   Thus, though the events and time periods in the four works

overlap, they give a representative sample of approaches and interpretive differences in the study of modern Chinese history.

● *Fanshen: A Documentary of Revolution in a Chinese Village*
William Hinton
New York: Random House, 1968
637 pp. $2.95 Paper

This case study is a compelling account of events in one village undergoing land reform under the direction of the Communist party, based on the author's own observations there between March and August 1948. Some of Hinton's generalizations have been questioned, but his study is particularly valuable as a unique source of information on land reform and Communist leadership in rural China. *Fanshen* provides insight not only into the Communist rise to power, but also into the nature and problems of Communist rule in China, and their effects on individual Chinese peasants.

The Tragedy of the Chinese Revolution
Harold R. Isaacs
Stanford: Stanford University Press, 1966
392 pp. $3.75 Paper

This is a detailed account of the Kuomintang-Communist alliance in the 1920s and of the near-destruction of the Chinese Communist party in 1927 as a result of its adherence to Russian-dictated policies. The author, a journalist in China at the time, wrote from a Trotskyite viewpoint and therefore equally denounced the Kuomintang, the Comintern, and the rural-based Kiangsi Soviet of 1927–34. The book concentrates, however, on the period 1925–27, and describes in sanguinary detail the events of those years. An excellent story for anyone interested in the history of the Chinese Communist movement. André Malraux's *Man's Fate* (New York: Vintage Books, 1971) is a fictionalized account of events in the same period, and makes highly engrossing reading.

● *Chinese Communism*
Robert C. North

New York: McGraw-Hill, 1966
254 pp. $2.45 Paper
A general and easy-to-read survey of the origins and growth of Communism in China. Beginning with an outline of Chinese history in the late eighteenth and nineteenth centuries, Professor North goes on to summarize the history of the Chinese Communist party, specific periods of which are analyzed more fully in several other works listed in this section. The book also contains a brief sketch of the post-1949 period and many excellent photographs.

Chinese Communism and the Rise of Mao
Benjamin I. Schwartz
New York: Torchbooks (Harper & Row), 1962
258 pp. $2.45 Paper
A study of the Chinese Communist party in terms of its doctrines and internal political relations, this book traces the development of Chinese Communism from its origins in 1919 to the ascendancy of Mao Tse-tung in the 1930s. The author's conclusion, that the Maoist political strategy was not planned in Moscow and that circumstances forced the Soviets "to provide a facade of rationalization for this new experience," aroused heated controversy when the book first appeared in 1951. The controversy was pursued in a series of articles by Professor Schwartz and Karl A. Wittfogel in issues no. 1 and 2 of *The China Quarterly*, 1960.

The Yenan Way in Revolutionary China
Mark Selden
Cambridge, Mass.: Harvard University Press, 1972
311 pp. $3.50 Paper
Professor Selden provides a scholarly yet readable survey of the critical period in Chinese Communist history just after the Long March (1934) when a political power base was established in the province of Yenan. There, an ideology and program were forged which were to serve as the basis for their revolutionary success. The study illuminates an important component of Mao's strategy: how to effectively mobilize the masses on the side of national and social revolution through the "mass line," the most charac-

teristic single achievement of the Chinese Communists. The author also provides new data in support of the argument that social and economic revolution in the countryside was more important to Chinese Communist success than was the struggle against the Japanese.

In part, this book is a direct refutation of a work long held to be standard (although controversial) in the field: Chalmers A. Johnson, *Peasant Nationalism and Communist Power: The Emergence of Revolutionary China, 1937–1945* (Stanford: Stanford University Press, 1966, 256 pp., $2.95, paper).

● *Red Star over China*
Edgar Snow
New York: Grove Press, 1971
543 pp. $2.95 Paper

In 1936, the late Edgar Snow traveled to the blockaded Communist areas in northwest China, where he met and interviewed Mao Tse-tung and other Communist leaders. On the basis of his interviews and observations during three months in the northwest, Snow wrote the first substantive account of Mao's life and of the rural Communist movement to reach the outside world. First published in 1938, *Red Star* was initially a journalistic scoop, but has remained an invaluable source of information on the early years of Chinese Communism.

China: The Struggle for Power, 1917–1972
Richard Thornton
Bloomington: University of Indiana Press, 1973
403 pp. $12.50

Most recent studies of the rise and triumph of Chinese communism have focused primarily on the impact of domestic crises and the "revolutionary" situation within. Thornton, in this specialized study, looks at how external forces (Soviet, Japanese, and American foreign policies) have been important to the formation of the Chinese Communist movement. He concludes with an analysis of the Cultural Revolution, which he perceives as part of the Sino-Soviet dispute of the 1960s as well as of domestic leadership conflicts over developmental priorities.

The Long March, 1935: The Epic of Chinese Communism's Survival
Dick Wilson
New York: Avon Books, 1971
384 pp. $1.95 Paper

In 1935, the Chinese Communists were forced to retreat from an attack by Chiang Kai-shek's Nationalist forces. This retreat, which turned into a Long March of some five thousand miles, became a keystone in the history of the Chinese Communist movement; an epic of fortitude and survival still celebrated in story and song. Until now, there was no complete Western account chronicling this feat. Wilson describes the event in a lively and readable style, and the book is at once exciting, informative, and comprehensive.

7. FIRSTHAND IMPRESSIONS

China: Inside the People's Republic
Committee of Concerned Asian Scholars
New York: Bantam Books, 1972
433 pp. $1.50 Paper

In July 1971, fifteen members of the Committee of Concerned Asian Scholars, mostly graduate students and their spouses, became the first American scholars to visit the People's Republic of China in over twenty years. This book conveys their sympathetic impressions of China and attempts to evaluate the Maoist social experiment through discussions of communes, factories, urban life, schools, culture, women and child care, health programs, and foreign policy.

China Journal
Emmett Dedmon
Chicago: Rand McNally & Company, 1973
176 pp. $8.95

Dedmon effectively conveys the sense of excitement and discovery he felt during his October 1972 trip to the People's Republic. Vice-president and editorial director of the Chicago *Sun Times* and the Chicago *Daily News*, he gives the reader a "feel" for what it is like to travel in China as a foreign guest and, in his mind's eye, even to live there (in a chapter "If You Lived in China"). Every person visiting China returns with somewhat different perceptions, and in *China Journal*, as with most such travelogues, it is these cross-cultural musings about trends in China which are the most interesting aspects, for they tell us almost as much about the author as about China itself. A feature of this book is an appendix with tips for tourists.

A China Passage
John Kenneth Galbraith
Boston: Houghton-Mifflin Company, 1973
143 pp. $5.95

In the autumn of 1972 the author, in company with his two predecessor presidents of the American Economic Association, was invited to visit China for a look at the economy. But Mr. Galbraith had another idea—to go beyond economics and tell of everything a visitor to China does, sees, and thinks from the moment he leaves home until he returns. In diary form, the book is a relaxed and urbane account by an astute observer and writer. His conclusion: "The Chinese economy isn't the American or European future. But it is the Chinese future. And let there be no doubt: For the Chinese it works."

Daily Life in People's China
Arthur Galston with Jean S. Savage
New York: Thomas Y. Crowell, 1973
223 pp. $6.95

The account of a noted biologist of his visit to China during the summer of 1972, when he, his wife, and daughter lived for three months in the Marco Polo Bridge Commune outside Peking. *Daily Life in People's China* is a descriptive and pictorial record, reinforcing the impressions of many other recent travelers to China and contributing to our understanding of communal organization and peasant life. It is somewhat less valuable in its treatment of other aspects of Chinese society and politics.

● *China Day by Day*
Eileen Hsu-Balzer, Richard Balzer, and Francis L. K. Hsu
New Haven: Yale University Press, 1973
112 pp. $7.95 Paper

Firsthand Impressions   *179*

The excellent photographs in this book are matched by a perceptive commentary, recounting a 1972 trip by the authors, who saw their relatives throughout China and traveled unencumbered by guides and interpreters. They spent time in communes, factories, schools, universities, government offices, and workers' homes, meeting people from all walks of life. In the introduction, Francis Hsu, professor of anthropology at Northwestern University, discusses the old (pre-1949) and new in the value structure fostered by the Chinese government. A good description which stops short of a specific analysis of questions such as how China'a leaders have used or modified traditional values and what mechanisms have been developed to reinforce the new value system.

Love and Hate in China: A New Yorker's Chinese Notes
Hans Koningsberger
New York: McGraw-Hill, 1967
150 pp. $1.95 Paper
Despite the deceptive title, this is a reasonably balanced account of the author's observations during a brief trip to China in 1965. The author, a journalist, is not a specialist on China, and does not claim to have had access to all areas of the country, but he vividly describes the "typical" daily lives of people in communes and cities. His perceptive descriptions of the sights and sounds of Peking and Shanghai, the countryside as he viewed it from a Chinese train window, conversations with factory workers and farmers convey a sense of Chinese reality to the Western reader.

The Chinese Difference
Joseph Kraft
New York: Saturday Review Press, 1972
113 pp. $5.95
The author, a prominent journalist generally associated with a conservative viewpoint (particularly in relation to China), was evidently impressed with his visit to the People's Republic of China in 1972. These essays are a vivid description of his three-month stay in China during and after the Nixon visit. For Kraft, the "difference" in the book's title is the Chinese ability to

maintain a pragmatic attitude in implementing their political beliefs without compromising them in principle (a flexibility which allowed them to invite the President without abandoning their revolutionary views). He illustrates the "difference" in a series of vignettes on the lives of workers, peasants, and intellectuals, and wonders whether or not it has had an effect on the development of the "new socialist man." A well-written, sympathetic account.

China Observed
Colin MacKerras and Neale Hunter
New York: Praeger, 1968
194 pp. $6.50

A well-organized, concise, and readable report on China in the mid-1960s as seen by two Australians, each of whom taught English in China for two years—MacKerras in Peking (1964–66) and Hunter in Shanghai (1965–67). They present a general description of Chinese life as they observed it, first under "normal" circumstances and then during the Cultural Revolution. There are chapters on the family, students, religion, the arts, and the Cultural Revolution in Shanghai. Of special interest are the final chapters in which the authors reveal their own feelings about China. For an expanded account of the Cultural Revolution in Shanghai, see Neale Hunter's *Shanghai Journal* (New York: Praeger, 1969).

To Peking and Beyond: A Report on the New Asia
Harrison E. Salisbury
New York: Quadrangle Books, 1973
308 pp. $7.95

Based upon his visit to China and North Korea in 1972, this book makes an effort to understand Chinese development in terms of an intense application of past experiences to present modes of economic and social organization. Mr. Salisbury views the Cultural Revolution as one of the most complex phenomena of modern nation states: a power struggle and conflict of generations as well as an attempt to avoid the Soviet road to Communism by building a Maoist "new man."

Firsthand Impressions

Red China Today: The Other Side of the River
Edgar Snow
New York: Vintage Books (Random House), 1971
749 pp. $3.45 Paper

This is a revised and updated edition of *The Other Side of the River* (1961). It is a generally favorable panorama of China as the author saw it in 1960, written by the late American journalist who first interviewed Mao and the Chinese Communist leaders in 1936. Many of the chapters contain interesting accounts of daily life, and others examine China's economic and political development. Although diverse in content and somewhat rambling in style, this is a very readable mixture of travelogue, social analysis, and reminiscences about earlier days spent in China. The book contains a number of useful statistical appendixes.

● *800,000,000: The Real China*
Ross Terrill
New York: Laurel Press, 1972
250 pp. $1.50 Paper

Ross Terrill, an Australian scholar teaching at Harvard University, toured China for six weeks in 1971. This book, an expansion of two *Atlantic Monthly* articles, is a well-written and at the same time scholarly evaluation of contemporary Chinese life, covering work, education, politics, foreign policy, and many other issues. Drawing from conversations with Premier Chou En-lai, other high officials, and scholars, workers, and students across the country, the author presents an insightful and well-balanced account of what China is and is not.

An American in China
Jan C. Ting
New York: Paperback Library, 1972
190 pp. $0.95 Paper

A young graduate student's account of his two months and four thousand miles of unescorted travel in the P.R.C. During his stay, Ting visited twelve major cities, their factories, schools, and day-care centers. His knowledge of the language allowed him to talk directly with people as well as their leaders, and the book, written in a casual style, is a good general account.

Dawn Wakes in the East
Audrey Topping
New York: Harper and Row, 1973
163 pp. $17.50

With the burgeoning of first-hand accounts of China, there is welcome room for this visually pleasing and exciting photographic record. Audrey Topping has put together a handsome volume based on her several recent visits to China, admirably capturing lifestyles and work habits in the city and countryside, and depicting the cultural and historical legacies of Peking, Sian, Hangchow, and Yenan. In places, the commentary does little justice to the pictures; the occasional use of stereotypes to describe certain key figures and places seems inappropriate.

Notes from China
Barbara Tuchman
New York: Collier Books, 1972
112 pp. $1.25 Paper

A collection of newspaper articles written by the Pulitzer Prize-winning historian on her visit to China in 1972. She found changes since 1949 "striking" and convincing, but retains a critical tone throughout of the "mental monotone" which, in her view, has been imposed on the country. Good as a sober balance to the occasional over-glowing accounts of China today.

Unglazed China
J. Tuzo Wilson
New York: Saturday Review Press, 1973
336 pp. $9.95

On his first visit to China in 1958, the author, a Canadian geophysicist, had mixed feelings; in *One China Moon* he lauded their efforts to resolve economic and social problems but was unsure whether the Chinese could create the kind of economically and ideologically viable society they desired. The uncertainty of that book has given way to admiration in *Unglazed China*, and some of the most valuable sections in the book are Wilson's specific comparisons of Chinese society in 1958 and 1972. The book adds an unusual and valuable perspective in that the author explains his views on how science policy relates to the overall patterns of China's social and political development as well as to the future course of scientific education and research in the aftermath of the Cultural Revolution.

8. STATE AND SOCIETY

Communist China: Communal Progress and Individual Freedom
American Education Publications
Columbus, Ohio: The Education Center, 1968
63 pp. $0.45 Paper

This excellent booklet raises questions about the social and cultural relativity of values. It does this by examining the impact of the Chinese Revolution both in terms of its concrete achievements for the Chinese people and its relationship to larger questions of personal values. The first half of the booklet is adapted from *Fanshen* (William Hinton [New York: Random House, 1968], see section 5 of this chapter)—an amazing eye-witness account of the revolutionary changes which occurred in one Chinese village. Other sections include: "Student Experiences" and "Achievements of the Revolution," presented both by statistics and three personal reports of foreign visitors to China. It must be cautioned, however, that some of the materials are out of date, since all were written before the Cultural Revolution. The booklet can also serve as a curriculum unit (see chapter 4).

The Educational Revolution in China
Robert D. Barendsen
Washington, D.C.: U.S. Government Printing Office, 1973
52 pp. $0.65 Paper

Chinese Education and Society: A Bibliographic Guide, the Cultural Revolution and Its Aftermath
Stewart Fraser and Hsu Kuang-liang
White Plains, New York: International Arts & Sciences Press, 1972
204 pp. $15.00

● *Revolutionary Education in China: Documents and Commentary*
Peter J. Seybolt, ed.

White Plains, New York: International Arts & Sciences Press, 1973
408 pp. $15.00

These three books collectively provide a summary of how the Chinese view the role of education in society. The first, by Robert Barendsen, an East Asian specialist in the U.S. Office of Education, traces the uncertain history of China's educational development between 1966 and 1971. After evaluating the educational system, he discusses the main lines of reform in the early 1970s: decentralization, diversification, funding, and curriculum. Useful in its brevity, while reflecting little attempt at sympathetic understanding.

The Fraser and Hsu bibliography, intended for the specialist, contains brief annotations of Chinese studies on the Cultural Revolution, the different levels of education, teacher training, and youth programs.

Perhaps the best introduction to how the Chinese themselves see their educational system is provided by the Seybolt book, which draws on relevant articles from the *People's Daily* and *Red Flag* (the Party's theoretical journal). *Revolutionary Education* reviews the educational transformation since 1966, placing emphasis on the efforts to unite educational theory with practical work experience. A selection of documents on Communist educational practices during the Yenan Period (1936–45) appears at the end of the book and provides an interesting comparison with methods and regulations established during and since the Cultural Revolution.

Chinese Communist Politics in Action
A. Doak Barnett, ed.
Seattle: University of Washington Press, 1969
620 pp. $4.95 Paper

This volume consists of eleven essays originally presented at a 1967 conference on the Chinese political system. Although aimed primarily at a scholarly audience, the essays also are of value to the layman. Topics covered include the historical roots of current policies and political organization; the characteristics and problems of leadership at the local level; techniques of political control in the countryside; and policies toward youth, the bourgeoisie, and the workers. The volume, although now somewhat dated, is a contribution toward the understanding of social and political development in modern China.

Uncertain Passage: China's Transition to the Post-Mao Era
A. Doak Barnett
Washington, D.C.: The Brookings Institution, 1974
350 pp. $3.95 Paper

As China's leadership increasingly shows the signs of age (Mao is 81, Chou 76), China watchers speculate on the question: after Mao, who, and what? This book, a solid analysis, examines the forces which Professor Barnett feels may shape Chinese policies in the years ahead: development strategies, efforts to achieve ideological consensus, institutional stability, and China's interaction with other nations. Intended for the general reader and serious student alike.

A shorter work, more expressly for lay audiences, is Harry Harding's *China: An Uncertain Future* (Headline Series, Foreign Policy Association [No. 223], 79 pp., $1.25). This pamphlet is recommended for its clear elucidation of what Harding sees as the basis for the "uncertain future" of China: succession, modernization techniques, the maintenance of revolutionary ideology, and the political institutions. Harding sees Chinese leadership as divided over many of these issues, and he outlines some possible scenarios of succession.

China in Ferment: Perspectives on the Cultural Revolution
Richard Baum and Louise Bennett, eds.
New York: Prentice-Hall, 1972
245 pp. $2.95 Paper

Through a collection of articles by Western observers and Chinese Communist writers, the editors attempt to break down the "myths and half-truths" which they believe have clouded American understanding of the Cultural Revolution. For the China scholar, the essays contain close and detailed analysis, and the introduction provides a good overall survey for the layman. Another source of American scholarly interpretation of the period is afforded by the six contributors to Thomas W. Robinson, ed., *The Cultural Revolution in China* (Berkeley: University of California Press, 1971).

Red Guard: The Political Biography of Dai Hsiao-ai
Gordon A. Bennett and Ronald N. Montaperto
Garden City, N.Y.: Anchor Books, 1972
268 pp. $1.95 Paper
This unusual book is a record of the Cultural Revolution based on the personal narrative of a student activist from Canton. It traces Dai Hsiao-ai (a pseudonym) through his initial enthusiasm for Mao's Revolution, his trips across China for mass demonstrations in Peking, his growing role as a faction leader among competing Red Guards, and the ultimate disillusionment which led him to leave his family and friends and defect to Hong Kong. The editors have effectively integrated Dai's accounts and background material to make the book of great interest to scholar and layman alike.

Medicine and Society in the People's Republic of China
John Z. Bowers and Elizabeth Purcell, ed.
New York: Josiah P. Macy Foundation, 1974
328 pp. $7.50 Paper

Away with All Pests: An English Surgeon in People's China, 1954–1969
Joshua S. Horn
New York: Monthly Review Press, 1971
192 pp. $2.45 Paper

Serve the People: Observations on Medicine in the People's Republic of China
Victor W. Sidel and Ruth Sidel
New York: Josiah P. Macy Foundation, 1973
317 pp. $10.00 Paper

Public Health in the People's Republic of China
Myron Wegman, Lin Tsung-yi, and Elizabeth Purcell, eds.
New York: Josiah P. Macy Foundation, 1973
354 pp. $7.50 Paper

As concern about the distribution of health services in the United States continues to grow, books by specialists on how China delivers health care to a population of about 800 million, and on whether there may be some relevance in her experience for the U.S., are increasingly in demand. The topics considered in these books overlap—and in many ways complement—each other, all dealing with the organization of public health services, the role of the community in health care, and the training of health care personnel (administrators, physicians, technicians, and paraprofessionals). The books therefore differ more in organization and structure than in substantive observation.

The Sidels provide a book-length study of their recent visits to China, giving an excellent treatment of medical education and the integration of traditional remedies with modern medical science. The Bowers and Wegman books are collections of scholarly essays, the Wegman volume concentrating on the organization of the health care system and the prospects for health care, and the Bowers on the actual delivery of health care services.

Horn's book, although filled with Marxist clichés and some sociopolitical sermonizing, provides a personal account not only of medical care in China, but also of life in general during the Cultural Revolution period. Special attention is given to the more spectacular clinical success stories, the paramedical "barefoot doctors," and the role of politics in medicine.

Other notable works on this subject include: Joseph R. Quinn, ed. *Medicine and Public Health in the People's Republic of China* (Washington: Department of Health, Education, and Welfare, 1972), 305 pp. $4.50; and Ralph Crozier, *Traditional Medicine in Modern China: Science, Nationalism, and the Tensions of Cultural Change* (Cambridge: Harvard University Press, 1968), 612 pp., $10.00.

A Year in Upper Felicity: Life in a Chinese Village during the Cultural Revolution
Jack Chen
New York: MacMillan Company, 1973
383 pp. $8.95

Jack Chen, who has worked in, and reported on, China for most of his life, spent a "working holiday" in a farm commune during 1969 and 1970. The book reflects a sympathetic appreciation of the problems, life styles, and work habits of the villagers, especially how each of these relates to changes of seasons. A warm and personal account, it leaves the impression that the villagers seem to be interested primarily in economic matters relating to their lives and only peripherally in the ideological policies which decide how those lives are to be led.

A History of the Chinese Cultural Revolution
Jean Daubier
New York: Vintage Books, 1974
336 pp. $2.45 Paper

From 1966 through 1968, the author, a French citizen, worked in the People's Republic as a teacher and, by his account, participated in the Cultural Revolution. From his perception and analysis, the Cultural Revolution was more than a "struggle for power"; its fundamental goals were concerned much more with human socialist values and ideas.

Another foreign observer who has written a firsthand account of his experiences during the Cultural Revolution is Jean Emein, the *The Chinese Cultural Revolution* (New York: Anchor Books, 1973, paper).

Liu Shao-chi and the Chinese Cultural Revolution
Lowell Dittmer
Berkeley: University of California Press, 1974
373 pp. $12.95

China's Great Proletarian Cultural Revolution represented a "struggle between two lines" to determine the direction of national development at a crucial transition point. In this struggle, the Maoist forces were seen as representing the "proletarian revolutionary line'" opposing Liu Shao-chi (the discredited, and now deceased, former chairman of the People's Republic) and those taking the "bourgeois reactionary line." Professor Dittmer's study tries to explain this rift by combining an analysis of the Cultural Revolution with the basis for the Mao-Liu rupture as seen in the development of Liu's thought and political base. The author treats his subject partly in terms of "psycho-history" and concludes that "Liu's attempt to combine order with revolution overemphasized organizational constraints to the neglect of ideo-

State and Society 189

logical or normative incentives." Heavy going for anyone but serious students of the subject.

Hundred Day War: The Cultural Revolution at Tsinghua University
William Hinton
New York: Monthly Review Press, 1972
288 pp. $7.95

A sympathetic description, relying mostly on Chinese views, of the conflict between the values and objectives of students, workers, and military personnel at a leading Chinese university during the Cultural Revolution.

For an account of the same period at Peking University, see *The Cultural Revolution at Peking University*, by Victor Nee with Don Layman (New York: Monthly Review Press, 1969).

China in Crisis
Vol. 1, in two books: *China's Heritage and the Communist Political System*
Ping-ti Ho and Tang Tsou, eds.
484 pp. $3.95 Paper
Vol. 2, *China's Policies in Asia and America's Alternatives*
Tang Tsou, ed.
484 pp. $3.45 Paper
Chicago: University of Chicago Press, 1968

This two-volume work contains the writings of many of America's foremost China scholars. The articles and commentaries were originally prepared for two conferences held in February 1967 and are generally, although not exclusively, addressed to a scholarly audience. Book 1 of volume 1 focuses on the conditions which led to the Communist victory in China and examines the Communist political system within the context of Chinese political tradition. Book 2 includes analyses of the Chinese political system, the Cultural Revolution, and fluctuations in China's economic development. (Volume 2, dealing with China's foreign policy, is discussed in section 11.)

Ideology and Practice: The Evolution of Chinese Communism
James C. Hsiung

New York: Praeger, 1971
300 pp. $4.50 Paper
This book deals with the development of political thought in the People's Republic of China and its connections to the past. In the first section, Professor Hsiung examines the importance of ideology in premodern China. In the second, he traces the historical development of Chinese Communism before 1949 and deals with the basic questions of why and how Communism prevailed in China. The content and functions of Chinese Communist ideology, the goals of Mao's revolution, and the CCP leadership's application of ideology to the problem of ruling a modernizing state are discussed in part 3. A well-documented and creative book.

Understanding Modern China
Joseph M. Kitagawa, ed.
Chicago: Quadrangle Books, 1969
284 pp. $7.95
This collection of essays, which resulted from a conference sponsored by the Council on Religion and International Affairs, is intended to "help us develop a more adequate perspective for the West's understanding of the East and . . . for self-understanding." Four articles deal with China's domestic politics; others discuss geography, China's "Cultural Unity," the Taiwanese in Taiwan, and Chinese communities in Southeast Asia. Particularly valuable, however, are the introduction and the two concluding chapters dealing with the problem of China's and America's mutual perceptions. A useful collection of stimulating articles for the general reader.

The City in Communist China
John Wilson Lewis, ed.
Stanford: Stanford University Press, 1971
370 pp. $12.95
The first in a three-volume series on the Chinese city, this book examines urban life and.problems in China today (the others will study the city in late imperial China and during the Republican period). The book is a collection of eleven scholarly papers; each chapter deals with a specific urban crisis such as leadership, bureaucracy, law, and modernization. The book is well illustrated.

State and Society   *191*

Party Leadership and Revolutionary Power in China
John Wilson Lewis, ed.
Cambridge: Cambridge University Press, 1970
422 pp. $3.45 Paper
Twelve essays, written by British and American scholars for a 1968 conference on the Chinese Communist party are bound together by several central issues: the problems of political leadership, power, and revolution that have governed the development of the Chinese Communist party. Individual essays examine the influence of the past, the origins of the Maoist myth, factionalism within the Central Committee, leadership problems after land reform, policies toward intellectuals, and army-party relations in light of the Cultural Revolution. See also Professor Lewis's earlier study, *Leadership in Communist China* (Ithaca, N.Y.: Cornell University Press, 1963).

Thought Reform and the Psychology of Totalism: A Study of "Brainwashing" in China
Robert J. Lifton
New York: W. W. Norton, 1961
510 pp. $3.75 Paper
In this psychiatric study of "brainwashing," or thought reform, in China during the early 1950s, the author uses Western psychological concepts to analyze the reform process. The book is written in an easily comprehensible style appropriate for the general reader as well as the specialist. Although Professor Lifton's study would now benefit from an evaluation of the long-term effects of this mechanism of "social control and individual change," it remains the most important analysis of Chinese Communist thought reform techniques. Useful for above-average students willing to delve into somewhat specialized material.

China: Management of a Revolutionary Society
John M. H. Lindbeck, ed.
Seattle: University of Washington Press, 1971
391 pp. $4.95 Paper
This collection of articles by ten China scholars highlights some of the major features of China's political development during the last two decades. Part 1 deals with the relationship between

authority and the masses; part 2 describes relationships within the political hierarchies; part 3 delves into the problems of restructuring Chinese society; part 4 focuses on the subordination of foreign to domestic concerns; and part 5 is an essay on China and comparative politics.

Religious Policy and Practice in Communist China
Donald E. MacInnis
New York: Macmillan, 1972
392 pp. $3.95 Paper

This is a documentary collection of authoritative statements by leaders of the People's Republic of China on topics such as: general policy toward religion; religious policy in practice; and the religious analogies in Maoist ideology. Editorial introductions are kept to a minimum and are intended only for clarification. The author concedes there are few signs of religious life as known in the West and that Chinese Marxism is likely to become the religion of the people. His point of view is that he hopes China's leaders will allow adherents of all religions to freely and openly practice their faith.

The Origins of the Cultural Revolution
Vol. 1: *Contradictions among the People, 1956-57*
Roderick MacFarquhar
New York: Columbia University Press, 1974
439 pp. $14.95

This is the first of a projected three-volume study of the Cultural Revolution and the factors which influenced Mao Tse-tung's decision to launch it in 1965. British scholar MacFarquhar sees Mao's concern about making party members less bureaucratic and more responsive to the needs of the people as going back to the "Hundred Flowers" campaign (1956-57), and argues that Mao was not ready to sacrifice party unity or rely on his conception that people alone should determine the course of Chinese society until 1965. Future volumes in this series, which promises to be one of the most comprehensive looks at the last twenty years of Chinese history, will deal with the Great Leap Forward, the Socialist Education Movement, and the Cultural Revolution itself.

Report from a Chinese Village
Jan Myrdal
New York: Vintage Books, 1972
374 pp. $2.45 Paper
    In 1962 the author, a Swedish anthropologist, spent one month
in the village of Liu Ling in northern China. He and his wife Gun
Kessle (who took the excellent photographs that appear in the
book) conducted extensive interviews with villagers of all ages and
backgrounds. Myrdal's accounts have been criticized for having
an overly official ring, but they have also been viewed as an
understated description of revolutionary fervor. Some scholars
have found the book useful only as an indication of official
government policy as understood by the peasants and recounted
to foreign visitors. Others, however, argue that it realistically
weighs the problems and prospects of maintaining revolutionary
fervor necessary for radical social change. A sequel to this book,
China: The Revolution Continued (New York: Vintage Books,
1971, $1.95 paper), is based on a return visit to Liu Ling in 1970,
and in part addresses itself to some of the criticisms of the earlier
book.

China's Developmental Experience
Michel Oksenberg, ed.
New York: Praeger Publishers, 1973
227 pp. $2.95 Paper
    This book contains fifteen chapters (the results of a conference
of the same title held in 1972) on many aspects of China's
development: including agricultural development and technology; organization and application of science; ecology and environmental control; family life and care of the aging; the functions
and structure of schooling; bureaucracy and popular participation; and politically induced social change. Few of the essays
touch more than lightly the challenging question of whether or
not China's experience might be relevant to other societies;
however, the editor's introductory essay, entitled "Learning from
China," and the piece on educational policy are particularly good.

Every Fifth Child: The Population of China
Leo A. Orleans

Stanford: Stanford University Press, 1972
191 pp. $8.50

This is not a demographic textbook. It tries, rather, to tell the story of China's population by exploring areas where policy and daily life coincide: the schools, farms, and factories of a country that faces immense problems in urbanization, technological education, and manpower. It conveys a good sense of what we do and do not know about China's population, which recent Chinese statements have put at about 800 million.

Dr. Orleans, a Chinese Research specialist at the Library of Congress, has also written a report on China's population for the House Committee on Foreign Affairs (*China's Experience in Population Control: The Elusive Model*, Washington, D.C., U.S. Government Printing Office, 1974). The report predicts that China is likely to be the first sizable developing nation to reduce population growth to below one percent per year. He makes the point that although the Chinese actually have implemented many of the current family planning techniques known in the West, they have referred minimally to Western experience, preferring an approach to birth control that is "characteristically their own."

A free pamphlet on *Population and Family Planning in the P.R.C.* is available from the Population Crisis Committee (Washington, D.C., 1971).

Elites in the People's Republic of China
Robert A. Scalapino, ed.
Seattle: University of Washington Press, 1972
670 pp. $4.95 Paper

Fourteen prominent scholars examine the structure of political power in the People's Republic: who holds power at the national and local levels; how it is allocated and exercised; and what the results are in terms of policies, programs, and goals. Political, military, and ideological elites are covered. Primarily for the specialist readers, this is an important benchmark in scholarly analysis of the People's Republic of China.

Authority, Participation and Cultural Change in China
Stuart R. Schram, ed.

London and New York: Cambridge University Press, 1973
350 pp. $4.95 Paper
This is a collection of essays by prominent European China specialists on all aspects of Chinese society. The introduction by the editor is a particularly valuable contribution, outlining the political and ideological orientations of the Communists when they assumed power in 1949, and discussing those contradictions in their heritage (between Leninist elitism and popular participation, and between patient realism and hopes for immediate revolutionary achievement, for example) which have influenced China's subsequent development, especially since the Cultural Revolution. Other essays deal with Chinese social, economic, and educational policies, and a final chapter is on the transformation of familial and personal relationships.

Ideology and Organization in Communist China
Franz Schurmann
Berkeley: University of California Press, 1968
642 pp. $5.50 Paper
In this major study, first published in 1966, Professor Schurmann describes and analyzes the theory and form of organization in the People's Republic of China, with reference primarily to the 1950s. Chapters on the party, government, bureaucratic management, the control system, urban organization, and rural administration provide some of the best introductions to these topics now available. Of particular interest is the one-hundred-page supplement to the second edition in which the author elaborates upon insights gained from the Cultural Revolution and suggests that ideology and organization have proved less powerful in manipulating the society than he had originally thought. This highly regarded volume might be slow reading for those not familiar with the analytical categories and concepts of social science.
A new book by Professor Schurmann, *The Logic of Power: An Inquiry into the Origins, Currents, and Contradictions of World Power* (New York: Pantheon Books, 1974), is an outgrowth of the above study, and reflects his insightful views on the policymaking of the Great Powers, and their interaction in Southeast Asia.

China: Science Walks on Two Legs
Science for the People

New York: Avon Books, 1974
316 pp. $1.75 Paper

This is a sympathetic account of a 1973 visit to the People's Republic of China by a delegation from the organization Science for the People, a group of politically active American scientists and technologists. In addition to being a general report of their visit, the book serves as a good introduction to how the Chinese have tried to make science and education more relevant to the needs of the people.

Women and Child Care in China
Ruth Sidel
Baltimore: Penguin Books, 1973
207 pp. $1.25 Paper

A first-hand account of the attitudes toward women and child-rearing in today's China by an American social worker. Sympathetically tells how the Chinese woman today is free from the "bitter past" and is taking an active part in all aspects of the society. The author also looks at nurseries, nursery schools, and kindergartens, comparing them with child-rearing institutions in the Soviet Union and Israel and speculating on what aspects of the Chinese experience might be of value in the United States. A related book is the author's *Families of Fengsheng* (Penguin Books, 1974), which tells how the Chinese organize their city neighborhoods and provide social services to all.

Mao's Revolution and the Chinese Political Culture
Richard H. Solomon
Berkeley: University of California Press, 1971
604 pp. $5.95 Paper

A psychoanalytical perspective is used to assess Mao's contribution to Chinese politics and the manner in which he has sought to strengthen certain cultural characteristics and weaken others to promote revolutionary change. In the first section Solomon analyzes the socialization process in traditional Chinese society which, he argues, has shaped political views. In the third and fourth sections, which take up most of the book, the author applies his analysis to China's post-1949 political culture. This book is mainly for the serious student of China but can also be interesting for the nonspecialist as an application of "psycho-cultural" political analysis.

Political Participation in Communist China
James R. Townsend
Berkeley: University of California Press, 1969
233 pp. $2.65 Paper

In this careful and well-written study of Chinese efforts to organize mass political participation on a nationwide scale, Professor Townsend first defines the meaning of political participation in theory and practice and then examines the institutional forms, including the state structure and nongovernmental organizations, within which participation is exercised. In conclusion, he summarizes and evaluates the major elements of mass participation in the People's Republic: small group activities, direct contact between cadres and the people, political education, the execution of party policies, and the mass movement. A clear but dry introduction to political life in contemporary China.

● *Politics in China*
James R. Townsend
Boston: Little, Brown and Company, 1974
400 pp. $4.95 Paper

A succinct and lucid review, based on the latest and most complete interpretations available, of politics and political organization in the People's Republic of China. The book begins with a summation of events in China before 1949 and then analyzes the political trends of the People's Republic. Although designed for undergraduate courses in comparative politics, this book should also be of interest to the general reader.

Communist China, 1949–1969: A Twenty-Year Appraisal
Frank Trager and William Henderson, eds.
New York: New York University Press, 1970
356 pp. $9.50

In separate essays, fourteen China specialists make generally critical assessments of the principal political, economic, and social developments on the mainland since 1949. The essays deal with administration, education, ideology, party politics, the military, the economy, agriculture, literature and art, minority groups, and foreign relations. Unfortunately the time span of the book concludes with the Cultural Revolution, which perhaps inevitably receives a disproportionate share of attention. The annotated bibliography and chronology are particularly useful.

Canton under Communism: Programs and Politics in a Provincial Capital, 1949–1968
Ezra F. Vogel
New York: Torchbooks (Harper & Row), 1971
450 pp. $3.95 Paper

Professor Vogel, a sociologist at Harvard, presents a detailed study of politics and administration in the province of Kwangtung and its capital city, Canton. Originally published in 1969, this was the first major study to concentrate on a single local area rather than the generalized whole of People's China. The book reconstructs post-1949 political history from the take-over of Canton through land reform, the socialist transformation of the economy, the Great Leap Forward, and the Cultural Revolution. The author examines how basic programs and policies issued from above have been adapted by local leaders to conditions in Kwangtung. This unusually comprehensive book should remain a standard source of information for university classes for some time. It is clearly and carefully written, with minimal recourse to specialized social science terminology.

The Government and Politics of Communist China
Derek J. Waller
Garden City, N.Y.: Anchor Books (Doubleday), 1971
188 pp. $1.45 Paper

Through careful organization and clear, although occasionally turgid writing, Mr. Waller has compressed into one short volume the significant features of China's political history, institutions, and policies. The book, useful as a college text, is filled with basic information and provides a dry but balanced survey of many subjects—from the May Fourth movement to the Cultural Revolution. Although brief, this is not a superficial work; interpretative speculation is foregone in favor of a straightforward presentation of factual material based on reliable scholarly sources. Among the best of the brief paperback surveys of modern Chinese politics.

State and Society   *199*

● *Small Groups and Political Rituals in China*
Martin K. Whyte
Berkeley: University of California Press, 1974
271 pp. $12.50

In recent years, various social science disciplines have made their marks on China studies, and this book, by a young sociologist, is a detailed and thorough a study of how the Chinese have used small group political study and mutual criticism sessions—the basic unit of all politics in China—to bring about social order and to implement mass political campaigns. Whyte explores the significance of the small study groups in the lives of officials, students, workers, and peasants, and concludes that while they have been instrumental in promoting order, they have been less successful in effecting day-by-day change in basic sociopolitical attitudes.

The People's Comic Book
Endymion Wilkinson, trans.
New York: Doubleday Company, 1973
252 pp. $3.95 Paper

The seven serialized comics in this volume are cartoon renderings of popular films, plays, and novels in China, some reflecting the Communist interpretation of history, others concerned with what are seen as the more important struggles of the Chinese people in the contemporary period. Gino Nebiolo's introduction provides a brief account of the political and ideological uses to which the comics are put. Recommended as a readily accessible way of learning the values which the Chinese leadership seeks to imbue in the population.

● *Anatomy of China: An Introduction to One-Quarter of Mankind*
Dick Wilson
New York: Mentor Books (New American Library), 1969
304 pp. $1.25 Paper

This volume is among the best introductions to the People's Republic of China. Each of its three sections ("society," "economy," and "diplomacy") summarizes a range of topics. Section 1 includes discussions of the peasantry, the proletariat, the bourgeoisie, the intellectuals, family life, youth, and national minorities. Section 2 contains chapters on agriculture, population, industry, and science and technology, and section 3 deals with China's foreign relations. The book is a product of the author's experience in Hong Kong as editor of the *Far Eastern Economic Review*, and of his firsthand observations as a visitor in China.

● *Chinese Communist Society: The Family and the Village*
C. K. Yang
Cambridge, Mass.: MIT Press, 1965
276 pp. $3.95 Paper
  This volume contains two studies, *The Chinese Family in the Communist Revolution* and *A Chinese Village in Early Communist Transition*, published separately in 1959; both focus on the early years of Communist rule. The pre- and postrevolutionary contrast the book provides contributes to an understanding of the transformation in the two fundamental Chinese institutions. The book's value for the general reader is enhanced by the summaries which conclude each chapter.

Women in China: Studies in Social Change and Feminism
Marilyn B. Young, ed.
Ann Arbor: Center for Chinese Studies at the University of Michigan, 1973
259 pp. $3.50 Paper
  One of the important movements in China since 1900—and especially after 1949—has been the effort to improve the social and economic status of women. The essays in this book attempt to perceive this change within the framework of the broader social revolution. They pose an issue perhaps more crucial in the West than in China: does "women's liberation" require a distinct movement of its own? And, how successful can we be in analyzing one radical society from the perspective of "radicals" in another? Included with the essays by Western writers are short pieces by two prominent Chinese women, both conceding that female emancipation has encountered difficulties but also suggesting that the thinking leading to inequalities is being corrected.

9. ECONOMIC STUDIES

The Chinese Economy under Communism
Nai-Ruenn Chen and Walter Galenson

Chicago: Aldine-Atherton, 1969
250 pp. $7.95

Two economists from Cornell University provide a concise review of the mainland economy. In the absence of official Peking statistics since 1960, the authors have carefully interpreted recent economic developments from other sources but deal primarily with the policies and results, rather than the processes, of economic life in China. A long introductory chapter on "The Economic Heritage" before 1949 and an analysis of "Alternative Paths to Economic Development" are followed by chapters on the industrial sector, agriculture, population and employment, the control and allocation of resources, conditions of life and labor, foreign economic relations, and a concluding evaluation of "The Prospects for the Chinese Economy." Although billed as "readily comprehended by the non-economist," the book contains dozens of statistical tables and abundant economic data in the text, making it attractive primarily for the serious student of China or as a general reference.

China's Economic System
Audrey Donnithorne
New York: Praeger, 1967
592 pp. $13.50

This large volume remains the most comprehensive study of economic organization in the People's Republic. Covering the period 1949–63, but concentrating on events since 1957, the book can be heavy reading for the nonspecialist; but unlike most other studies, it deals extensively with the character and workings of economic institutions and thus provides unusual insights into China's development. Beginning with an analysis of collective agriculture, the author devotes subsequent chapters to water conservation and electric power, industry and industrial labor, mining, transport, internal and foreign trade; the fiscal system, price policies, and economic planning also receive separate treatment. The succinct statement of the author's "Conclusions" is a valuable overview for the general reader.

Communist China's Economic Growth and Foreign Trade
Alexander Eckstein

New York: McGraw-Hill, 1966
366 pp. $8.50

Dr. Eckstein, professor of economics at the University of Michigan, presents a lucid, scholarly discussion of the Chinese economy, its pattern of development, and, most specifically, of China's foreign economic relations and trade potential. Portions of the book are fairly technical, but chapter 2 provides a clear summary of China's developments up to 1966. Recommended for the layman and economist alike.

Iron Oxen: A Documentary of Revolution in Chinese Farming
William Hinton
New York: Vintage Books (Random House), 1971
225 pp. $1.95 Paper

In this extension of his earlier work, *Fanshen*, Mr. Hinton describes the preliminary steps in agricultural mechanization during the Chinese Revolution. Hinton is uniquely qualified to write about rural conditions in China, having made four extended stays there between 1937 and 1971. In 1947 he went to China as a tractor technician for the United Nations Relief and Rehabilitation Administration and stayed until 1953, teaching courses in English and mechanized agriculture. His postscript to the book contains a brief but excellent theoretical interpretation of how the political struggle between the "two lines," revealed in the Cultural Revolution, affected agricultural development.

The Chinese Worker
Charles Hoffman
Albany: State University of New York Press, 1974
252 pp. $15.00

One of the only studies in existence on how Maoist economic ideas have affected the well-being and productivity of the individual worker. Professor Hoffman concludes that while industrial development may have taken place at a somewhat slower rate than had been hoped, the emphasis on social motivation and the increased participation of workers in factory decisions have strengthened the possibilities for a genuinely classless and egalitarian society.

Economic Studies   *203*

People's Republic of China: An Economic Assessment
Joint Economic Committee, U.S. Congress
Washington, D.C.: U.S. Government Printing Office, 1972
382 pp. $1.75 Paper
   This is a compendium of reports submitted to the Joint
Economic Committee of Congress by a variety of China special-
ists. The ten papers offer data and interpretation on the state of
China's domestic economy, her efforts at economic development,
and her economic relations with the rest of the world. Serves to
update an earlier work released by the Committee, *An Economic
Profile of Mainland China* (1970).

A Concise Economic History of Modern China (1840–1961)
Frank H. H. King
New York: Praeger, 1968
243 pp. $7.50
   Designed for the general reader, this is a useful introduction to
China's economic history during the past century and a guide to
other relevant monographs. Professor King begins with a discussion of the reasons for China's failure to modernize, and then
outlines major aspects of the traditional economy and the
Western impact (1840–95) upon it. Succeeding chapters cover
China's attempts at economic modernization from 1896 to 1936,
the great inflation of 1937–49, and economic problems and
policies of the People's Republic. The volume concludes with a
survey of economic development in Taiwan.

The Idea of China: Myth and Theory in Geographic Thought
Andrew L. March
New York: Praeger Publishers, 1974
167 pp. $8.50
   After reviewing the traditional geographic approaches (environmental determinism, population pressures, and so on) which
have traditionally been considered natural barriers to China's
development, the author concludes— in consonance with Chinese
ideology—that collective human effort can surmount the barriers
which nature poses to economic development. Dr. March, a
professor of geography at the University of Denver, also examines

how Chinese conceptions of politics have affected their thinking about the environment. An interesting, different, and provocative perspective.

Agricultural Development in China: 1368–1968
Dwight H. Perkins
Chicago: Aldine-Atherton, 1968
395 pp. $12.50

This valuable study of the relationship between population growth and the evolution of agricultural techniques fills a major gap in English-language scholarship on Chinese economic history. It lays a foundation for understanding China's traditional agricultural problems and the solutions now being devised to cope with them. The most technical portions are concentrated in two hundred pages of appendixes; the first half of the volume is appropriate for anyone with an interest in the subject. For a detailed study of the agricultural development of the People's Republic of China, see Kang Chao's *Agricultural Production in Communist China* (Madison: University of Wisconsin Press, 1970).

The Political Economy of Communist China
Jan S. Prybyla
Scranton, Pa.: International Textbook Company, 1970
605 pp. $6.95 Paper

Professor Prybyla offers a comprehensive survey of China's economy from 1949 to 1969. Organized in thirteen chronological chapters, this book seems most useful as a university text, one which describes the changes in economic policies brought on by shifts in political power. The book is well documented, containing a number of helpful charts and practical data. However, like other economists studying China, the author was handicapped by the lack of meaningful official statistics on recent economic development. Although he acknowledges in the preface that he has "certain reservations about totalitarian systems as vehicles of human advancement," he does present a fairly balanced view.

Economic Studies   *205*

China's Trade with the West: A Political and Economic Analysis
Arthur A. Stahnke, ed.
New York: Praeger Publishers, 1972
234 pp. $16.50

The book is the compilation of papers given at a conference in March 1971—shortly before the advent of ping-pong diplomacy. It features a general essay on the interrelationship of politics and trade, and then analyzes the pattern of trade with the U.S., Germany, Japan, and Hong Kong. Unfortunately superficial, it reflects how little prepared American experts were for the impending "normalization" of relations.

The Chinese Road to Socialism: Economics of the Cultural Revolution
E. L. Wheelwright and Bruce McFarlane
New York: Monthly Review Press, 1971
256 pp. $2.95 Paper

This is a collaborative work by two Australian academics, both of whom have worked in China; one is a political scientist and the other an economist. The book is a sympathetic but somewhat superficial treatment of Chinese economic policies and their impact on the economy since 1957. Major emphasis is placed on the Cultural Revolution period from 1966 to 1968. The authors restrict themselves to qualitative analysis, and, unlike many other writers, approach their subject from the viewpoint of the policymakers in the People's Republic.

Doing Business with China: American Trade Opportunities in the 1970s
William Whitson, ed.
New York: Praeger Publishers, 1974
593 pp. $21.50

A compendium of essays (and as such, of uneven quality) on every aspect of trading with the People's Republic of China—from how to approach China's foreign trade corporations to the proper social and negotiating etiquette. Some of the sector reports are particularly valuable (e.g., for automobiles), and it contains some interesting accounts by individuals actually involved in the China trade.

A spate of "how-to" books in this field has emerged, including:

Boarman and Mugar, eds. *Trade with China* (Praeger Publishers, 1974), now seriously dated; JETRO, *How to Approach the China Market* (John Wiley and Sons, 1972); and, *Trading with the People's Republic of China* (the May 1973 edition of the U.S. Department of Commerce's "Overseas Business Reports").

10. MILITARY STUDIES

The Chinese Communist Army in Action: The Korean War and Its Aftermath
Alexander L. George
New York: Columbia University Press, 1967
255 pp. $2.75 Paper

As part of a Rand Corporation study for the U.S. Air Force in 1951, the author interviewed approximately three hundred Chinese captured during the Korean War. The objective of the inquiry was to determine "what motivated the Chinese soldiers and enabled them to fight so well." The book analyzes in detail the effectiveness of political commissars in maintaining the superiority of "men over weapons" in the Chinese army. In the last chapter Dr. George describes the "swing to professionalism" which followed the Korean War and the political difficulties faced by the People's Liberation Army during the 1960s. A good case study in military sociology, informative for both laymen and scholars.

The Role of the Chinese Army
John Gittings
New York: Oxford University Press, 1967
331 pp. $9.50

Covering the period 1946–65, this volume examines the transformation of the Chinese Communist guerrilla forces into a professional army of national defense, and its later swing back toward the revolutionary model. The special emphasis on the political and social roles of the armed forces, together with chapters on military leadership, should be of interest to the general reader and scholar alike.

The Chinese People's Liberation Army
Samuel B. Griffith

New York: McGraw-Hill, 1967
398 pp. $10.95

In the first section of this book, one in a series on China commissioned by the Council on Foreign Relations, General Griffith traces the growth of the People's Liberation Army from its origins through the end of the Korean War, highlighting the influence of the Chinese Communist party. In the second section he evaluates the capabilities, both qualitative and quantitative, of the Chinese armed forces. The book also contains brief (and now rather dated) biographies of the marshals of the People's Republic. See also General Griffith's *Peking and People's Wars* (New York: Praeger, 1966) which includes major statements by Lin Piao and Lo Jui-ching, two of China's deposed military leaders. The author also translated Mao Tse-tung's essays on guerrilla warfare (*Mao Tse-tung on Guerrilla Warfare*, New York: Praeger, 1961).

The People's Liberation Army and China's Nation Building
Kao Ying-mao
White Plains, New York: International Arts & Science Press, 1973
407 pp. $15.00

A group of documents drawn from the official organ of the People's Liberation Army brought together to illustrate the problem of uniting Mao's revolutionary theories with practical military needs. The documents focus on the army's interaction with other forces of society and its involvement in government activities. Of particular value are two translations of Mao's views on the army written during the 1920s and 1930s (over the extent to which the army should be involved in nonmilitary affairs), views which appear to have remained largely unchanged in theory but whose implementation in practice have caused problems.

● *The Chinese High Command: A History of Communist Military Politics, 1927–71*
William Whitson
New York: Praeger Publishers, 1973
650 pp. $25.00

This is as close to a "definitive" book on the Chinese army and its inseparable role in politics as is likely to appear for some time. An inclusive and encyclopaedic account of the development of the Chinese Communist armies, the factionalism which has had such an important role in military as well as general domestic politics in the last twenty years, and an overall view of the role and organization of the People's Liberation Army.

Another recent monograph, by Angus Fraser, *The People's Liberation Army* (Crane, Russak, 1973, 63 pp. $2.95 Paper), evaluates the P.L.A. in terms of the preoccupation with preparations for defense and retaliation should the Soviet Union attack along the disputed border territories.

11. TAIWAN

China and the Question of Taiwan: Documents and Analysis
Hungdah Chiu, ed.
New York: Praeger Publishers, 1973
395 pp. $18.50

A combination of scholarly articles and documents covering Taiwan's history and political and economic development, as well as an essay by the editor on the legal aspects of the Chinese attitude towards the island. He concludes that China has a legitimate claim to the island on the basis of historical records and the principles of international law, particularly those of occupation and prescription.

Hsin Hsing, Taiwan: A Chinese Village in Change
Bernard Gallin
Berkeley: University of California Press, 1966
324 pp. $11.00

For sixteen months during 1957–58 the author and his wife lived in the Taiwanese village of Hsin Hsing. In this study, written in a more academic and less personal style than *The House of Lim* by Margery Wolf (listed in this section), Mr. Gallin examines the general patterns of village life, including the agricultural process, land tenure, family and kinship, personal relationships within and beyond the village, and religion and magic. Emphasizing the impact of social and cultural change, the author analyzes the manner in which rural Taiwanese are increasingly brought into contact with areas beyond their own village.

Formosa: A Study in Chinese History
W. G. Goddard
East Lansing: Michigan State University Press, 1966
229 pp. $7.50

This is one of the few English-language works available on the history of Taiwan. Beginning his narrative with a description of the earliest settlement and the geography of the island, Goddard devotes each succeeding chapter to a major period in Formosan history: "The Dutch Interlude," "The Age of Unrest," "Liu Ming-ch'uan the Master Builder," "The Japanese Occupation," "Formosa since 1945." The author, an Australian who appears highly sympathetic to the Nationalist (KMT) point of view, writes in a rather romantic style. The book is a useful introduction to Taiwan for the nonspecialist.

Formosa: Licensed Revolution and the Home Rule Movement, 1895–1945
George H. Kerr
Honolulu: University Press of Hawaii, 1974
265 pp. $12.50

Kerr concerns himself primarily with Formosan reactions to Japanese colonial rule during a fifty-year period that ended in 1945. A central theme is Formosa's long struggle for autonomy and self-government. "With reversion to continental Chinese control at the end of WW II, Formosans expected to conserve and enhance gains made during the Japanese era. Bitter disappointment promptly led again to rebellious relations" with the newly imposed government of Chiang Kai-shek. The author believes that Peking faces a formidable task in converting the island into a fully integrated province.

Formosa Today
Mark Mancall, ed.
New York: Praeger, 1964
171 pp. $5.75

This is a collection of thirteen articles, most of which first appeared in *The China Quarterly* (July-September 1963). More than half the contributors had studied, worked, or lived in Taiwan; their essays were intended to present a cross section of knowledge and opinion then current among scholars and journalists. Topics covered include an outline of Taiwanese history, aspects of Taiwan's economic growth, Taiwan as a diplomatic issue, the position of intellectuals, and the Taiwanese independence movement. Although the essays are now somewhat dated and, as the editor acknowledges, often "highly personal," the volume nevertheless is one of the few major sources of information and insight about the seat of Nationalist government.

● *The House of Lim: A Study of a Chinese Farm Family*
Margery Wolf
New York: Prentice-Hall, 1968
148 pp. $3.80 Paper
Engagingly told, this story of a Taiwanese family was written from data gathered between 1959 and 1961 when the author and her husband lived in the Lim household. Intended first as a case study for the social scientist, second as an account of village life for the China specialist, and third simply as a good story, the book is woven out of Mrs. Wolf's interviews and conversations with family members, relatives, and neighbors. Mrs. Wolf vividly portrays for the Western reader the gossip, humor, and temperament characteristic of daily life in a Chinese household, and illustrates the strains inherent in a large family which is the ideal rather than the norm of Chinese society.

12. CHINA IN WORLD POLITICS

China and Russia: The "Great Game"
O Edmund Clubb
New York: Columbia University Press, 1972
578 pp. $3.95 Paper

The Sino-Soviet Conflict, 1956–1961
Donald S. Zagoria
New York: Atheneum, 1964
484 pp. $4.95 Paper

The Sino-Dispute Dispute
G. F. Hudson, Richard Lowenthal, and Roderick MacFarquhar

New York: Scribner and Sons, 1969
120 pp. $2.45 Paper

The Sino-Soviet Rift
William E. Griffith
Cambridge, Mass.: MIT Press, 1964
508 pp. $3.95 Paper

Sino-Soviet Relations, 1964–1965
William E. Griffith
Cambridge, Mass.: MIT Press, 1967
504 pp. $3.95 Paper

Survey of the Sino-Soviet Dispute: Commentary and Extracts from the Recent Polemic, 1963–1967
John Gittings
New York: Oxford University Press, 1968
410 pp. $14.25

The Arms Race and Sino-Soviet Relations
Walter C. Clemens, Jr.
Stanford: Hoover Institution on War, Revolution and Peace, 1968
335 pp. $7.50

War between Russia and China
Harrison E. Salisbury
New York: Norton Books, 1969
224 pp. $4.95 Paper

   These eight volumes, listed in rough chronological order by the periods they cover, provide a general survey of Sino-Soviet relations. The first, and most recently published, is a major scholarly study which spans three and a half centuries of relations between the two powers. Beginning with the first "meeting of empires," Mr. Clubb, an American diplomat with wide experience in East and Central Asia, traces events through to the present Sino-Soviet "Cold War." Special emphasis is placed on events since 1850 in this detailed but very readable book. Professor Zagoria's analytical study and the volume by Hudson et al. outline the period from 1956 to 1961, with special attention to developments during 1960 when the rift initially came into the open. The bulk of the second work consists of major documents through which the dispute has been publicized, reprinted with helpful annotations.

The Sino-Soviet Rift, by Professor Griffith, analyzes and documents developments in Sino-Soviet relations from late 1962 through November 1963, a period of hardening disagreement between the two Communist powers. Writing for both the general reader and the specialist, Griffith examines the Cuban missile crisis, the Sino-Indian border war, the signing of the atomic test ban treaty, and the fragmentation of the world Communist movement as factors in the dispute. Some two hundred pages of supporting documents are included. In *Sino-Soviet Relations, 1964–1965*, Griffith picks up the discussion where his earlier work left off. He includes chapters on Soviet and Chinese policies toward the Third World and specifically toward North Vietnam and North Korea. Also discussed are the effects on Sino-Soviet relations of the Vietnam War, the Indo-Pakistani conflict, and the 1965 coup in Indonesia.

Perhaps the most generally informative is Gittings's *Survey of the Sino-Soviet Dispute*. Although emphasizing the years 1963–67, the book begins with a brief survey of the historical background of the dispute and a review, based on recent disclosures, of relations between the Soviet Union and China during 1953–59.

Professor Clemens's book focuses specifically on the problems of disarmament and arms control as key elements in the Sino-Soviet dispute. He provides an analytical history of arms control and related issues from the early 1950s to the mid-1960s, including the Soviet-American nuclear test ban treaty, the non-proliferation negotiations, and their implications for Western policy vis-à-vis the Communist world generally.

Finally, Salisbury's *War between Russia and China* takes us full circle, being an eminent journalist's study of their relations from the Mongol invasion of Russia in the thirteenth century up to and including events of 1969. After the short historical sketch of relations between the two nations through the nineteenth century, and then between the two Communist parties from the 1920s through the post-Stalin years, Mr. Salisbury moves to a discussion of the most recent conflicts: political, military, and ideological. He describes the military buildup on both sides of the Sino-Soviet border and by the Russians in Mongolia, and suggests that although war is not inevitable, it will become so if events continue on their present (1969) course. In closing, he speculates on how U.S. efforts might sway the pattern of events away from the brink of nuclear war.

People's China and International Law: A Documentary Study
Jerome Alan Cohen and Hungdah Chiu
Princeton: Princeton University Press, 1974
1791 pp. $60.00 2 volumes
A significant compilation of treaties, cables, government statements, and other documents which illuminates China's position on international law. In the introduction, the authors discuss the experience of previous Chinese governments with international law, and the relationship of China's domestic public order and its foreign policy to its views of international law. For various scholarly interpretations of Chinese views on this subject, see the author's other volume, Jerome Cohen, ed., *China's Practice of International Law* (Cambridge: Harvard University Press, 1972), 417 pp., $10.00.

China and the Overseas Chinese: A Study of Peking's Changing Policy, 1949-70
Stephen FitzGerald
Cambridge and New York: Cambridge University Press, 1973
268 pp. $19.50
A study by Australia's current ambassador to Peking (and a longtime China scholar) which examines the policy that the People's Republic of China has pursued toward the overseas Chinese. The author suggests that Peking has discouraged activities which might be unacceptable and embarassing to the "host" states.

Communist China in World Politics
Harold C. Hinton

Boston: Houghton Mifflin, 1966
527 pp. $9.95

Professor Hinton's history of China's foreign relations from 1949 to 1965, somewhat controversial among scholars for its inferences based largely on speeches and events, emphasizes China's dealings with its Asian neighbors. Extensive data and numerous citations make the volume more useful as a reference work than as a general introduction to China's foreign policy. A more general book, covering China's relations with all of the world and updating some of the themes in the above, is the author's *China's Turbulent Quest* (New York: Macmillan, 1970).

The Security of China: Chinese Approaches to Problems of War and Strategy
Arthur Huck
New York: Columbia University Press, for the Institute of Strategic Studies, London, 1970
93 pp. $1.95 Paper

This essay is the product of the author's two visits to China in 1965 and 1966, discussions at the Institute for Strategic Studies in London, and a culling of official Chinese statements. The book deals with the Chinese view of the country's strengths and weaknesses and of strategic threats to China's security; the significance of Lin Piao's important 1965 essay on people's war; the relationship between military matters and politics; and the differences between Chinese doctrines ("the atom bomb is a paper tiger") and actions with respect to nuclear weapons. Professor Huck concludes with some speculative comments on the direction that China might take in international affairs after Mao. On the whole, a balanced interpretation for the general reader.

How Communist China Negotiates
Arthur Lall
New York: Columbia University Press, 1968
301 pp. $2.95 Paper

This carefully written volume is primarily a case study of Peking's methods and approaches in international negotiation, as observed at the fourteen-nation foreign ministers' conference on Laos held at Geneva in 1961–62. The author, now a professor of government at Columbia University, was formerly India's ambassador to the United Nations and its representative at the Geneva negotiations on Laos. He has combined information from published documents with his own private records to shed light not only on Peking's negotiating style, but on those of London, Washington, and Moscow as well. He concludes that "ideological bombast" should not be taken as the key determinant of China's attitudes on foreign affairs: "When it comes to negotiation they will eventually talk in terms that are related to their national interests, their sense of a viable balance, and the desirability in some cases of the nonalignment and neutralization of areas."

India's China War
Neville Maxwell
New York: Doubleday, 1972
475 pp. $2.95 Paper

The *London Times* Southeast Asian correspondent Neville Maxwell provides a closely documented history of the Sino-Indian border war of November 1962. The documents cited contradict the usual Western view of the war by indicating that India was responsible for the outbreak of hostilities and refused to negotiate the disputed borders. China is seen as reasonable and willing to compromise, responding with force only in defense against India's "forward policy." This book provides well-reasoned support for the thesis that the People's Republic of China is not an aggressive nation.

Chinese Foreign Policy in an Age of Transition
Ishwer C. Ojha
Boston: Beacon Press, 1969
234 pp. $3.95 Paper

In this interpretative essay, Mr. Ojha examines China's foreign policy from the nineteenth century through the establishment of the People's Republic. He places great weight on internal developments as well as on the international circumstances which shape and limit China's orientation toward other nations. The author, an Indian scholar teaching at Boston University, examines China's relations with the Soviet Union, the U.S., and the Third World, including her various border disputes. Lucid analysis together with the book's moderate length and readable style make it one of the more useful contributions toward an understanding of China's foreign policy.

Revolution and Chinese Foreign Policy: Peking's Support for Wars of National Liberation
Peter Van Ness
Berkeley: University of California Press, 1971
266 pp. $3.25 Paper

This volume is a major step toward understanding the relationship between what the Chinese Communists say and what they actually do in promoting revolutionary wars. Professor Van Ness, who teaches at the University of Denver, examines both the theory and practice of China's support for wars of liberation, primarily in the countries of the Third World. China's relations with these countries are examined with particular emphasis on the period 1965-67. The analysis suggests that Chinese foreign policy continues to be motivated more by national interests than by ideological pretensions to leadership of world revolution.

China and the Great Powers: Relations with the United States, the Soviet Union, and Japan
Francis O. Wilcox, ed.
New York: Praeger Books, 1974
103 pp. $10.00

This slim volume holds an empty promise. Developed out of the Christian Herter Lecture Series at the Johns Hopkins School of Advanced International Studies in 1973, it unfortunately often provides superficial views of a most important subject. The essays by Senator Mike Mansfield and Professor Jerome Cohen, the better papers in the book, suggest possible options for the U.S. government in seeking to improve and normalize the Sino-American relationship.

The Future of the Overseas Chinese in Southeast Asia
Lea E. Williams
New York: McGraw-Hill, 1966
143 pp. $5.50

Professor Williams provides a short, well-written assessment of the position of the approximately thirteen million Chinese living in Southeast Asia. Overseas Chinese communities, economically and often politically among the most important segments of the population, have been a continuing source of friction in the region's new nations. Professor Williams, who lived in Southeast Asia for four years, analyzes the orientation of these expatriate Chinese communities toward both the People's Republic and the Nationalist government on Taiwan and suggests that they are not, as has often been claimed, a "disciplined instrument for subversion." This study was one in the China series commissioned by the Council on Foreign Relations.

13. UNITED STATES–CHINA RELATIONS

U.S. China Policy and the Problem of Taiwan
William M. Bueler
Boulder, Colo.: Colorado Associated University Press, 1971
143 pp. $6.95

Mr. Bueler reviews U.S. policy toward China since 1948 as it developed under each president. He relates this to an inquiry into the wishes of the Taiwanese people, and concludes that they desire independence and that the U.S. should help them to attain self-determination (a position which both the Communists and Nationalists excoriate).

A similar argument has been developed by Chu Lung-chu and Harold Lasswell in *Formosa, China and the United Nations* (New York: St. Martin's Press, 1967). Chu, closely identified with the Formosan Independence Movement, traces the "China Question" in the UN through 1966 and then argues proposals for the emergence and development of an independent Formosa through a UN plebiscite. A provocative and more scholarly study, done through interviews with native Formosans living in Japan, is *The Politics of Formosan Nationalism* by Douglas Mendel (Berkeley: University of California Press, 1970).

• *The Witness and I*
O. Edmund Clubb
New York: Columbia University Press, 1975
308 pp. $9.95

Like John Service, John Patton Davies, and others, O. Edmund

Clubb was a State Department China expert (and last U.S. Consul in Peking), whose career became embroiled in the conflicts and passions of the McCarthy era. In this well-written book, he recalls that era, and the background of America's China policy in the 1930s and 1940s. The book is a cautionary story of the dangers of separating America from an important and growing world power and in creating the atmosphere of fear and suspicion in our foreign policy bureaucracy. See also John S. Service in Joseph W. Esherick, ed., *Lost Chance in China*, reviewed in this section.

Taiwan and American Policy: The Dilemma in U.S.-China Relations
Jerome A. Cohen, Edward Friedman, Harold Hinton, and Allen S. Whiting
New York: Praeger, 1970
192 pp. $2.50 Paper
In the papers and proceedings of a 1971 conference convened by the National Committee on United States–China Relations and the League of Women Voters Education Fund, leading China scholars, businessmen, government officials, and representatives of various public affairs organizations debate the U.S. relationship with Taiwan and the Republic of China government. The principal papers deal with "The Real Interests of China and America in the Taiwan Area," "Morality, Taiwan, and U.S. Policy," and "U.S. Policy Options." A brief introduction outlines the social and political setting on Taiwan, and identifies basic questions for discussion. A useful chronology is also appended.

America's Response to China
Warren I. Cohen
New York: John Wiley & Sons, 1971
242 pp. $4.25 Paper
This interpretative history of Sino-American relations focuses on American responses to China within the context of our overall foreign policy. The author argues that while generally seeing our role as redemptive, we oscillated between poles of attraction and rejection, resulting in a negative policy which looked foolish to the Chinese; challenges to our stated policy goals were often met with

United States–China Relations   *219* weakness and indecision. The book includes a section on the tribute and treaty-port systems, describes the U.S. role in nineteenth- and twentieth-century Asia and the motivations behind it, and then traces our policy through the Japanese invasion of China and the establishment of the People's Republic.

China and United States Far Eastern Policy, 1945-1966
Congressional Quarterly, Washington, D.C., 1967
348 pp. $4.95 Paper
The most useful portions of this reference book are a 184-page chronology of events in U.S.-East Asian relations since 1945 and a documentary section containing excerpts from both the 1947 Wedemeyer Report and the 1966 Senate Foreign Relations Committee hearings on China. The book also contains biographies of Chinese and American officials important in foreign affairs and a list of U.S. associations, pressure groups, and lobbies concerned with China policy since 1945. A recent updating of this volume, to the eve of Nixon's China visit, is now available (*China: U.S. Foreign Policy*, 1971, 92 pp., $4.00 paper).

● *Lost Chance in China: The World War II Despatches of John S. Service*
Joseph W. Esherick, ed.
New York: Random House, 1973
409 pp. $12.95
During and after the Second World War, a handful of American foreign service officers had opportunities for close-up observation of the confrontation between the Chinese Communists and Nationalists which ultimately led to the founding of the People's Republic of China in 1949. Because some of these men were later held partly responsible for our "loss" of China, their work became controversial, and some, like John Service, were dismissed from their government posts. Service has already told of his successful struggle for reinstatement in the State Department in *The Amerasia Papers* (Berkeley: University of California Press, 1971). Now, his original memoranda and despatches during the Chinese civil war have been published, and they provide a unique look at American policy in the 1940s and at the determinants of American and Chinese actions in this period. The editor has

provided a valuable introduction, setting the context in which the despatches were written, and provides excellent annotations which help to identify many of the leading personalities in both China and America at the time.

China Perceived: Images and Policies in Chinese-American Relations
John K. Fairbank
New York: Alfred A. Knopf, 1974
254 pp. $7.95

Fairbank, "dean of American China studies," has collected seventeen of his own essays going back to 1946 that develop the theme that "American relations with China have reached a difficult phase. We can't just *do* something, we have to think." The essays, which seek to help us understand the Chinese as well as giving us a perspective on ourselves, are grouped under five broad headings: (1) Before and After the Revolution [1949]; (2) Perspectives and Politics; (3) The Mediation of Contact and Mutual Images; (4) American Experience and Chinese Life; and, (5) Studying China. Intended and recommended for the general reader.

● *The United States and China*
John K. Fairbank
Cambridge, Mass.: Harvard University Press, 1971
500 pp. $3.50 Paper

This is the third revised and enlarged edition of the now classic introduction to Chinese history and politics, first published in 1948. Based on the assumption that a successful U.S. China policy "must take full account of China's own process of social change," Professor Fairbank presents a general survey of China's historical development and political traditions. The contemporary Communist regime is analyzed in the immediate context of its rise to power and against a backdrop of Chinese history from ancient times to the present.

America's Asia: Dissenting Essays on Asian-American Relations
Edward Friedman and Mark Selden, eds.

New York: Vintage Books (Random House), 1971
458 pp. $2.45 Paper

This collection of ten essays, written by members of the Committee of Concerned Asian Scholars, challenges what they consider to be the inadequate and biased scholarship of America's leading Asian specialists. The essays in the first two sections attempt to redefine America's past and present interests in Asia and also include an essay criticizing secondary school units on China. The final section deals with Maoist economics, the Chinese and Vietnamese revolutionary experience, and Chinese industry, finding in China both inspiration and practical applications for solving general human problems.

Sino-American Detente and Its Policy Implications
Gene T. Hsiao, ed.
New York: Praeger Publishers, 1974
319 pp. $6.95 Paper

Events in Sino-American relations have moved so rapidly that some of the essays in this book—the results of a conference in June 1973—by now have limited use in assessing the implications of the future. The ones analyzing the recent past, and thus contributing to the historical record, are the more successful (Iriye: America's role as an Asian power; Karnow: Media coverage of the Nixon visit; Cohen: China trade and the problems involved). Other essays on how the Nixon-Kissinger visits have affected American-Chinese bilateral relations, and on how various countries view this new connection in terms of their own interest, are generally well done.

The Cold War in Asia: A Historical Introduction
Akira Iriye
Englewood Cliffs: Prentice-Hall, Inc., 1974
214 pp. $4.50 Paper

This book is an interpretive history of Asian-Pacific international relations and U.S.-East Asian relations during the watershed period of the 1940s—"a decade that was of crucial importance in shaping the subsequent history of Asia and America's role in it." Based on documents in British and American archives (many available only since 1971), it is a fresh and critical approach, with the conclusion that the cold war should not serve as a framework for analyzing events in the 1970s. A balanced treatment of interest both to the scholar and the layman. (The author has also written an excellent history of U.S.-Asian relations in terms of mutual images: *Across the Pacific: An Inner History of American-East Asian Relations*, New York: Harcourt, Brace and Jovanovich, 1967.)

● *Images of Asia: American Views of China and India*
Harold R. Isaacs
New York: Harper & Row, 1962
416 pp. $1.95 Paper
Originally published in 1958 under the title *Scratches on Our Minds*, the book is based on 181 interviews conducted during the mid-1950s, and on analyses of U.S. books, newspapers, and films. It examines the many images that Americans have had about Asia in general and China and India in particular. Although now somewhat dated, the book is a unique contribution to a little-studied problem. The author, a wartime correspondent in China and now professor of political science at MIT, attempted not only to retrieve and describe the diverse impressions about Asia which have existed in this country, but also to place them within the historical settings which inspired them. He thus traces the "natural history" of American feelings about China and things Chinese through six stages, the most recent of which are the Age of Admiration (1937–44), the Age of Disenchantment (1944–49), and the Age of Hostility (1949–).

The China Lobby in American Politics
Ross Y. Koen
New York: Harper & Row, 1974
280 pp. $3.25 Paper
In the 1940s and 1950s, a strong "China lobby," consisting of well-financed Nationalist Chinese officials and a fringe of conservative American political elites, was active in giving vocal and financial support to Chiang Kai-shek and his goals of mainland recovery. Strongly supporting the economic blockade and political isolation of the People's Republic, the lobby was a potent force in American politics (e.g., the McCarthy era) until the early 1970s.

This book, long suppressed by another publisher, is the thorough and documented story of its activities.

Sino-American Relations, 1949–1971
Roderick MacFarquhar, ed.
New York: Praeger, 1972
244 pp. $2.95

A set of important documents concerning the foreign policy of China since 1949 is supplemented by articles from three China scholars: A. M. Halperin writing on China's foreign policy since the Cultural Revolution, Morton Halpern on the impact of Nixon's new China policy in America and Asia, and Donald Klein on the men behind China's foreign policy.

American–East Asian Relations: A Survey
Ernest R. May and James C. Thomson, Jr., eds.
Cambridge: Harvard University Press, 1972
445 pp. $15.00

A collection of essays which attempt a reconsideration of how American foreign policy has interacted with the domestic policies of various countries in East Asia. Each essay reviews previous historical interpretations of the American–East Asian relationship in certain periods and then poses questions which ought now to be considered in light of newly emerged facts and changing times.

Remaking China Policy: U.S.–China Relations and Governmental Decision Making
Richard Moorstein and Morton Abramowitz
Cambridge, Mass.: Harvard University Press, 1971
136 pp. $5.95

The unique contribution of this book is its ordering of general knowledge available on China into "usable" and "policy relevant" information needed by government decision-makers. The authors, the first a RAND consultant, the other a foreign service officer, analyze almost brutally the complexity, the uncertainties, the political constraints and risks involved in the "options" open to policymakers. Their recommended "opening moves" have been superseded by events (e.g., that we follow a "one China but not now" policy in the UN), but in general, it would be difficult to find a clearer exposition of the basic issues in our relations with China.

The Amerasia Papers: Some Poblems in the History of U.S.-China Relations
John S. Service
Berkeley: Center for Chinese Studies, 1971
220 pp. $4.00 Paper

A former foreign service officer, John Service was one of the principal victims of the Senate Internal Security Subcommittee's purge of China specialists in the early 1950s. In this monograph, Service counters an interpretation of the "Amerasia" case recently written by Professor Anthony Kubek (*The Amerasia Papers: A Clue to the Catastrophe of China*, Washington: U.S. Government Printing Office, 1971) with his own account, and analyzes the problems involved in the struggle for power between Chiang Kai-shek and the Chinese Communists in 1944 and 1945. A thoughtful and deeply personal book about a critical period in U.S.-China relations.

The American People and China
A. T. Steele
New York: McGraw-Hill, 1966
325 pp. $2.45 Paper

A journalist in China before 1949, Mr. Steele discusses traditional American attitudes toward China, outlines the key features of the U.S. alliance with the Chiang Kai-shek government during and after World War II, and evaluates current American thinking about China. The author tries to pinpoint American attitudes by geographic region, social and economic group, and branch of the U.S. government. An appendix contains the results of a survey conducted by the Survey Research Center of the University of Michigan in 1963 and 1964, in which 28 percent of the persons interviewed were unaware that China had a Communist government. Although public attitudes appear to have changed considerably, this book remains of value to anyone interested in the evolution of Sino-American relations.

While China Faced West: American Reformers in Nationalist China, 1928-1937
James C. Thomson, Jr.
Cambridge, Mass.: Harvard University Press, 1969
310 pp. $8.50

Professor Thomson explores an important chapter in the history of America's relationship with pre-Communist China. He examines the efforts of American church and foundation representatives to bring radical change to rural Chinese society and to achieve reform without the presumed violence and godlessness of the Communist alternative. The author examines the work of the National Christian Council in Kiangsi province and of various missionaries aiding Chiang Kai-shek's New Life Movement, and analyzes the ultimate futility of these efforts. A well-written and informative study.

America's Failure in China
Tang Tsou
Chicago: University of Chicago Press, 1963
614 pp. in two vols.
Vol. 1: $2.95 Paper
Vol. 2: $2.45 Paper

This historical study by an American-trained political scientist analyzes the men and events which led to the failure of U.S. China policy after World War II, in terms of America's own "objectives, intentions, and interests." Professor Tsou's major hypothesis is that liberal idealism and a reluctance to give direct military support account for America's inability to respond effectively to its policy commitments.

China in Crisis: Vol. 2, *China's Policies in Asia and America's Alternatives*
Tang Tsou, ed.
Chicago: University of Chicago Press, 1968
484 pp. $3.95 Paper

This book, the second of two volumes on modern China, deals with China's foreign policy (for vol. 1, see section 7 under Ping-ti Ho). In fifteen separate articles, scholars and other specialists analyze China's foreign policy objectives, capabilities, and relations with her neighbors in Asia. In addition, Hans Morgenthau, Robert Scalapino, and George Taylor examine three alternative courses for American China policy. The articles are generally of a scholarly nature, but include much to interest the general reader.

Stilwell and the American Experience in China, 1911-1945
Barbara Tuchman
New York: Bantam Books, 1972
794 pp. $2.25 Paper

Barbara Tuchman possesses a rare ability to weave solid research and historical data into an interesting story. To an entire generation of Americans, Chiang Kai-shek was a hero whose courage, steadfastness, and close cooperation with the Allies were a major factor in the Pacific War victory. By focusing on the life of General Joseph Stilwell, one of America's most eccentric soldiers, who was liaison officer with the Nationalist government, Mrs. Tuchman suggests otherwise. She tells of the deterioration of relations between the Chinese and U.S. governments during the 1940s and presents a new and persuasive interpretation of the "loss" of China to the Communist forces.

The China White Paper
U.S. Department of State
With a new Introduction by Lyman P. Van Slyke
Vol. 1: 519 pp.
Vol. 2: 560 pp.
Stanford: Stanford University Press, 1967
$7.50 (the set) Paper

Originally issued in August 1949 by the U.S. Department of State, *The China White Paper* continues to be a major source of information on America's policies toward China during the controversial period before the Communist victory. These two volumes consist principally of documents and extracts thereof, with particular emphasis on the years 1947 and 1948. This new edition, containing a well-written introduction by Professor Lyman P. Van Slyke which serves as a guide for those unfamiliar with the issues raised in the documents, is a valuable resource for understanding America's subsequent postures toward the People's Republic.

Negotiating with the Chinese Communists: The United States Experience, 1953–1967
Kenneth T. Young
New York: McGraw-Hill, 1968
461 pp. $3.95 Paper

Mr. Young, a former U.S. Ambassador to Thailand, surveys the history, style, and machinery of Sino-American contacts and negotiations since the Korean armistice of July 1953. In the absence of official diplomatic records and documents (which are still classified), this survey commissioned by the Council on Foreign Relations is based largely on secondary sources but remains the most comprehensive account of these contacts yet available. The book is devoted principally to the "ambassadorial talks" conducted in Europe for more than a decade and reflects the official American perspective of the time. The author explains why the talks were worthwhile despite minimal concrete results and advocates a policy of contact and conciliation with modifications in the U.S. policy of containment. Toward that end he outlines a six-point program aimed at a gradual, incremental liberalization of U.S. relations with the People's Republic.

14. CHINESE IN AMERICA

● *East Meets West*
George Goldberg
New York: Harcourt Brace Jovanovich, 1970
136 pp. $4.50

A dramatic, absorbing account of the Chinese and Japanese in California who first came to this country in the nineteenth century and experienced a difficult period of alienation familiar to many immigrant groups. This is a story of the American ideal of freedom preached, ignored, attacked, and finally triumphant, as the Chinese and Japanese overcame their hardships and gradually achieved acceptance into the mainstream of American life.

Americans and Chinese: Purpose and Fulfillment in Great Civilizations
Francis L. K. Hsu
New York: Natural History Press (Doubleday), 1970
493 pp. $5.95

The author is an anthropologist who grew up in China and has

228

Books

lived in the United States for more than twenty years. He examines two vital civilizations and the inherent weaknesses and strengths of each. Professor Hsu argues that in Chinese culture, the individual knows his place in society and is secure in his relationships with others, whereas in America the individual is highly mobile and self-reliant and finds close personal ties difficult to maintain. The author looks at history, politics, human relationships, religion, and art from these two different perspectives and suggests lines of change that China and America might take in the future.

The Heathen Chinee: A Study of American Attitudes toward China, 1890–1905
Robert McClellan
Columbus: Ohio State University Press, 1971
272 pp. $10.00
This study explores the background of American attitudes toward the Chinese in America and illuminates the image which was shaped at the turn of the century as a result of the confrontation between this nation and an emerging China. A thorough study of a hitherto largely silent—yet extremely important—minority. For another perspective, see James W. Loewen, *The Mississippi Chinese: Between Black and White* (Cambridge, Mass.: Harvard University Press, 1971).

The Unwelcome Immigrant
Stuart Creighton Miller
Berkeley: University of California Press, 1974
259 pp. $3.25
This is a study of the American image of Chinese from 1785 to 1882. Although a focus on this one historical period may limit its appeal, the book is a well-researched study of the basis for our subsequent images of Chinese and China, and is the fullest analysis now available of our impressions as recorded during that first century of contact.

● *Longtime Californ'*
Victor G. and Brett de Bary Nee

Chinese in America   *229*

New York: Pantheon Books, 1973
410 pp. $10.00

Through interviews with members of the Chinese-American community in San Francisco, the Nees present a vivid picture of what it has meant to be a person of Chinese origin in the United States since the gold rush days of the 1840s. The result, history written from the collective memory of the living (with aid from the archives), is a mixture of humor and bitterness about the efforts to feel at home in America—some by embracing "white" values, others by retaining their ethnic identities, and still others trying to be both Chinese and American and finding acceptance in either community difficult.

The Anti-Chinese Movement in the United States
Elmer Clarence Sandmeyer
Champaign-Urbana: University of Illinois Press, 1939, 1973
132 pp. $2.25 Paper

The first modern account of an important episode in the development of organized racism in the western United States, this book, originally published in 1939, is still timely and accurate. Drawing from pamphlets, newspapers, government documents, and the periodical press, the author establishes clearly how anti-Chinese sentiment coalesced into a movement that triumphed successively on the local, state, regional, and finally national level.

Chinese Americans: A Brief History
Larry Stevens
Stockton, California: Relevant Instructional Materials, 1973
84 pp. $0.75 Pamphlet

This booklet briefly sketches Chinese immigration into the United States, their contributions to our history, the struggle against poor working conditions and prejudice, and the organizational structure of the Chinese community. The author also notes the remnants of traditional Chinese culture in American life, the acculturation process, and the struggle for civil rights. The brevity of the pamphlet unfortunately precludes discussion of these issues in depth, leaving little understanding of the context in which they took place. Still, it is a good introduction to Chinese-American history.

The Story of the Chinese in America
B. L. Sung
New York: Collier Books, 1971
341 pp. $2.95 Paper
   This readable account presents a well-rounded picture of the history of the Chinese in America and discusses many aspects of Chinese society and culture. Unlike many other accounts, this book does not emphasize the strange and exotic (tong wars, opium dens, yellow peril, and so on), but gives a straight, factual account stripped of myth and mystery. See also Rose Hum Lee, *The Chinese in the United States of America* (Hong Kong, 1961).

"Chink!" A Documentary History of Anti-Chinese Prejudice in America
Wu Cheng-tu, ed.
New York: The World Publishing Company, 1972
290 pp. $3.95 Paper
   A collection of documents taken from newspapers, journals, and other archives which trace the history of the Chinese in America from 1852 to the present. The documents are divided topically and chronologically and are an excellent sampling for the researcher or the person wishing to supplement other readings. In the book, which is part of the publisher's "Ethnic Prejudice in America" series, the author takes the unusual step of disowning the picture put on the front cover—which he correctly asserts is in itself a stereotype.

7. Periodicals

1. INTRODUCTION

The periodicals chapter of this edition is a restructuring and consolidation of several chapters in the first edition of this guide. It is divided as follows:

2. General
3. Newsletters and Association Bulletins
4. Scholarly Journals
5. Monographs and Papers
6. Trade Journals
7. Publications from and about Taiwan

Periodicals of particular interest to the general reader are marked with a •.

2. GENERAL

These publications are written for a nonspecialist audience and generally provide brief, informative articles of potential interest to community education organizations, teachers, and students.

Asia
The Asia Society
112 East 64th Street
New York, New York 10021
Five times a year plus supplements
Cost: Free to members
        $6.00 nonmembers

The Society's newsletter reports on activities and programs and occasionally includes brief reviews of new books and other educational material. The supplements (usually two per year) are reprints of lectures given at the Asia Society or other special topics.

Asian Affairs: An American Review
American Educational Exchange, Inc.
88 Morningside Drive

New York, New York 10027
William Henderson III, ed.
Bimonthly
Cost: $12.00 per year
  The magazine's editorial policy is to devote "special attention to the Free World autonomies in Asia—South Korea, Taiwan, South Vietnam and the Indian Ocean area." Written for high school and college social studies teachers, the 72-page magazine includes articles on both domestic and international politics.

Atlas
Atlas Magazine
1180 Avenue of the Americas
New York, New York 10036
Monthly
Cost: $10.00 per year
  This magazine, recently revived, translates and excerpts articles from the world press, and almost every issue contains some news about China. Approximately 80 pages.

● *Bridge*
Bridge: The Magazine of Asians in America
22 Catherine Street, 3rd Floor
New York, New York 10038
Six times per year
Cost: $5.00 per year
      $4.00 student
  A one-of-a-kind magazine that makes a special contribution by focusing on the concerns of Americans of Asian descent, *Bridge* contains general articles, interviews, reports, creative writing, research materials, and school notes for teachers. This 52-page magazine is highly recommended.

China News Analysis
P.O. Box 13225
Hong Kong, B.C.C.
Weekly
Cost: $96.00 plus $8.00 for airmail
  An interpretive newsletter, anticommunist in tone, used by

scholars and written by a long-time observer in Hong Kong. Each issue of this 7-page magazine focuses on a particular topic.

● *China Notes*
National Council of Churches
East Asia Department
475 Riverside Drive, Room 612
New York, New York 10027
Quarterly
Cost: $2.00
Book reviews and short articles, often reprinted from other publications, which concern education, ideology, social change, and church-related issues in contemporary China. Approximately 15 pages.

China Report
Committee for Free China
1735 DeSales Street, NW
Washington, D.C. 20036
Monthly
Cost: Free
This newsletter carries conservative political opinion on many issues in U.S.–China relations reprinted from the general press.

● *Far Eastern Economic Review*
P.O. Box 160
Hong Kong, B.C.C.
Weekly
Cost: $45.00 airmail
An outstanding newsmagazine (often referred to as the "*Time* magazine of Asia") with comprehensive coverage of current political, social, and economic developments in all of Asia. Good coverage of China, from various writers, often with firsthand reports. Includes book reviews, business outlook, and feature sections on particular topics and countries. The *Review* also publishes an annual yearbook. Approximately 75 pages.

● *Focus on Asian Studies*
Service Center for Teachers of Asian Studies
Ohio State University
29 West Woodruff Avenue
Columbus, Ohio 43210
Cost: $2.00 per year (four issues)
   The *most essential single resource* available for teachers. A newsletter especially designed for elementary and secondary teachers including essays, book reviews, and announcements of conferences, publications, multimedia materials, and summer programs. No mere listing, it has a distinct and attractive character and flavor.

Getting Together
P.O. Box 26229
San Francisco, California 94126
Bimonthly
Cost: $3.50 individual
      $5.00 institutions
   Tabloid of news articles affecting the Chinese-American community, radical in tone. Bilingual, approximately 16 pages.

● *New China*
U.S.-China People's Friendship Association
41 Union Square West, Room 1228
New York, New York 10003
Quarterly
Cost: $4.00
   A visually attractive magazine for the general reader, featuring notes on the activities of the national and local U.S.-China People's Friendship Associations, articles on China today, interviews, photo essays, and reports by recent visitors to China, all generally sympathetic to the Chinese point of view.

Ta Kung Pao
China Arts and Crafts, Ltd.
33 Hastings Street
Vancouver, B.C. Canada

General   *235*

Weekly
Cost: $9.50 for six months
Since the *People's Daily* is printed only in Chinese, this weekly synopsis of news in English relating to the People's Republic, published in Hong Kong by the publisher of one of the largest Chinese language dailies generally reflecting P.R.C. views, is an excellent way of keeping up to date on events in China from that point of view. Includes most of the important speeches given by Chinese leaders as well as documents, photos, and general news.

3. NEWSLETTERS AND ASSOCIATION BULLETINS

The following publications are written primarily for scholars in the China field and others concerned with the activities of related professional associations. Teachers, however, might find these newsletters helpful in locating potential speakers or learning about upcoming conferences, publications, and academic programs on China in their own locality and throughout the country.

American-East Asian Relations Newsletter
American Historical Association
Committee on American-East Asian Relations
745 Holyoke Center
Cambridge, Massachusetts 02138
Irregular
Cost: free
Approximately 4 pp.
Information concerning fellowships and grants, conferences, and summer language study programs.

American Universities Field Staff Reports
American Universities Field Staff
P.O. Box 150
Hanover, New Hampshire 03755
Sixty reports per year
Cost: $35.00
      $1.00 per issue
Pagination varies
These reports are written by knowledgeable American observers all over the world and cover a wide range of topics. Each

report usually focuses on a particular political or economic issue in the respective country or region. Special subscriptions are available for the East and Southeast Asia series, 20 issues at $15.00 per year.

Asian Studies Professional Review
Association for Asian Studies
1 Lane Hall
University of Michigan
Ann Arbor, Michigan 48104
Ray A. Moore, ed.
Semiannual
Cost: $3.00 (nonmembers)
        free to members
Approximately 150 pp.
The review reports on association activities, government research, doctoral dissertations, conferences, bibliographic and archival materials, academic programs, professional activities, and some materials and programs useful to teachers.

Asian Studies Newsletter
Association for Asian Studies
1 Lane Hall
University of Michigan
Ann Arbor, Michigan 48104
Myrna Adkins, ed.
5 times per year
Cost: $2.00 nonmembers
        Free to members
Announcements of grants, fellowships, summer programs, conferences, employment opportunities, personals, and a list of foreign scholars in the U.S. and Canada. Material designed to be more timely and topical than the association's "Professional Review" which is also available to members of the association without charge.

China Exchange Newsletter
Committee on Scholarly Communication with the P.R.C.

2101 Constitution Avenue, NW
Washington, D.C. 20418
Quarterly
Cost: Free
This newsletter reports on developments in U.S.-China scholarly exchanges, particularly as they relate to the field of science and medicine. Also reviews books and materials available on related topics, and notes China's exchange program with other countries.

CCAS Newsletter
Committee of Concerned Asian Scholars
c/o Carl Jacobson
1737 Cram Circle, Apt. 5
Ann Arbor, Michigan 48104
Irregular
Cost: $5.00 nonmembers
         $2.00 unemployed or low-income
         Free to members
Short articles, correspondence, and lists of conferences, committee activities, publications, and information on activities of this organization of scholars who have generally opposed U.S. policies in Asia and the "traditional" role of academic Asia specialists.

Notes from the National Committee
National Committee on United States-China Relations
777 United Nations Plaza, 9-B
New York, New York 10017
(212) 682-6848
Quarterly
Cost: $2.00 (nonmembers)
Approximately 8 pp.
Reports on Committee programs, activities of other organizations, educational resources, book reviews, and brief articles about China and U.S.-China relations. Free to members, civic organizations and libraries, $2.00 contribution requested by others.

Understanding China Newsletter
801 Miner
Ann Arbor, Michigan 48103
Bimonthly
Cost: $3.00 suggested
   Brief background and analytic articles, generally sympathetic to the P.R.C., on contemporary China and American policy. Also includes resources for teachers.

U.S.-China Friendship Association Newsletter
   With the recent establishment of many local U.S.-China Friendship Associations came a series of newsletters covering their activities, reporting on recent trips to China, and so on. Information about these newsletters can be obtained from individual associations, or the regional chapters:

407 South Dearborn, Suite 1085
Chicago, Illinois 60605

50 Oak Street, Room 502
San Francisco, California 94102

41 Union Square West
New York, New York 10003

4. SCHOLARLY JOURNALS

These publications are written primarily for scholars and university students in the China field, but can also be useful in the precollegiate classroom for reference material and in-depth studies of particular issues.

Asia Major
12 Bedford Square
London, WC-1, United Kingdom
Semiannual
Cost: $13.50
   A journal of Far Eastern studies containing scholarly monographs on premodern historical and literary subjects. Includes

book reviews and lists of new publications. Approximately 250 pages.

● *Asian Survey*
University of California Press
Berkeley, California 94720
Monthly
Cost: $12.00 general
    $6.00 student
Scholarly articles of general academic interest dealing with political, economic, and social developments in contemporary Asia. Articles on China appear regularly. Approximately 95 pages.

● *Bulletin of Concerned Asian Scholars*
Bay Area Institute
604 Mission Street
San Francisco, California 94105
Quarterly
Cost: $10.00 Institutions
    $6.00 General
    $4.00 Student
Articles, book reviews, and correspondence concerning contemporary Asia and China. Generally critical of established policies and traditional American approaches to Asia. The chief outlet for "radical" scholarship on China available to American academics. Approximately 120 pages.

● *The China Quarterly*
Research Publications Services, Ltd.
Victoria Hall
East Greenwich
London S.E. 10 ORF, United Kingdom
Quarterly
Cost: $10.00 general
    $5.00 student
The preeminent scholarly journal devoted chiefly to articles about the People's Republic of China and the history of Chinese

Communism. Includes book reviews and a chronology and documentation of recent events. Approximately 250 pages.

China Report
China Study Center
29 Rajpur Road
Delhi 6, India
Bimonthly
Cost: $12.00 Institutions
       $10.00 Individual
       $4.00 student
A 60-page journal of academic interest on topics in Chinese politics, society, and economics. Although technically an international journal, it predominantly reflects the views of Indian writers.

Journal of Asian Studies
Association for Asian Studies
1 Lane Hall
University of Michigan
Ann Arbor, Michigan 48104
Quarterly
Cost: $20.00 (Includes A.A.S membership)
       $10.00 Fulltime students
The principal historically oriented American scholarly journal dealing with Asia (comparatively little on China); includes a comprehensive book review section. Subscribers also receive the annual *Bibliography of Asian Studies*, a definitive listing of articles and books; it can be purchased separately for $8.00. Approximately 215 pages.

Journal of Chinese Studies
American Association of Teachers of Chinese Language and Culture
c/o The Western College
Oxford, Ohio 45056
Quarterly
Cost: $8.00

This interdisciplinary journal features articles and symposia on China and Chinese culture with special emphasis on problems and methods of language teaching. Bibliographies, book reviews, monograph listings, scholarly articles, and doctoral dissertations are all listed as a regular feature.

Modern China
SAGE Publications
P.O. Box 3006
Beverly Hills, California 90212
Quarterly
Cost: $12.00 Individual
       $9.00 Student
A new forum for scholarly articles from various disciplinary standpoints based on the journal's stated purpose of promoting scholarship "free of those assumptions that underlie the 'enemy watching' and 'China watching' work of the past."

Pacific Affairs
University of British Columbia
Vancouver 8, Canada
Quarterly
Cost: $10.00
An international scholarly review of contemporary Asia and Pacific affairs, with frequent articles on China. Includes a book review section.

Problems of Communism
U.S. Information Agency
Superintendent of Documents
U.S. Government Printing Office
Washington, D.C. 20402
Bimonthly
Cost: $6.90
       $1.20 single copy
Articles by scholars and specialists for both the lay reader and scholar, with analysis and background on communist countries, often including China.

5. MONOGRAPHS AND PAPERS

Most of the major centers for Chinese and Asian studies, both in the United States and abroad, publish mongraphs and occasional papers by scholars associated with them. Although such publications are usually designed for a specialized, scholarly audience, they often can be of general interest for personal background study.

For a directory of these centers, see:

Area Studies on U.S. Campuses
World Study Data Bank, 1974
680 Fifth Avenue
New York, New York 10019
(212) 265-3350
Cost: $9.50

6. TRADE JOURNALS

With the expansion of U.S.-China trade, a number of magazines have appeared to serve the interests of businessmen. The primary source of information for U.S.-China trade is the National Council for U.S.-China Trade, 1100 Seventeenth Street, NW, Washington, D.C., 20036. The principal trade journals are:

China Trade Briefing
500 North Michigan Avenue
Chicago, Illinois 60611
Monthly
Cost: $250.00

An 8-page, tabloid-size compendium of articles of interest to the trader, including political analysis and background articles on particular sectors of Chinese industry.

● *China Trade Report*
Far Eastern Economic Review
P.O. Box 47
Hong Kong, B.C.C.
Monthly
Cost: $150.00

A comprehensive, 15–20-page monthly analysis of market trends and commercial policies, giving detailed information on trade policies, commercial transactions, and developments in China's commercial relations with other countries, including the United States.

● *China's Foreign Trade*
Guozai Shudian
Peking, People's Republic of China
Quarterly
Cost: $3.00
Indispensable for those wishing to know China's general position on international trade. Includes articles on general trade policy, descriptive pieces on China's industry and particular products, and advertising for Chinese products. Those looking for detailed trade statistics and specific sector reports will be disappointed, however.

● *Jetro China Newsletter*
Japan External Trade Organization
2 Akasaka Aio-Cho
Minato-ku
Tokyo, Japan
Bimonthly
Cost: Apply to JETRO
A complete compendium of Japanese business activities with China.

● *U.S.-China Business Review*
National Council for U.S.-China Trade
1100 Seventeenth Street, N.W.
Washington, D.C. 20036
Bimonthly
Cost: $60.00
    Free to Council members
The authoritative U.S. magazine on trade developments with the People's Republic. Contains important information for the American trader, including well-researched sector reports on different aspects of China's foreign trade.

7. PUBLICATIONS FROM AND ABOUT TAIWAN

Asian Outlook
P.O. Box 22992
Taipei, Taiwan
Monthly
Cost: $2.00 Surface
$5.00 Airmail
Official statements and short articles on current developments in Asia.

Echo of Things Chinese
P.O. Box 36–427
Taipei, Taiwan
Monthly
Cost: $17.50
A colorful magazine covering a wide variety of cultural topics—from Chinese astrology to a guide to Taiwan's restaurants.

Free China Review
Chinese Information Service
159 Lexington Avenue
New York, New York 10016
Monthly
Cost: $3.00
This review contains articles, brief reports, and a month-in-review summary of events on Taiwan. Also prints documents and analysis of events in the People's Republic.

Free China Weekly
Chinese Information Service
159 Lexington Avenue
New York, New York 10016
Weekly
Cost: $2.50
This short newspaper (4 pages) reports on current events in Taiwan as well as commenting on events and reportage of the People's Republic.
The Chinese Information Service (an organ of the Nationalist

Government) also prepares daily press releases about Taiwan and U.S.-China and U.S.-Taiwan relations, as well as other information.

Issues and Studies
P.O. Box 3377
Taipei, Taiwan
Monthly
Cost: $14.00
   A publication of the Taiwan Institute for International Studies, this 120-page monthly carries scholarly articles and analysis of events both in the People's Republic and on Taiwan. Often includes translations of documents not available elsewhere.

Vista
P.O. Box 36–427
Taipei, Taiwan
Bi-monthly
Cost: $1.80 surface
   A human-interest and "showcase" pictorial of life in Taiwan.

8. Resources

1. INTRODUCTION

The following section, which has been consolidated in this edition for easier usage, includes three parts: resource centers, published materials for general background use, and packets for the classroom. Of particular interest are the local and regional resource centers which have increased in number in the past several years and offer the teacher a valuable source of advice and consultation on curriculum development, teaching methods, and the use of materials in the classroom.

Another major resource which should not be overlooked by the layman is the various university centers specializing in Asian studies. These universities not only afford personal contact with scholars (who are increasingly aware of and sympathetic to the problems of secondary educators), but also provide rich resources through their libraries (which contain most of the journals and books mentioned in this guide), seminars, and special programs. At several universities, specific programs have been established to deal with the promotion of Asian studies in secondary education.

A directory of colleges and universities with area study programs is available (see p. 243).

2. RESOURCE CENTERS

American Association of Teachers of Chinese Language and Culture
Sun Yat-sen Hall
St. John's University
Jamaica, New York 11432
Paul K. T. Shih, executive secretary

The purposes of the association are to encourage the study and teaching of Chinese language and culture, to advance such study and teaching through the exchange of information and scholarship across disciplinary lines, and to promote understanding and communication between Chinese and Western scholars involved in China studies. Annual membership dues are $5.00.

The Asia Society
112 East 64th Street
New York, New York 10021
Bonnie R. Crown, director of Educational Resources
The Asia Society sponsors a variety of activities for its members, including art exhibitions, performances by Asian performing artists and dance troupes, art tours of Asia, lectures, conferences, and seminars. The society also translates works of Asian writers and provides curriculum advice to teachers. A textbook review project of secondary materials covering Asia is currently underway.

Bay Area China Education Project (BAYCEP)
P.O. Box 2373
Stanford, California 94305
David Grossman, project director
BAYCEP is a regional project designed to coordinate university-based specialists and resources with precollegiate educators in the San Francisco Bay Area. A model center for providing materials and advice on China to school teachers, it offers consultation on curriculum development, as well as workshops on teaching about China. The project has produced a Guide to Bay Area Resources ($1.50 per copy), listing the services, organizations, libraries, museums, and film centers dealing with China in the San Francisco area. Lists of recommended materials and sample classroom units are also available.

Center for International Programs and Comparative Studies
State Education Department
99 Washington Avenue
Albany, New York 12210
Ward Morehouse, director
The center is involved in developing materials, organizing in-service programs for teachers, and assisting schools and colleges in New York State in strengthening teaching and research about third-world cultures. Materials on China, including comprehensive slide sets, are available.

Center for Teaching International Relations
University of Denver
Denver, Colorado 80210
William Welch, director
  Sponsored by the Center for War/Peace Studies and the
University of Denver, the C.T.I.R. serves Colorado and Rocky
Mountain teachers by working with schools and school districts in
the area and developing pre-service teacher training for teaching
"global perspectives."

Center for War/Peace Studies
218 East 18th Street
New York, New York 10003
Robert Gilmore, president
  Stressing the development of "global perspectives," the center
provides assistance to educators by producing and evaluating
curriculum materials, providing in-service education through
workshops and demonstration classes, and through publications
(e.g., *Intercom*; the September 1971 issue was on China, and one
on teaching about China in elementary schools is forthcoming).
  For a list of current projects, including regional projects in the
East, West, and Midwest, write the center's New York headquarters.

China Institute of America
125 East 65th Street
New York, New York 10021
F. Richard Hsu, president
  The China Institute sponsors lectures, conferences, seminars,
special forums, and publications for the understanding and
appreciation of Chinese culture. Its School of General Studies, in
cooperation with the Board of Education of the City of New York,
offers courses on Chinese history, politics, language and culture
for the general public. Its cultural programs feature exhibitions of
traditional Chinese art, as well as musical and theatrical presentations.

Chinese Culture Center of San Francisco
750 Kearny Street
San Francisco, California 94108
The center offers a comprehensive program for its members on traditional Chinese and contemporary Chinese-American culture, including lectures, workshops, seminars, language and art classes, film programs, and story-telling hours. It maintains an information center and a research and reference library, and sponsors performances by Chinese performing artists. The center is also planning a museum and art gallery.

Chinese-Russian Studies Center
Toledo Public Schools
3301 Upton Avenue
Toledo, Ohio 43610
Norman Klee, director
This center was established to initiate Russian and Chinese language teaching, and has issued several bibliographies and course syllabi for more general courses on China. It also publishes a newsletter.

Committee of Concerned Asian Scholars
Building 600-T
Stanford University
Stanford, California 94305
The committee operates a speaker's bureau and publishes materials on Asia and America's presence there. Its branches, at most major universities across the country, engage in activities such as lectures, seminars, film showings, and so on, which are generally critical of both America's political role in Asia and traditional scholarship on the subject.

Education Development Center
15 Mifflin Place
Cambridge, Massachusetts 02138
Peter Dow, director
The Social Studies Program of EDC, a nonprofit corporation, has been developing new programs, approaches, and curri-

culum units for social studies teaching in junior and senior high schools. Materials it has produced have focused on the social problems of our time.

Foreign Area Materials Center
60 East 42nd Street
New York, New York 10017
Ward Morehouse, director
The Foreign Area Materials Center (FAMC) is part of the Center for International Programs and Comparative Studies of the New York State Education Department. Under the latter's direction, the FAMC has compiled bibliographies, syllabi, a curriculum unit, and various guides suitable primarily for college but also for secondary level teaching. A catalog, and the periodic publication "Intercultural Studies Information Service," are available free of charge.

Great Lakes Colleges Association: Center for East Asian Studies
103 Bosworth Hall
Oberlin College
Oberlin, Ohio 44074
Halsey L. Beemer, Jr., coordinator for Chinese Studies
A consortium of twelve private colleges and universities in Ohio, Michigan, and Indiana which has a joint office at the Center for East Asian Studies. In addition to serving the academic needs of the consortium's membership, the center provides teacher training seminars, speakers, and films to other schools and organizations in the three states and in neighboring states. A list of the center's Chinese resources is available on request.

Midwest Ecumenical China Center
American Lutheran Church Headquarters
422 South 5th Street
Minneapolis, Minnesota 55415
Douglas Swendseid, chairman
The center, under development at the time of this writing, will coordinate China resources for the church judiciaries—colleges, seminaries, and concerned citizen groups in the Minneapolis

Resource Centers   *251* area. Research projects will be carried out on topics of regional interest, a library will be maintained, and community outreach programs will include symposia, seminars, consultations, workshops and teaching units for high school teachers, and general publications.

Pacific and Asian Affairs Council
Pacific House
2004 University Avenue
Honolulu, Hawaii 96822
John H. Maier, program specialist
The council serves the Hawaiian Islands as an Asian resource center with programs aimed primarily at precollegiate audiences. There are PAAC school clubs, state-wide conferences, in-service teacher training programs, children's magazine, and a speaker's program. It is currently in the process of launching a systematic survey of Asian studies throughout Hawaii's secondary school system.

Project on Asian Studies in Education (PASE)
300 Lane Hall
University of Michigan
Ann Arbor, Michigan 48104
Margaret Carter, Mike Fonte, Jody Hynes, staff
The principal aim of PASE is to improve the teaching of Asian Studies in secondary schools and colleges and to help increase understanding and appreciation of Asia among the general public. PASE sponsors workshops on China, Japan, and South Asia, has a mobile resource center, provides in-service training (including summer courses), and produces film guides and learning packages. Also sponsors a speakers bureau.

National Committee on United States–China Relations
777 United Nations Plaza 9-B
New York, New York 10017
Arthur H. Rosen, President
The National Committee, a private, nonprofit, organization, encourages public interest in, and understanding of, China and its relations with the United States through cultural exchanges

with the People's Republic of China and related educational programs. National Committee Field Staffs at eleven universities throughout the country consist of professors and advanced graduate students who volunteer their time both as speakers and educational advisors to high schools and community groups. A listing of Field Staffs, many of which have strong outreach programs and publish materials such as guides to resources in their areas, and a National Committee "Publications and Resources" brochure are available upon request.

Service Center for Teaching of Asian Studies
Ohio State University
29 West Woodruff Avenue
Columbus, Ohio 43210
Franklin R. Buchanan, director
 The center, directed by one of this country's foremost advocates and developers of Asian studies in secondary education, was established by the Association for Asian Studies in 1971. It serves primarily as a clearinghouse, identifying the existing and continually emerging print and non-print materials on Asia for the precollegiate level, and giving guidance to teachers about the best available materials for the needs of a given teacher or school situation. To help fulfill this function, the Center publishes an invaluable thrice-yearly newsletter, *Focus on Asian Studies*, and a series of "Service Center Papers on Asian Studies" (see chapter 7, section 3).

Understanding China Committee
American Friends Service Committee
980 North Fair Oaks Avenue
Pasadena, California 94108
 The Committee operates a speakers' bureau for teachers and cooperates with other organizations in the Los Angeles area in providing services for teachers, including a resource kit on China, a curriculum guide, and several other publications.

3. FOR CLASSROOM USE: PUBLISHED MATERIALS FOR THE TEACHER

Asian Studies in American Secondary Education
U.S. Government Printing Office

Washington, D.C.
119 pp. $0.75 1971

This publication is the outgrowth of two conferences, sponsored jointly by the Association for Asian Studies and the U.S. Office of Education in 1970. The conferences, reported in this booklet, focused on existing programs, proposals for curriculum change, and problems of introducing change into the school system. While informative, this publication covers much old ground and largely reflects the needless reinvention of the wheel.

China and U.S. Foreign Policy
Congressional Quarterly, Inc.
1735 K Street, N.W.
Washington, D.C. 20036
91 pp. $4.00 1971

A summary of America's policy to China through 1971, including maps, charts, and presidential statements. The Congressional Quarterly's research service regularly puts out books and pamphlets on major issues in the news.

China Information Library
Newsbank, Inc.
P.O. Box 645
Greenwich, Connecticut 06830
$750 per year   Microfiche

Taking advantage of the evolution of the microfiche, this service provides libraries and institutions with reproductions of secondary source materials relating to China from a great number of journals, newspapers, monographs, periodicals, and other published material. Organized under six headings (agriculture, commerce, politics, international relations, social developments, and resources for teachers), the file is updated for subscribers every two months with a detailed index.

China Series
MSS Information Corporation
655 Madison Avenue
New York, New York 10021
$1.20 single copy

A series of articles on different aspects of China's development (public health, communes, and so on), edited by Gerald Tannebaum, an American who lived for some twenty years in the People's Republic. Designed for use in secondary schools, these articles generally convey the Chinese perspective on progress and problems in these areas.

"Contemporary Chinese Writing for the Masses"
Social Education, January 1973
National Council for the Social Studies
1201 16th Street, N.W.
Washington, D.C. 20036
$1.50 single copy
    This issue contains selections from contemporary Chinese literature, along with a U.S. Department of State briefing on the People's Republic. The literary materials—poems, playlets, articles—are ideally suited for classroom adaptation.

Current History
4225 Main Street
Philadelphia, Pennsylvania 19127
$1.00 single copy
    The September issue of this journal is annually devoted to a summary of China's foreign and domestic policies and events. Articles are written by leading scholars in a style suitable for nonspecialists.

"Education in the Land of Mao"
Learning, November 1973
Education Today, Inc.
530 University Avenue
Palo Alto, California 94301
$1.00 single copy
    Doreen Croft, a specialist in early childhood development, and Albert Yee, an educational psychologist, report on Chinese schools as they observed them during their 1973 visits. In addition, there is an excellent section for the teacher suggesting classroom projects and teaching approaches.

Focus on Asian Studies
Service Center for Teachers of Asian Studies
Ohio State University
29 West Woodruff Avenue
Columbus, Ohio 43210
Cost: $2.00 per year (four issues)
   The *most essential single resource* available for teachers. A newsletter especially designed for elementary and secondary teachers including essays, book reviews, and announcements of conferences, publications, multimedia materials, and summer programs. No mere listing, it has a character and flavor that is infectious.

Report on the National Inventory Conference on Learning Resources Related to China
Great Lakes College Association
Center for East Asian Studies
Earlham College
Richmond, Indiana 47374
Free
   This is the report of a conference held in 1974 to discuss resources and resource centers available for assisting precollegiate educators. Helpful in identifying the resources and projects now underway in this area.

Service Center Papers on Asian Studies
Ohio State University
29 West Woodruff Avenue
Columbus, Ohio 43210
$1.00 each
   A series of papers designed especially to aid the secondary teacher in different aspects of the curriculum. Current titles available are:
   No. 1 — "A Critical Guide to Four Published Asian Studies Curriculum Programs," by Daniel Davis
   No. 2 — "The Dynamics of Modernization, A Study of Comparative History by C. E. Black: Some Suggestions for Classroom Use," by Daniel Davis
   No. 3 — "Introducing Asian Studies in Elementary Education: China and India," by James Hantula

No. 4 — "Levels of Conceptualization in the Teaching of Asian Studies in the Schools," by Donald Johnson

No. 5 — "Problems and Opportunities in Improving Secondary Education About China," by H. Thomas Collins

No. 6 — "Where is the Flowery Kingdom?" by James Hantula

No. 7 — "Modern Japanese Novels in English," by Nancy Beauchamp

No. 8 — "Recent Materials on China and U.S.-China Relations: An Annotated Bibliography," by Robert Goldberg

Wingspread Conference Reports
The Johnson Foundation
Racine, Wisconsin 53401
Free

These reports reflect conferences held at Wingspread, the Johnson Foundation's conference center. The reports on China, done in cooperation with the National Committee on U.S.-China Relations, are:

"Education in the People's Republic of China" (April 1973)
Recent visitors, China scholars and educators assess China's present education policies and progress and suggest fruitful areas of inquiry for future visitors.

"Science in the People's Republic of China" (May 1973)
A review of China's progress in various fields of science and an assessment of the prospects for more extended scholarly exchanges.

"Health Care in the People's Republic of China" (November 1973)
Sixteen recent visitors and twenty other health professionals discuss China's contributions in this field.

"The Prospects for U.S.-China Relations" (May 1974)
The factors likely to shape U.S.-China relations in the months ahead, with a view to identifying some of those issues especially deserving public attention.

"Women in China: American Perspectives" (June 1974)
The role of women in China.

4. PACKETS FOR CLASSROOM USE

China Pac
Orbis Books, Maryknoll Publications

Maryknoll, New York 10545
Cost: $4.95 student pac
       $1.00 leader's pac
This field-tested educational unit and resource packet is designed for both high schools and community groups. Includes role-plays, short dramatic presentations, stereotyping exercises, and other learning activities from new and old China, along with some two hundred pages of documentation, bibliographies, three paperbacks, and a "Little Red Book" of five of Mao's essays.

China—Prelude to Chaos
China—Age of the Warlords
Time-Life Multimedia
100 Eisenhower Drive
Paramus, New Jersey 07652
Cost: $0.50; minimum order 25
These reprints from past *Life* magazine files are a remarkable photo essay. Each reprint is 20 pages, and a teacher's guide comes free with every 25 of the same title. An interpretive essay by Professor John K. Fairbank completes the set.

China: Teacher's Starter Kit
Social Studies School Service
10,000 Culver Boulevard
Culver City, California 90230
Cost: $10.50
A collection of basic readings, resource materials, and teaching units prepared by the Center for War/Peace Studies. Contains paperbacks, reprints, visual materials, and lesson plans designed to provide introductory background for teaching about China. The paperbacks include: Hellerman and Stein, *Readings in the Middle Kingdom*, Tudisco's *Confucianism and Taoism*, and Vogel's *Social Change: The Case of Rural China*.

The Ch'ing Game: Simulation and the Study of History
Foreign Area Materials Center
60 East 42nd Street
New York, New York 10017
Cost: $2.00

This book is primarily aimed at history teachers in secondary schools and colleges, and is designed to introduce students to traditional Chinese history as participants in a simulated Chinese society.

Modern Chinese: A Basic Course
Dover Publications
180 Varick Street
New York, New York 10014
Cost: $3.50
An adaptation of the course in basic Mandarin Chinese designed by the faculty of Peking University in China. The book—accompanied by three records for an additional $12.50—assumes no previous training, and thus the course lends itself to a self-study program of the Chinese language.

People and Systems: Cuba, China, Tanzania
Friendship Press
7820 Reading Road
Cincinnati, Ohio 45237
Cost: $6.95 complete packet
        $1.75 China unit
A Church Study Packet of five units, analyzing how five countries cope with five universal issues. The countries are China, Cuba, Tanzania, Canada, and the United States; the issues are education, health care, religion, work, and the role of women.

Syllabi for Use in Mandarin Chinese Language
Chinese-Russian Study Center
Toledo Public Schools
3301 Upton Avenue
Toledo, Ohio 43613
Cost: Free
The four syllabi for Chinese language are intended for use in a four-year high school Chinese language course on a schedule of five fifty-five minute periods per week. One of the five periods every week is to be devoted to the study of Chinese history and culture based on a topical outline presented in the last half of each volume. Each of the four volumes has a seventeen-unit

lesson plan which is correlated to three textbooks by John DeFrancis and *Read Chinese*, by Fred Wang.

Teaching about Asia
Shelter Institute
540 Santa Cruz Avenue
Menlo Park, California 94025
Cost: $3.75
This visually and substantively rewarding packet is a good introduction to teaching about Asia. Billed as a "non-book," it is a listing of sources and resources, film annotations, bibliographies, and discographies. Five short pamphlets—from how to survive your first course on Asia to the diversity of the Asian experience—round out the packet.

Part III   Materials from the People's Republic of China

9. Materials from the People's Republic of China

1. INTRODUCTION

For Americans, it has been particularly difficult to grasp the meaning, if not the value, of the dramatic social and political changes under way in the People's Republic of China. The "loss of China" twenty-five years ago and the resulting U.S. attempt to isolate the People's Republic politically and economically, coupled with a natural tendency to judge any foreign culture by our own values and standards, served to increase our misunderstanding and inability to evaluate China on its own terms.

With the reopening of relations between the two countries has come the opportunity to reevaluate our views. In particular, the increased availability of materials from China—books, magazines, films, art works—now allows us to approach the study of China by considering how the Chinese themselves describe their society and to some degree, how the people view their own lives.

This chapter has been added to the guide, therefore, in part because the increased availability of materials warrants a special listing, but also as an attempt to encourage the careful use of such materials for public education and in the classroom. The very nature of these materials, precisely because they often are clearly "propagandistic" in their tone and purpose, can tell us a great deal about a society from which we have been isolated for a generation.

Suggestions for use of these primary sources can be found in the individual sections of this guide. They can be used to supplement most or all of the books for the general reader, as well as the textbooks, curriculum units, and lesson plans commercially available. A short story from *Chinese Literature*, for example, can give an excellent idea of what values are important in the society today. *Historical Relics*, a film on the relics unearthed in the last few years, not only shows the beauty of the artifacts of ancient China, but will also be a quick lesson in how that art is related to the politics and society of today. The Chinese find in both their past and their present a great number of lessons: what are they? what do they tell us about the people and their goals? Such a spirit of inquiry, supplemented by the more standard and Western scholarly materials, can greatly strengthen a learning experience about the People's Republic of China.

2. PUBLICATIONS

Periodicals in English from the People's Republic of China provide a wealth of material that can be adapted to classroom use. Short magazine articles, accompanied by photographs and drawings, can give students a feel for the Chinese experience and lead to lively discussions comparing that experience with their own. They are useful in providing insights into literary, journalistic, and political approaches and for improving skills of both critical analysis and general reading. With imaginative guidance, students can use periodicals from China to better understand living and working conditions, the Chinese view of themselves and others, the impact of Mao Tse-tung's thought upon society, and the stated aspirations of the Chinese government and people.

All publications listed in this section are available directly from China: Guozi Shudian, Peking, People's Republic of China. In addition, they are readily available in this country from the three branches of China Books and Periodicals:

2929 24th Street
San Francisco, California 94110

125 Fifth Avenue
New York, New York 10003

210 W. Madison Street
Chicago, Illinois 60606

China Books and Periodicals, in addition to carrying the periodicals mentioned in this section, has English translations of various Chinese literary and political works, language study materials, postcards, posters, papercuts, films, recordings of Chinese music, and postage stamps. A free catalogue is available upon request.

Principal publications follow in this section.

China Pictorial
Cost: $ 4.00 surface mail
$16.00 airmail
A large-format, glossy magazine with good photographs and short articles, covering China's progress in all fields of life, the daily life of the people, and contact with people of other countries.

China Reconstructs
Cost: $3.00 airmail
An illustrated monthly news magazine featuring general articles and reports on such topics as politics, economics, education, public health, science, literature, art, women, children, history, geography, and China's foreign relations. An interesting feature is the Language Corner with short lessons in the Chinese language for self instruction. Probably the most valuable general magazine for exploring how the Chinese view themselves and others, as well as how they in turn wish to be viewed.

The editors have also published *Some Basic Facts about China* ($0.45), a small booklet which provides answers to questions about communes, women's liberation, education, medical care, and other issues most often asked by readers of *China Reconstructs*.

Chinese Literature
Cost: $ 4.00 per year, surface mail
$14.00 airmail
A monthly literary magazine reflecting the current focus of China's literary arts on social revolution and construction. Regular features include short stories, poems, plays, critical articles, and reproductions of art works. Among other things, it is useful for seeing how China uses models (workers, communes, youth, etc.) to build collective values in the society.

Peking Review
Cost: $4.50 airmail
The authoritative political weekly dealing with China and world affairs. Carries documents and reports on current political campaigns in China and her views on international questions.

Also contains theoretical articles, and is most useful to the serious student.

3. FILMS

Films from the People's Rupublic of China must be viewed as part of the total picture of China's new art and culture. They provide insight into Chinese efforts to use the visual arts both to provide cultural enrichment and to convey a political message; for China today, these two elements seem inseparable.

Several organizations are currently distributing 16 mm. films made and produced in the People's Republic. Catalogues and detailed information on rental costs (which may vary) can be obtained from the following:

U.S. China People's Friendship Association
41 Union Square West
New York, New York 10003

407 S. Dearborn, Suite 1085
Chicago, Illinois 60605

619 S. Bonnie Brae
Los Angeles, California 90057

50 Oak Street, Room 502
San Francisco, California 94102

International Corporation of America
1300 Army-Navy Drive, Suite 409
Arlington, Virginia 20008

Contemporary Films–McGraw Hill
Princeton Road
Hightstown, New Jersey 08520

Third World Newsreel
26 West 20th Street
New York, New York 10011

Films listed in this section were available for distribution in January 1975—others may subsequently be added by additional distributors. Descriptions for each are provided to aid in selection, although there has been no attempt to critically evaluate the films in terms of content or technical worth. Unless otherwise specified, the narration is in English, translated in the P.R.C.

Acupuncture Anesthesia
16 mm, 28 minutes, color
Eight different operations are recorded in vivid detail in this film depicting surgical procedures performed under acupuncture anesthesia. One of the operations shows a patient, himself a surgeon, talking with the operating team while having a part of his lung removed. Narrated by the American ear specialist Dr. Sam Rosen, who discusses some of the theories explaining acupuncture and its effects.

Afro-Asia Table Tennis Friendship Tournament
16 mm, 60 minutes, black and white
"Friendship first, competition second" is the theme of China's sports men and women, and it is echoed in this film, which is a record of the Afro-Asia tournament held in Peking in November 1971. The visitors are seen playing matches and touring factories, agricultural communes, and Peking's historic environs.

Arts and Crafts of China
16 mm, 30 minutes, color
Four specialties of China's arts and crafts—ivory carving, embroidery, cloisonne and jade carving—are depicted in this film, with a detailed look at how the raw material is turned into finished craft.

Away with All Pests
16 mm, 60 minutes, black and white
Insight into life in China today by the English surgeon Joshua Horn, who worked there from 1954 to 1969 organizing medical resources and "barefoot doctors."

A Brilliant Spectacle
16 mm, 120 minutes, color
Ping-pong teams from eighty districts and countries in Asia,

Africa, and Latin America are entertained by their Chinese hosts. Part of the film is devoted to ping pong matches, while the remainder records the teams' travels through scenic China and shows the dances and theatricals performed for them.

Children of China
16 mm, 60 minutes, color
A view of how children from birth through middle school are cared for and of the services provided. Extensive shots of a children's hospital, special medical-care services, nurseries, kindergartens, children at play, constructive leisure-time activities and work projects.

China Today
16 mm, 10 minutes, color
This documentary records the economic progress of China. It consists of a series of short vignettes describing specific agricultural developments across the country, with special emphasis on the status of China's ethnic minority groups.

China's Ping Pong Team Visits the U.S.
16 mm, 40 minutes, color
This film, in its Chinese-language version, was shown throughout China. Through it, the Chinese people were able to look at the visit of China's table tennis team to the U.S. in 1972, and have a filtered look at the American people and their culture. Beyond its value as a documentary, the film indicates what aspects of American life the Chinese considered worth reporting.

Chinese Delegation Visits Hanoi
16 mm, 60 minutes, color
At the invitation of the government in Hanoi, a Chinese delegation headed by Premier Chou En-lai pays a visit to North Vietnam in 1971.
Chinese soundtrack.

The Cock Crows at Midnight
16 mm, 18 minutes, color
A children's cartoon about a landlord who wakes his rooster before the sun rises so that he can get more work out of the peasants, but is caught in the act. This animated film describes the resolution of the problem to the betterment of all.

Down with the New Tsars
16 mm, 65 minutes, black and white
Documents the Sino-Soviet border dispute, specifically in the areas of the Wusuli and Heilung Rivers.

The East is Red
16 mm, 150 minutes, color
A modern opera-epic combining elements of traditional Chinese opera with modern revolutionary songs, music, costumes, and staging. This portrayal of the Chinese Revolution begins with descriptions of exploitation and misery in the pre-Communist period and the birth of the Communist party in 1921. The theme is the struggle of Chinese workers, peasants, and soldiers against foreign and domestic enemies, and builds upon events such as the Long March, the war against the Japanese, land reform in the liberated areas, and the victory of 1949.
This film is available only from Contemporary Films–McGraw Hill.

Fishing on the South China Sea
16 mm, 20 minutes, color
The scenery, sea resources, and fishing life in a village in South China are depicted.

Flowers Greeting the Sun
16 mm, 25 minutes, black and white
Nine sequences about children in China. Shows school activities in various parts of China including a floating school on Lake Weishan, a tent school in Inner Mongolia, and science projects at

the Shanghai Children's Palace. The film illustrates the combining of practical training with theoretical study.

Chinese soundtrack; English narration available on separate cassette.

Good News from Industry
16 mm, 15 minutes, color
Coverage of the progress in China's industrial development.

Han Tomb Find
16 mm, 28 minutes, color
This documentary shows the ancient artifacts recently discovered in a tomb of the Han Period. The 2000-year-old female corpse for whom this tomb was made was found to be in a remarkable state of preservation, and the film is a record not only of the tomb itself, but also of the exhumation of the corpse.

Chinese sound track; English narration available on separate cassette.

Historical Relics Unearthed during the Great Cultural Revolution
16 mm, 60 minutes, color
A montage including much of the excavation work carried out all over China since the Cultural Revolution. The artifacts are an overwhelming testimony to the greatness of Chinese civilization and the commentary recounts the price in exploitation paid by the working masses.

Chinese sound track with English narration on separate cassette. Available only from the International Corporation of America.

Hsui-Lin's Diary
16 mm, 10 minutes, color
A children's cartoon in three sequences showing how peasant children in China help commune members and each other.

New Face of China
16 mm, 60 minutes, black and white

Documentary on various aspects of life in China, including industry, agriculture, housing, medical care, and so on.

Prince Sihanouk Visits South China
16 mm, 60 minutes, color
A record of the visit of Sihanouk, living in exile in China, to Hangchow, Shanghai, Suchow, Wuhsi, and Nanking in the spring of 1971.
Chinese soundtrack.

Red Blossoms on Tien Shan Mountains
16 mm, 120 minutes, color
Story of a woman who becomes the first woman brigade-leader of her commune's production unit and her struggle against feudal ideas.

Red Detachment of Women
16 mm, 120 minutes, color
A revolutionary dance drama about the creation and development of a company of Chinese women workers and peasants fighting for the People's Liberation Army on Hainan Island, in 1929–37. The style of the ballet is a combination of traditional Western ballet, Peking opera, folk dance, and Chinese acrobatics.

Red Flag Canal
16 mm, 45 minutes, black and white
One of China's major construction efforts in recent years has been to increase agricultural productivity. This film shows how the peasants of Lin Hsien County in North Central China, against enormous odds, cut through mountains to build an irrigation canal, and in ten years transformed a barren, drought-stricken area into a flourishing farmland.

Rent Collection Court Yard
16 mm, 12 minutes, black and white
A dramatic animation film which uses about one hundred

life-size sculptured figures created by a cooperative team of artists. The film depicts the abject misery of the peasants of Tayi at the hands of the local despots before the 1949 liberation.

Spring Comes to Our Land
16 mm, 20 minutes, color
   Documentary on all aspects of life in an agricultural commune in southern China.

Spring Everywhere
16 mm, 30 minutes, color
   A montage of cultural performances by art troupes and theatrical groups from different parts of China, including national minority regions.

Two Heroic Sisters of the Grassland
16 mm, 45 minutes, color
   In this animated cartoon, two sisters, aged nine and seven, are left to guard the commune's flock of sheep. A violent blizzard isolates the girls from their flock. Rather than save themselves, the two girls brave cold and hardship to find the flock and stay with it until help arrives.
   Available only from Third World Newsreel.

The White Haired Girl
16 mm, 120 minutes, color
   Originally a folk story from Hopei province, *The White Haired Girl* was first written as an opera in 1945, then revised and produced as a revolutionary ballet in the late 1960s. It depicts the class conflict in a North China village, in the winter of 1935, during the Sino-Japanese War. The heroine, Hsi-erh, daughter of a poor peasant, learns first-hand the cruelty of landlord oppression and of war. She flees into the mountains, where hardship and hunger turn her hair white. She is finally rescued by her sweetheart, who meanwhile has joined the Eighth Route (Communist) Army, and, in the final scene, she joins in the victory against her family's former landlord.

Wu Shu
16 mm, 17 minutes, color
This is a colorful film of the fast-moving sport of Wu Shu (martial arts), as practiced by young students at Peking's Amateur School of Athletics. The students demonstrate stick-fighting, saber, spear, and sword fighting, and other martial arts while touring famous Peking scenic spots.
Chinese narration.

4. OTHER TEACHING MATERIALS

The following two kits from the People's Republic of China are available from China Books and Periodicals (see section 2 of this chapter for address).

Elementary Chinese, Part 1
Cost: $12.50 four cassettes, 3½ hours
        $1.25 text of lessons
Chinese language tapes produced by the People's Broadcasting station of Peking, designed to give a basic knowledge of Chinese.

Introductory Classroom Kit on China
Cost: $6.30
A wide-ranging selection of books, posters, cutouts, records, and magazines from the People's Republic specifically designed to be helpful in the classroom and as a "sampler" of materials available.

5. AMERICAN TRANSLATIONS OF CHINESE MEDIA

China Program
Plenum Publishing Company
227 West 17th Street
New York, New York 10011
An ongoing project of translating of major scientific and technological journals (excluding medicine) from the People's Republic; largely for specialist, scholarly use. Contact publisher for complete listing.

China Review
International Arts & Sciences Press

901 North Broadway
White Plains, New York 10603
Quarterly
Cost: $12.00
  A translation journal, appearing quarterly, covering the social sciences and related fields: education, law, government, economics, sociology, history, philosophy, literature, and linguistics. For both specialists and nonspecialists.

Chinese Education
Chinese Economic Studies
Chinese Law and Government
Chinese Sociology and Anthropology
Chinese Studies in History
Chinese Studies in Philosophy
International Arts & Sciences Press
901 North Broadway
White Plains, New York 10603
Quarterly
Cost: $65.00 institutions
      $15.00 individuals
  Each of these journals, edited respectively by Peter Seybolt, George C. Wang, Kau Ying-mao, Sidney Greenblatt, Li Yunning, and Cheng Chung-ying, contains unabridged translations from Chinese scholarly journals and published collections of articles. Each issue focuses on a particular topic.

Current Background
National Technical Information Service
U.S. Department of Commerce
Springfield, Virginia 22151
15–30 issues per year
Cost: $275.00
  Selections from press of the People's Republic of China, with each issue focusing on a particular topic. Available at most university libraries with an East Asia department.

Daily Report
Foreign Broadcast Information Service

National Technical Information Service
U.S. Department of Commerce
Springfield, Virginia 22151
Daily
Cost: $125.00
A unique publication offering the most comprehensive coverage of China's national, international, and regional affairs as translated by U.S. monitoring of Chinese radio broadcasts. Also available at most major university libraries.

Hsinhua Selected News Items
Hsinhua News Agency
Hong Kong
Weekly and daily
Cost: $57.00
This is not an American translation, but the official Chinese translation of major stories from their official news agency.

Selections from People's Republic of China Magazines (SPRCM)
National Technical Information Service
U.S. Department of Commerce
Springfield, Virginia 22151
Weekly
Cost: $130.00
Selections from China magazines as translated and compiled by the American consulate in Hong Kong. A major source for research into all aspects of Chinese life. Also included in this series is a digest of daily press (*Selections from People's Republic of China Press*).

Appendix 1
List of Publishers

Abelard-Schuman Ltd.
  257 Park Avenue South
  New York, New York 10010
  (212) 533-9000

Abingdon Press
  55 East 55th Street
  New York, New York 10022
  (212) 752-6118

Ace Books
  1120 Avenue of the Americas
  New York, New York 10036
  (212) 867-5050

Addison-Wesley
  Reading, Massachusetts 02720
  (617) 944-3700

Aldine-Atherton, Inc.
  529 South Wabash Avenue
  Chicago, Illinois 60605
  (312) 939-5190

Allyn & Bacon, Inc.
  470 Atlantic Avenue
  Boston, Massachusetts 02210
  (617) 482-9220

American Council on Education
  1 Dupont Circle N.W.
  Washington, D.C. 20036
  (202) 833-4724

American Education Publications
  Education Center

Columbus, Ohio 43216
(614) 253-0982

American Friends Service Committee
112 South 16th Street
Philadelphia, Pennsylvania 19102
(215) 563-9372

American Heritage Publishing Co., Inc. (Subs. of McGraw–Hill)
1221 Avenue of the Americas
New York, New York 10020
(212) 997-1221

Anchor Books (Imprint of Doubleday & Co.)
245 Park Avenue
New York, New York 10010
(212) 953-4580

Apollo Editions, Inc. (Division of Thomas Y. Crowell Co.)
666 Fifth Avenue
New York, New York 10019
(212) 489-2200

Appleton-Century-Crofts
440 Park Avenue South
New York, New York 10016
(212) 689-5700

Atheneum Publishers
122 East 42d Street
New York, New York 10017
(212) 661-4500

Avon Books
959 Eighth Avenue
New York, New York 10019
(212) 262-6252

Bantam Books, Inc.
666 Fifth Avenue
New York, New York 10019
(212) 765-6500

Barre Publishers
South Street
Barre, Massachusetts 01005
(617) 355-2914

Basic Books
404 Park Avenue South
New York, New York 10010
(212) LE2-0110

Beacon Press, Inc.
25 Beacon Street
Boston, Massachusetts 02108
(617) 742-2110

Belknap Press of Harvard University Press
79 Garden Street
Cambridge, Massachusetts 02138
(617) 868-7600

Bobbs-Merrill Co., Inc. (Division of ITT)
4 West 58th Street
New York, New York 10029
(212) 688-6350

Brookings Institution
1775 Massachusetts Avenue, N.W.
Washington, D.C. 20036
(202) 797-6258

Cambridge University Press
32 East 57th Street
New York, New York 10022
(212) 688-8885

Children's Press
1224 West Van Buren Street
Chicago, Illinois 60607
(312) 666-4200

China Books and Periodicals
(East)

125 Fifth Avenue
New York, New York 10003
(212) 677-2650
(Midwest)
210 W. Madison Street
Chicago, Illinois 60606
(312) 782-6004
(West)
2929 24th Street
San Francisco, California 94110
(415) 282-2994

China Research Monographs
Center for Chinese Studies
2168 Shattuck Avenue
University of California
Berkeley, California 94704
(415) 642-6000

P. F. Collier Inc.
866 Third Avenue
New York, New York 10022
(212) 935-2000

Colorado Associated University Press
University of Colorado
1424 15th Street
Boulder, Colorado 80302
(303) 443-2211

Columbia University Press
562 West 113th Street
New York, New York 10025
(212) 865-2000

Comstock Editions (Subsidiary of Ballantine Books)
3030 Bridgeway Blvd.
Sausalito, California 94965
(415) 332-3216

Congressional Quarterly, Inc.
1735 K Street N.W.

Washington, D.C. 20006
(202) 296-6800

Coward, McCann & Geoghegan, Inc.
200 Madison Avenue
New York, New York 10016
(212) 883-5500

Criterion Book Co., Inc.
257 Park Avenue South
New York, New York 10010
(212) 533-9000

Thomas Y. Crowell Co.
666 Fifth Avenue
New York, New York 10019
(212) 777-2600

Dell Publishing Co.
245 East 47th Street
New York, New York 10017
(212) 832-7300

Denoyer-Geppert
5235 Ravenswood Avenue
Chicago, Illinois 60640
(312) 561-9200

Doubleday & Company, Inc.
501 Franklin Avenue
Garden City, New York 11530
(516) 294-4561

E. P. Dutton and Company
201 Park Avenue South
New York, New York 10003
(212) 674-5900

East Asian Research Center
1737 Cambridge Street
Harvard University

Publishers

Cambridge, Massachusetts 02138
(617) 495-1000

Evergreen Books (Imprint of Grove Press)
53 East 11th Street
New York, New York 10003
(212) 677-2400

Farrar, Straus & Giroux, Inc.
19 Union Square West
New York, New York 10003
(212) 675-3000

Fawcett Publications, Inc.
1515 Broadway
New York, New York 10036
(212) 869-3000

Follett Educational Corporation
1010 West Washington Boulevard
Chicago, Illinois 60607
(312) 666-5858

Foreign Area Materials Center
60 East 42d Street
New York, New York 10017
(212) 972-9877

Foreign Language Press
Peking
People's Republic of China

Foreign Policy Association
345 East 46th Street
New York, New York 10017
(212) 697-2432

Friendship Press
7820 Reading Road
Cincinnati, Ohio 45237
(513) 761-2100

Garrard Publishing Co.
    1607 North Market Street
    Champaign, Illinois 61820
    (217) 352-7685

Ginn and Company
    191 Spring Street
    Lexington, Massachusetts 02173
    (617) 816-1670

Grove Press Inc.
    53 East 11th Street
    New York, New York 10003
    (212) 677-2400

G. K. Hall
    70 Lincoln Street
    Boston, Massachusetts 02111
    (617) 423-3990

Harcourt Brace Jovanovich, Inc.
    757 Third Avenue
    New York, New York 10017
    (212) 572-5000

Harper & Row, Publishers
    10 East 53d Street
    New York, New York 10022
    (212) 593-7000

Hart Publishing Co., Inc.
    719 Broadway
    New York, New York 10003
    (212) 260-2430

Harvard University Press
    79 Garden Street
    Cambridge, Massachusetts 02138
    (617) 868-7600

Publishers   *283*

Harvey House, Inc., Publishers
c/o E. M. Hale & Co.
1201 South Hastings Way
Eau Claire, Wisconsin 54701
(715) 832-8303

D. C. Heath & Company
125 Spring Street
Lexington, Massachusetts 02173
(617) 862-6650

Holt, Rinehart & Winston, Inc.
383 Madison Avenue.
New York, New York 10017
(212) 688-9100

Hoover Institution Press
Stanford University
Stanford, California 94305
(415) 497-2300

Houghton Mifflin Company
2 Park Street
Boston, Massachusetts 02107
(617) 423-5725

International Arts and Sciences
901 North Broadway
White Plains, New York 10603
(914) 428-8700

International Textbook Company
257 Park Avenue
New York, New York 10017
(212) 533-9000

John Day Company, Inc.
257 Park Avenue South
New York, New York 10010
(212) 533-9000

Alfred A. Knopf, Inc.
201 East 50th Street
New York, New York 10022
(212) 751-2600

Kodansha International Ltd., distributed by:
Harper & Row Publishers, Inc.
Keystone Industrial Park
Dunmore, Pennsylvania 18512
(717) 343-4761

Laidlaw Brothers (Division of Doubleday & Co., Inc.)
Thatcher and Madison Streets
River Forest, Illinois 60305
(312) 369-5320

J. B. Lippincott Co.
521 Fifth Avenue
New York, New York 10017
(212) 687-3980

Little, Brown and Company
60 East 42d Street
New York, New York 10017
(212) 687-1135

Lothrop, Lee & Shepard Co., Inc.
105 Madison Avenue
New York, New York 10016
(212) 889-3050

MIT Press
28 Carleton Street
Cambridge, Massachusetts 02142
(617) 864-6900

McCormick-Mathers Publishing Co., Inc.
450 West 33d Street
New York, New York 10001
(212) 594-8660

Publishers   *285*

McGraw-Hill, Inc.
  1221 Avenue of the Americas
  New York, New York 10019
  (212) 997-1221

David McKay Co., Inc.
  750 Third Avenue
  New York, New York 10017
  (212) 661-1700

Macmillan Co.
  866 Third Avenue
  New York, New York 10022
  (212) 935-2000

Josiah P. Macy Foundation
  1 Rockefeller Plaza
  New York, New York 10020
  (212) 246-8830

Maryknoll Communications (Friendship Press)
  Orbis Press
  Maryknoll, New York 10545

Mentor Books (Imprint of the New American Library, Inc.)
  1301 Avenue of the Americas
  New York, New York 10019
  (212) 956-3800

Michigan State University Press
  1405 South Harrison Road
  25 Manly Miles Building
  East Lansing, Michigan 48823
  (517) 355-1855

Monthly Review Press
  116 West 14th Street
  New York, New York 10011
  (212) 691-2555

William Morrow & Co., Inc.
  105 Madison Avenue

New York, New York 10016
(212) 889–3050

Natural History Press (Division of Doubleday)
245 Park Avenue
New York, New York 10017
(212) 953-4561

New American Library, Inc.
1301 Avenue of the Americas
New York, New York 10019
(212) 956-3800

New York University Press
Washington Square
New York, New York 10003
(212) 598-2882

Noonday Press (Imprint of Farrar, Straus)
19 Union Square West
New York, New York 10003
(212) 675-3000

W. W. Norton & Co., Inc.
55 Fifth Avenue
New York, New York 10003
(212) 255-9210

Ohio State University Press
2070 Neil Avenue
Columbus, Ohio 43210
(614) 422-6930

Oxford University Press, Inc.
200 Madison Avenue
New York, New York 10016
(212) 679-7300

Paperback Library
315 Park Avenue South
New York, New York 10010
(212) 677-1000

Publishers

Pantheon Books, Inc.
201 East 50th Street
New York, New York 10022
(212) 751-2600

Parents' Magazine Press
52 Vanderbilt Avenue
New York, New York 10017
(212) 685-4400

Pelican Books (Division of Penguin Books, Inc.)
7110 Ambassador Road
Baltimore, Maryland 21207
(301) 944-8600

George Philip & Son Ltd.
Victoria Road
Willesden Junction
London NW10, England

Pica Press (Division of Universe Books)
381 Park Avenue South
New York, New York 10016
(212) 689-0276

Pocket Books (Division of Simon and Schuster, Inc.)
630 Fifth Avenue
New York, New York 10020
(212) 245-6400

Population Crisis Committee
1835 K Street N.W.
Washington, D.C. 20006
(202) 659-1833

Praeger Publishers, Inc.
111 Fourth Avenue
New York, New York 10003
(212) 254-4100

Prentice-Hall, Inc.
Rt. 9W

288   Appendix 1

Englewood Cliffs, New Jersey 07632
(201) 947-1000

Princeton University Press
Princeton, New Jersey 08540
(609) 452-4900

G. P. Putnam's Sons
200 Madison Avenue
New York, New York 10016
(212) 883-5500

Quadrangle/The New York Times Co.
10 East 53d Street
New York, New York 10022
(212) 593-7800

Rand McNally & Co.
Box 7600
Chicago, Illinois 60680
(312) 673-9100

Random House, Inc.
201 East 50th Street
New York, New York 10022
(212) 751-2600

St. Martin's Press, Inc.
175 Fifth Avenue
New York, New York 10010
(212) 674-5151

Saturday Review Press
380 Madison Avenue
New York, New York 10017
(212) 883-8000

Scholastic Book Services
50 West 44th Street
New York, New York 10036
(212) 867-7700

Publishers

Scott, Foresman and Company
1900 East Lake Avenue
Glenview, Illinois 60025
(312) 729-3000

Charles Scribner's Sons
597 Fifth Avenue
New York, New York 10017
(212) 486-2700

Signet Books (Division of the New American Library, Inc.)
1301 Avenue of the Americas
New York, New York 10019
(212) 956-3800

Stanford University Press
Stanford, California 94305
(415) 323-9471

State University of New York Press
Albany, New York 12203
(518) 457-3300

Stein & Day Publishers
7 East 48th Street
New York, New York 10017
(212) 753-7285

Time-Life Books (Time, Inc.)
Time and Life Building
Rockefeller Center
New York, New York 10020
(212) 586-1212

Torchbooks (Division of Harper & Row)
10 East 53d Street
New York, New York 10022
(212) 593-7000

Charles E. Tuttle Co.
Rutland, Vermont 05701
(802) 773-8930

Appendix 1

United Nations Association of the U.S.A. Inc.
345 East 46th Street
New York, New York 10017
(212) 697-3232

U.S. Government Printing Office
Superintendent of Documents
Washington, D.C. 20402
(202) 541-3000

University of Arizona Press
Box 3398
Tucson, Arizona 85721
(602) 884-1441

University of California Press
2223 Fulton Street
Berkeley, California 94720
(415) 642-4247

University of Chicago Press
5801 Ellis Avenue
Chicago, Illinois 60637
(312) 753-3344

University of Illinois Press
Champaign/Urbana, Illinois 61801
(217) 333-0950

University of Indiana Press
Bloomington, Indiana 47401
(812) 337-4203

University of Michigan
Center for Chinese Studies
Ann Arbor, Michigan 48104
(313) 764-1817

University of Toronto Press, orders to:
33 East Tupper Street
Buffalo, New York 14208
(716) 852-0342

Publishers

University of Washington Press
Seattle, Washington 98105
(206) 543-4050

University Press of Hawaii
Honolulu, Hawaii 96825
(808) 536-6051

Viking Press, Inc.
625 Madison Avenue
New York, New York 10022
(212) 755-4330

Vintage Books (Division of Random House)
201 East 50th Street
New York, New York 10022
(212) 751-2600

Henry Z. Walck, Inc.
19 Union Square West
New York, New York 10003
(212) 924-7650

Washington Square Press (Division of Simon and Schuster)
630 Fifth Avenue
New York, New York 10020
(212) 245-6400

Franklin Watts, Inc. (Subsidiary of Grolier Inc.)
845 Third Avenue
New York, New York 10022
(212) 751-3600

Westminster Press
Witherspoon Building
Philadelphia, Pennsylvania 19107
(215) 735-6722

Weybright and Talley, Inc.
750 Third Avenue
New York, New York 10017
(212) 490-1155

John Wiley & Sons, Inc.
605 Third Avenue
New York, New York 10016
(212) 867-9800

World Publishing Co.
110 East 59th Street
New York, New York 10022
(212) 759-9500

Yale University Press
92A Yale Station
New Haven, Connecticut 06520
(203) 432-4969

Young Scott Books (Imprint of Addison-Wesley)
Reading, Massachusetts 01867
(617) 944-3700

Appendix 2
List of Audiovisual Distributors

ACI Films, Inc.
    35 West 45th Street
    New York, New York 10036
    (212) 582-1918

AIMS Instructional Media Services
    P.O. Box 1010
    Hollywood, California 90028
    (213) 467-1171

AFC-UCLA
    Instructional Media Library
    Royce Hall, Room 8
    405 Hilgard Avenue
    Los Angeles, California 90024
    (213) 825-0755

American Society for Eastern Arts
    2640 College Avenue
    Berkeley, California 94704
    (415) 548-7777

AV-ED Films
    7934 Santa Monica Boulevard
    Hollywood, California 90046
    (213) 654-9550

Avon Productions, Inc.
    200 West 57th Street
    New York, New York 10019
    (212) 581-4460

BEE Cross Media
    36 Dogwood Glen
    Rochester, New York 14625
    (716) 381-5554

B.F.A. Educational Media
2211 Michigan Avenue
Santa Monica, California 90404
(213) 829-2901

Black Star Company
450 Park Avenue South
New York, New York 10016
(212) 679-3288

Broadcasting Foundation of America
52 Vanderbilt Avenue
New York, New York 10017
(212) 684-2505

Carousel Films
1501 Broadway
New York, New York 10036
(212) 524-4126

CBS Educational and Publishing Group
383 Madison Avenue
New York, New York 10017
(212) 688-9100 Extension 795

China Books and Periodicals
(East)
125 Fifth Avenue
New York, New York 10003
(212) 677-2650
(Midwest)
210 W. Madison Street
Chicago, Illinois 60606
(312) 782-6004
(West)
2929 24th Street
San Francisco, California 94110
(415) 282-2994

Chinese Information Service
159 Lexington Avenue

Audiovisual Distributors

New York, New York 10016
(212) 725-4950

Contemporary Films–McGraw-Hill
(East)
Princeton Road
Hightstown, New Jersey 08520
(609) 448-1700
(Midwest)
828 Custer Avenue
Evanston, Illinois 60202
(312) 869-5010
(West)
1714 Stockton Street
San Francisco, California 94133
(415) 362-3115

Current Affairs Films
24 Danbury Road
Wilton, Connecticut 06897
(203) 762-0301

Tom Davenport Films
Pearlstone
Delaplane, Virginia 22025
(703) 592-3701

Denoyer-Geppart Audio-Visuals
5235 Ravenswood Avenue
Chicago, Illinois 60640
(312) 561-9200

Doubleday Multimedia
1371 Reynolds Avenue
Santa Ana, California 92705
(714) 540-5550

Eastfoto-Sovfoto Agency
25 West 43d Street
New York, New York 10036
(212) 279-8846

296   Appendix 2

Educational Audio Visual, Inc.
  Pleasantville, New York 10570
  (914) 769-6332

EMC Corporation
  180 East 6th Street
  St. Paul, Minnesota 55101
  (612) 227-7366

Encyclopaedia Britannica
  1822 Pickwick Avenue
  Glenview, Illinois 60025
  (312) 321-7311

Eye Gate House
  146-01 Archer Avenue
  Jamaica, New York 11435
  (212) 291-9100

Film Images
  17 West 60th Street
  New York, New York 10023
  (212) 279-6653

Films Incorporated
  1144 Wilmette Avenue
  Wilmette, Illinois 60091
  (312) 256-4730

Guidance Associates
  757 Third Avenue
  New York, New York 10017
  (212) 754-3700

Handel Film Corporation
  8730 Sunset Boulevard
  West Hollywood, California 90069
  (213) 657-8990

Harper and Row
  Audio-Visual Department

Audiovisual Distributors   *297*

10 East 53d Street
New York, New York 10022
(212) 593-7000

Harvard University Press
79 Garden Street
Cambridge, Massachusetts 02138
(617) 495-2606

Impact Films
144 Bleecker Street
New York, New York 10012
(212) 674-3375

International Corporation of America
1300 Army-Navy Drive, Suite 409
Arlington, Virginia 22202
(703) 979-8888

International Film Foundation
475 Fifth Avenue, Room 916
New York, New York 10017
(212) 685-4998

The Johnson Foundation
Wingspread
Racine, Wisconsin 53401
(414) 639-3211

Macmillan Audio Brandon
(East)
34 MacQuestern Parkway South
Mount Vernon, New York 10550
(914) 664-5051
(Midwest)
8400 Brookfield Avenue
Brookfield, Illinois 60513
(312) 485-3925
(West)
3868 Piedmont Street
Oakland, California 94611

(415) 658-9890
(South)
2512 Program Drive
Dallas, Texas 75220
(214) 357-6494
(Southwest)
1619 North Cherokee
Los Angeles, California 90028
(213) 463-0357

Magnum Photo
15 West 46th Street
New York, New York 10036
(212) 541-7570

Martin Mayer Productions
900 Federal Avenue East
Seattle, Washington 98102
(206) 322-9308

Multi-Media Productions
P.O. Box 5097
Stanford, California 94305
(415) 968-1061

NBC Educational Enterprises
30 Rockefeller Center
New York, New York 10020
(212) 247-8300

NET Service
Audio-Visual Center
Student Service Building
Indiana University
Bloomington, Indiana 47401
(812) 337-2103

A. J. Nystrom and Company
3333 Elston Avenue
Chicago, Illinois 60618
(517) 688-3056

Audiovisual Distributors   *299*

Ohio State University
Film Library
Department of Photography and Cinema
156 West 19th Avenue
Columbus, Ohio 43210
(614) 422-5966

Oxford Films
1136 North Las Palmas Avenue
Los Angeles, California 90038
(213) 461-9231

Pictura Films Distributing Company
43 West 16th Street
New York, New York 10011
(212) 691-1730

Shostal Associates, Inc.
60 East 42d Street
New York, New York 10017
(212) 687-0696

Social Studies School Service
10,000 Culver Blvd.
Culver City, California 90230
(213) 839-2436

Society for Visual Education
1345 Diversey Parkway
Chicago, Illinois 60614
(312) 525-1500

Spoken Arts, Inc.
310 North Avenue
New Rochelle, New York 10801
(914) 636-5482

Sterling Films
600 Grand Avenue
Richfield, New Jersey 07657
(201) 943-8200

Syracuse University
Film Rental Library
1455 East Colvin Street
Syracuse, New York 13210
(315) 479-6631

Teaching Resource Films
Station Plaza
Bedford Hills, New York 10506
(914) 241-1350

Third World Newsreel
26 West 20th Street
New York, New York 10011
(212) 243-2310

Time-Life Films
100 Eisenhower Drive
Paramus, New Jersey 07652
(201) 843-4545

U.S. China People's Friendship Association
(East)
41 Union Square West
New York, New York 10003
(212) 255-4727
(Midwest)
407 South Dearborn, Suite 1085
Chicago, Illinois 60605
(312) 922-3414
(West)
619 South Bonnie Brae
Los Angeles, California 90057
(213) 484-8140

Universal Education and Visual Arts
100 Universal City Plaza
Universal City, California 91608
(213) 985-4321

University of California Extension
   Media Center
   Berkeley, California 94720
   (415) 642-0460

University of Rochester
   The East Asian Center
   Rush Rhees Library, Room 555
   Rochester, New York 14627
   (716) 275-2521

Westinghouse Learning Corporation
   100 Park Avenue
   New York, New York 10017
   (212) 983-5077

Index

This index is divided into the following categories: Books and Authors; Audiovisual Materials; Periodicals; and Other Resources and Materials. Materials both on and from the People's Republic of China are included.

Index

Hunter), 181
China on Stage (Snow), 164
China Passage (Galbraith), 179
China Perceived (Fairbank), 221
China Reader (Schurman et al.), 154
China Shakes the World (Belden), 172
China Today (Cohen and Cohen), 163
China White Paper (Van Slyke), 227
China's Changing Map (Shabad), 155
China's Development Experience (Oksenberg), 194
China's Cultural Tradition (Bodde), 155
China's Economic System (Donnithorne), 202
China's Experience in Population Control (Orleans), 195
China's Gentry (Fei), 156
China's Struggle to Modernize (Gasster), 174
China's Three Thousand Years (Heren et al.), 157
China's Trade with the West (Stahnke), 206
China's Turbulent Quest (Hinton), 215
Chinese Americans (Stevens), 230
Chinese Civilization (Eichhorn), 156
Chinese Communism (North), 175
Chinese Communism and the Rise of Mao (Schwartz), 176
Chinese Communist Army in Action (George), 207
Chinese Communist Politics in Action (Barnett), 185
Chinese Communist Society (Yang), 201
Chinese Cultural Revolution (Emein), 189
Chinese Difference (Kraft), 180
Chinese Economy under Communism (Chen and Galenson), 201
Chinese Education and Society (Fraser and Hsu), 184
Chinese Foreign Policy in an Age of Transition (Ojha), 216
Chinese High Command (Whitson), 208
Chinese Literature: An Anthology from the Earliest Times to the Present Day (McNaughton), 169
Chinese Literature: Popular Fiction and Drama (Chang), 169
*Chinese Painting (Weitzman), 31
Chinese People's Liberation Army (Griffith), 207
*Chinese Popular Fiction (Weitzman), 34
Chinese Road to Socialism (Wheelright and McFarlane), 206
Chinese Thought from Confucius to Mao Tse-tung (Creel), 155
Chinese View of China (Gittings), 71, 152
Chinese Worker (Hoffman), 203
Chinese Writing (Creel), 163
"Chink!" A Documentary History of Anti-Chinese Prejudices in America (Wu), 231
Chiu, Hungdah, ed., *China and the Question of Taiwan*, 209
Chou En-lai (Hsu), 167
Chu Lung-chu and Lasswell, Harold, *Formosa, China and the United Nations*, 218
City in Communist China (Lewis), 191
Clemens, Walter, *Arms Race and Sino-Soviet Relations*, 212, 213
Clubb, O. Edmund, *China and Russia*, 211, 213; *Twentieth Century China*, 173; *The Witness and I*, 218
Cohen, Jerome A., and Chiu, Hungdah, *People's China and International Law*, 214
Cohen, Jerome A., and Cohen, Joan L., *China Today*, 163
Cohen, Jerome A., et al., *Taiwan and American Policy*, 219
Cohen, Warren I., *America's Response*

306

China, 221

Families of Fengsheng (Sidel), 197

Fanshen (Hinton), 175

Fei Hsiao-tung, China's Gentry, 156

Fitzgerald, C. P., Communism Takes China, 174; Horizon History of China, 163

FitzGerald, Stephen, China and the Overseas Chinese, 214

Folktales from China (Eberhard), 166

Fontein, Jan, and Tung, Wu, Unearthing China's Past, 162

*Food and Survival in Asia (McKeown), 40

Formosa: A Study in Chinese History (Goddard), 210

Formosa: Licensed Revolution and the Home Rule Movement, 1895–1945 (Kerr), 210

Formosa, China and the United Nations (Chu and Lasswell), 218

Formosa Today (Mancall), 210

Forrester, James, China: Man and His World, 152

Fraser, Angus, The People's Liberation Army, 209

Fraser, Stewart, and Hsu Kuang-liang, Chinese Education and Society, 184

Fremantle, Anne, ed., Mao Tse-tung, 167

Friedman, Edward, and Selden, Mark, eds., America's Asia, 221

Froncek, Thomas, ed., The Horizon Book of the Arts of China, 163

Fullard, Harold, China in Maps, 152

Future of the Overseas Chinese in Southeast Asia (Williams), 217

Galbraith, John K., A China Passage, 179

Gallin, Bernard, Hsin Hsing, Taiwan, 209

Galston, Arthur, Daily Life in People's China, 179

Gasster, Michael, China's Struggle to Modernize, 174

George, Alexander L., The Chinese Communist Army in Action, 207

Gernet, Jacques, Daily Life in China on the Eve of the Mongol Invasion, 157

Gittings, John, A Chinese View of China, 71, 152; The Role of the Chinese Army, 207; Survey of the Sino-Soviet Dispute, 212, 213

Goddard, W. G., Formosa: A Study in Chinese History, 210

Goldberg, George, East Meets West, 228

Government and Politics of Communist China (Waller), 199

Graff, Edward, *China, 47

Greenblatt, Miriam, and Chu, Donchean, *The Story of China, 63

Griffith, Samuel B., The Chinese People's Liberation Army, 207; Peking and People's War, 208; Mao Tse-tung on Guerilla Warfare, 208

Griffith, William E., The Sino-Soviet Rift, 212; Sino-Soviet Relations, 1964–65, 212

Grousset, Rene, The Rise and Splendour of the Chinese Empire, 157

Guide to Chinese Poetry and Drama (Bailey), 165

Guide to Chinese Prose (Paper), 166

Harding, Harry, China: An Uncertain Future, 186

Harrison, James P., The Long March to Power, 174

Heathen Chinee (McClellan), 229

Hellerman, Leon, and Stein, Alan L., China: Readings on the Middle Kingdom, 153

Heren, Louis, et al., China's Three Thousand Years, 157

Hinton, Harold, An Introduction to Chinese Politics, 174; Communist China in World Politics, 214; China's Turbulent Quest, 215

Index

Index

Index   *315*